Perspectives on resource management T.O'Riordan

Pion Limited, 207 Brondesbury Park, London NW2 5JN

Library edition   SBN 85086 024 5
Student edition   SBN 85086 025 3

Set on IBM 72 Composers by Pion Limited, London.
Printed in Great Britain by J.W.Arrowsmith Limited, Bristol.

Preface

The field of resource management is nowadays more commonly identified with the widespread concern for environmental quality. This area of research and opportunity is receiving increasing attention from all kinds of academic disciplines and is changing very rapidly indeed. As a result, there is no current comprehensive textbook on the subject, nor any general statement of its aims and methodology. This book is therefore written in an attempt to fill this void. It is designed to guide undergraduates and graduates who are taking introductory courses in resource management to significant concepts in the field, to stimulate them to develop existing lines of research and to develop new avenues. Above all, it has been my intention to provide as comprehensive a bibliography as possible from the viewpoint of the social sciences in order to assist the reader in exploring the extensive literature in the resources field.

The book is devoted to three major themes. Firstly, an analysis of the concept of resource and resource management; secondly, the problems of resource allocation and particularly the question of identifying and measuring the important extra-market effects of resource decisions; and thirdly, the decision-making process whereby resources are evaluated and allocated both by the professional resource manager and by the individual citizen.

I am indebted to my colleague Shue Tuck Wong, who made many valuable suggestions for improving an early draft of the manuscript. Naturally the faults that remain are mine, but I immensely enjoyed writing this book and hope that it sparks the imagination and academic interest of some of its readers.

T.O'Riordan
Department of Geography, Simon Fraser University

Acknowledgements

The author wishes to express his gratitude for the permissions received to reproduce the following material:

Her Majesty's Stationery Office, London. Extract on page 67 from the Fifth Annual Report 1968, Water Resources Board.

Iowa State University Press, Ames, Iowa. Poem on page 36 from K. E. Boulding, 1964, *The Economist and the Engineer; Economic Dynamics of Water Resource Development.*

The Johns Hopkins Press, Baltimore, Maryland. Tables 2.1, 2.2, 2.3, 2.4, and Figures 8.1 and 8.2, all of which were published by the Johns Hopkins Press for Resources for the Future, Inc.

National Academy of Sciences—National Research Council, Washington, D.C. Figure 2.4, Table 4.2, and extract on page 110 from a report 1968, by the Committee on Water.

Penguin Books Ltd., Harmondsworth, Middlesex. Extract on page 61 from R.Arvill, 1967, *Man and Environment: Crisis and the Strategy of Choice.*

Contents

List of Figures

List of Tables

Resources and management—a historical perspective

Introduction

The purpose of this monograph is to bring together some of the more important of the many diverse threads of research that constitute the general field of resource management. Unfortunately, this procedure involves a certain degree of subjectivity in the selection of, and emphasis given to, the various research themes chosen, but the subject matter is now so vast and the relevant literature so voluminous that some degree of screening is necessary. The selection of relevant research themes was not easy. Discussion will centre around attempts to improve the efficiency and accuracy of resource allocation procedures between individuals and groups over time and space, the efforts to quantify or at least to rationalise the inclusion of intangibles or nonmonetary values (such as beauty, uniqueness, harmony, symbolism), the recent work done on the social appraisal of environmental influences (such as hazard impact, public attitudes), and the analysis of the various forces and influences acting upon the process of choice (a central theme in resource management) and upon the decision-makers themselves. However, the aim is not so much to concentrate on a number of significant yet isolated findings and review these purely upon their merits, as to gather these together to provide the perspective for a broad framework for analysis.

The emphasis throughout is upon the holistic approach, though it is readily conceded that the total view is exceedingly difficult to grasp and even more awkward to translate into operational terms. Nevertheless, it is becoming increasingly apparent that we, as a society, are faced with various groupings of problem complexes that extend beyond the bounds of casual comprehension and the limited purview of specific fields of specialisation into the vast and somewhat uncharted territories of the total environment. Such problems have been named 'meta-problems' by Chevalier and Cartwright (1966). Examples of meta-problems include racial and ethnic strife, poverty and hunger, unequal regional economic and social opportunity, the urban malaise, and environmental pollution.

The view taken here is that the broad field of resource management acts as an integrating focus for a number of meta-problems. Thus resource management itself should not be visualised as a meta-problem, but rather as a rational framework of analysis within which various meta-problems can be anchored. Figure 1.1 attempts to portray this relationship schematically. It is evident that many of the world's most pressing social, economic, and political problems are valid topics for resource management analysis.

While meta-problems are not mutually exclusive (for example, one cannot dissociate environmental pollution from the question of poverty), nevertheless, they all contain certain fundamental distinguishing features.

The first of these is the problem of definition. Because, by their very nature, meta-problems embrace a totality of approaches, it is very difficult for any single individual, no matter how well trained, to conceive them in their entirety. The result is that the interpretation, appraisal, and search for solution differs for each individual concerned, depending on his value systems, his experience, and his training. Such differences in conception are usually fundamental, frequently contradictory, and often shift in emphasis and content over time.

The absence of a consensus as to the very nature of the problem we are trying to overcome introduces a second dimension to the question of developing an optimum social policy towards meta-problems, namely the question of goals identification. For, in addition to imperfect comprehension, there is incomplete agreement over what kind of society and what quality of environment we want and how we propose to achieve these. In other words, social aims are ambiguous, inconsistent, and conflicting, and the search for feasible solutions lacks singleness of purpose and tends to be timid, inconclusive, and called constantly to question.

A third feature of the meta-problem is that it can only be satisfactorily appraised through the collaborative attention of a number of disciplines. The geographer often visualises himself as playing the role of an integrator, whereas, in fact, he is but one member of a team, each of whom has a fundamental contribution to make. Again, there are a number of factors here which tend to inhibit the proper analysis and solution of meta-problems, among which should be included the need to develop cross-disciplinary understanding (Kates, 1966b), the readiness to listen to and to comprehend many other viewpoints, the ability to stand back and to adjust focus, and, finally, the determination to seek and find solutions even at the expense of overriding personal prejudices.

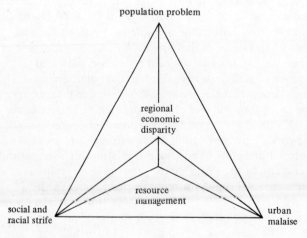

Figure 1.1. Resource management—a framework for the analysis of meta-problems.

Meta-problems continue to exist for the obvious reason that they cannot easily be solved. We shall find that the solutions lie not so much in the new technological or fiscal policies (though these play their part), as in the need to change the more delicate yet more rigid social and institutional impediments described above, and to reassess ourselves as a society—our values, our aspirations, and our conscience. The approach here is public-policy orientated, for it is believed that the major focus of attention for the geographer interested in resource management should be to clarify the various issues involved in order to provide a clearer basis for public judgement and social action.

The concept of a resource

As has already been implied, there is no satisfactory definition of a resource; nor has any given set of definitions remained generally acceptable over time. Hunker (1964), paraphrasing Zimmermann (1951), has pointed out that a resource can no longer be conceived as a tangible object, but a *functional relationship* that exists between man's wants, his abilities, and his appraisal of his environment. The definition of a resource is thus a culturally defined abstract concept, which hinges upon man's perception of the means of attaining certain socially-valued goals by manipulating selected elements of the biophysical environment. We shall look at this man–nature theme in some detail later (Chapter 5). Suffice it to say here that the biophysical environment offers *opportunities* [which Zimmermann (1951) called resources], yet imposes certain *restrictions* or *resistances,* whose inhibiting effects will vary depending upon their biophysical nature, the scientific and technological capacity and inventiveness of the group in question, the social pressures to achieve desired aims, society's assessment of economic feasibility, and the nature of the laws and administrative–institutional arrangements into which the managing group is organised to guide policy and to focus action (Firey, 1960).

The rather complex relationship between man and his appraisal of resources is presented in a simplified schematic form in Figure 1.2. Resources *become*, as Zimmermann (1951) put it, to satisfy man's *wants* which are both biological (food, shelter, comfort) and cultural (values, aspirations) in nature, and exist both at the individual and social levels. To create these resources, man employs his technological and organisational abilities, though his actions are restrained by *ecological resistances,* which demand that a harmonious equilibrium be maintained between man and nature. The actual decision to utilise a resource depends upon supply and demand and relative *economic scarcity,* which in turn influences choice of strategy (Firey, 1960).

Of particular value to the geographer is the fact that the concept of a resource is intimately related to the interaction between man's cultural and biophysical environments, and thus varies over space and time, depending upon the myriads of possible combinations of these two highly complex variables. This fundamental relationship has traditionally consumed the geographical discipline, and indeed still provides one of its basic tenets (Spoehr, 1956; Thomas, 1956; Lowenthal, 1961; Glacken, 1967). However, it is a concern not unique to geographers and has been extensively discussed by ecologists (Sears, 1966, 1969; Dasmann 1964, 1966a, 1966b), conservationists (Leopold, 1949; Darling and Milton, 1966, Darling 1967a, 1967b), and anthropologists (Malinowski, 1935; Meggers, 1958; Frake, 1962, 1964; Porter, 1965).

While no definition of such a complex concept as a resource will prove entirely satisfactory, we can summarise the above discussion by concluding that a resource is an attribute of the environment appraised by man to be of value over time within constraints imposed by his social, political, economic, and institutional framework.

Traditional approaches toward the classification of resources

In the past the concept of resource has always been associated with what is commonly known as 'natural resources', that is those tangible elements of the biophysical environment necessary for the production of certain basic commodities (land, forest, fish, minerals, fuels, and so on). And, until recently, most of the textbooks dealing with resource conservation (Highsmith *et al.*, 1969; Parson, 1964; Smith, 1965; Allen and Leonard, 1966) were devoted to extensive statements with regard to the supply, demand, and methods of management of each of these factors. The emphasis was primarily economic, with few concessions towards ecology, cultural appraisal, or public policy. The results were often rather sterile inventories of natural resource locations, quantities, and uses, which failed to provide meaningful insights as to how resources were valued, managed, and allocated. In addition, the traditional 'natural resource' viewpoint

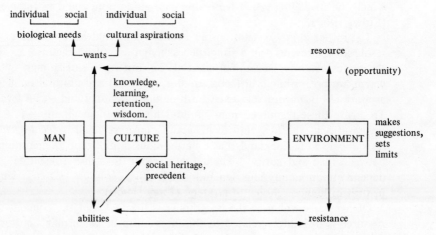

Figure 1.2. The bio-cultural process of resource appraisal (after Zimmerman, 1959).

led to a number of misconceptions regarding the nature of resources: namely, that they were tangible, single-purpose, and static in their value over time (Hunker, 1964).

Though many of the authors recognised the cultural component of resource appraisal, early classifications of resources rested essentially upon assumptions of availability for man's use in relation to geological and biological time scales (Table 1.1). The basic distinction was based upon the concept of renewability or natural substitutability of the resource in relation to man's perceived needs over time. Where resources were not naturally replaced (or did not replace themselves) they were termed *stock* or *nonrenewable* resources. Examples include fossil fuels such as coal and oil. Where the resource was capable of replenishing itself (such as forests, soil), or of being replenished by natural processes (water) within a time scale that was meaningful to man, the classification of *fund* or *renewable* resources was applied. A third category pertained to resources that remained essentially unchanged after man's use and were constant in supply (for example tides, sunlight).

Historical approaches to resource allocation
Such a classification is rather misleading (though not entirely invalid), since the concept of a resource has changed in meaning as man's appraisal of his environment has altered and his social institutions have become adjusted to reflect these new values.

Zobler (1962) has portrayed these changing concepts admirably. He visualises resources, as others have done before him (see Barnett and

Table 1.1. Traditional classification of resources

Resources	Examples
Flow resources—depending upon management these can either be *depleted, sustained,* or *increased*	soil, forests, wildlife, fish, and water
Stock resources—these are of two kinds:	
(1) totally physically exhaustible	coal, oil, natural gas, and nuclear fuels
(2) depletable, but capable of reuse	most metals and rubber
Continuous resources—these are of two kinds:	
(1) availability endless, but independent of man's action	solar energy and tidal energy
(2) availability endless, but affected by man's action	landscape amenity, site space, air, and water

(Adapted from Highsmith *et al.*, 1969)

Morse, 1963), as the land element in the three classical factors of production—land, labour, and capital. Over time, each of these three factors shifts in its significance, depending upon its relative perceived scarcity and cost. Such scarcities are relative in the sense that changing social, economic, and institutional factors may alter the very nature of the production system.

In preindustrial societies resources were absolutely abundant, but relatively scarce as man's ingenuity for resource appraisal and his ability for resource exploitation was poorly developed. Resources were prised from nature at a heavy cost of labour, institutions of exchange were poorly organised, and resources were allocated on a social rather than economic basis. Transactions were made in kind, not money, and elaborate cultural institutions and symbolic rituals were developed to permit orderly exchange. Resources were perceived as segmental and time-invariant: during periods of apparent abundance populations increased, thus maintaining subsistence living standards and relative resource scarcity.

With the onset of the industrial age, resources were perceived as being both absolutely and relatively abundant as the new technical prowess unlocked a vast storehouse of untapped goods. With industrial expansion came a dramatic shift in social values and attitudes. Social controls over resource appraisal and allocation gave way to the 'laissez faire' and the freedom of rights of the individual. Competition set the rules and the weak were automatically eliminated. This view culminated in the philosophy of social Darwinism under Spencer (1890–1920), and the extraordinary centralisation of economic power in vast monopolies. The market place dominated the resource allocation process, and the entrepreneur with his profit maximisation incentive and his myopic time horizon was lauded with high social status. Resources were there to be consumed, and waste was acceptable if there was no profit to be gained by preventing it. As we have shown, the delicate and vital interlinkages between resource uses were at best poorly perceived.

It was inevitable that this period of relentless misuse of resources would result in some form of intellectual and social reaction. The intellectual reaction came with the work of Marshall and Pigou (Zimmermann, 1951), who realised that private gain did not necessarily lead to improved social welfare, and indeed contributed largely to the detriment of the public good, and that some formal theory should be developed to link the act of an individual to its effects upon society. The outcome was the body of theory known as welfare economics, where public intervention and social control were deemed necessary to regulate the excesses of private action in the public interest. Thus the market place gave way to the quasi-political forum as the rationale for the allocation of resources.

The development of the conservation philosophy

We have noted that, up till the turn of the century, shifts in the relative values of land, labour, and capital led to changes in the system of resource allocation away from social and ritual controls to 'laissez faire' and emotionalism. Rationality was not yet evident: resources were 'developed' rather than 'managed', for their production and consumption depended primarily upon willingness to pay and the maximisation of net private gain, rather than upon the optimisation of net social benefits. As resources were not yet considered relatively scarce, costs were related only to the tangible costs of production, rather than to the intangible costs of environmental disruption and impending scarcity. Thus resources were valued largely in terms of the benefits that they realised.

It has been well said that it is only out of the darkest gloom that the first glimmer of light shines. The period preceding the turn of the century displayed the very antithesis of conservation. However, time was ripe for social change and it was out of this that the conservation movement developed. True, the philosophy of man–nature harmony dates back to classical times (Glacken 1967), and certainly a number of notable conservationists had appeared before this time (Marsh, 1864; Udall 1963), but no organised social and political ideology existed until after 1890. The reasons for the growth of the First Conservation Movement (1890–1920) (Hays, 1959) are not too difficult to imagine.
1. Resource scarcity was beginning to be perceived as being absolute. Barnett and Morse (1963) describe the views of the leading economists of the time, notably Malthus, Ricardo, and Mill. Each of these men visualised land as the only finite factor of the production triad, but while Malthus visualised land as a fixed commodity, both Ricardo and Mill realised that, as land became more scarce, so increasing amounts of labour and/or capital would be employed to reduce its relative importance in the production function. Nevertheless, the myth of superabundance was shattered, and some control over the private exploitation of public resources was considered necessary.
2. Man began to realise his capability for destroying his environment and that ultimately his own survival was at stake. Man's power over Nature's forces had been considered before, particularly in the writings of Marsh (1864) (see Lowenthal, 1958), but it took 40 years for this fact to carry social and political significance. Action and reaction are equal and opposite: in the social laws of physics the ability to destroy produces a desire to conserve.
3. The conservation movement was propelled by the powerful force of contemporary social reform. The turn of the century was also associated with the progressive principle which in essence fought for the wise use of resources for the many rather than for the powerful and selfish few. In effect this was a reaction against big business and centralised economic power, a reaction which is possibly being reincarnated at the present time.

With the reaction against social Darwinism came a desire for the control of resources by the people for the people (McConnell, 1965).
4. This period also marked the beginning of scientific rationality and the interaction between the elected decision-maker and the nonelected professional expert (Hays, 1959). There was a reaction against unthinking exploitation in favour of the principles of sound management and wise use. These ideas began with forests, but spread to parks, water, soils, and even human resources (Nash, 1968).

The changing concept of conservation
Conservation is a philosophy which is directed at the manner and timing of resource use, and has been subject to various interpretations of an economic and political nature. The literature surrounding the development and meaning of conservation is voluminous and notably diffuse (Ciriacy-Wantrup, 1952; Price, 1955; Scott, 1955; Jarrett, 1958; Herfindahl, 1961; Nash, 1968). The word itself stems from the practice of the British in India, where forest areas called 'conservancies' were protected to provide sufficient cover for the maintenance of soil stability and the control of surface runoff (Pinchot, 1947). Since then the term has been used to identify various periods of political activity either when public policy was directed at better management of resources, or when the political interests of certain resource-using groups were threatened. The history of the conservation movement in the United States illustrates this point. The emergence of various 'conservation eras' coincided with public alarm over specific environmental crises, the emergence of a technical elite, and the dominance of a powerful and sympathetic President (Udall, 1963) (Table 1.2). The focus of conservation policy has shifted from protection of the public domain (1890–1920) Hays, 1959; Griffith, 1958) through regional multiple resources planning (1935–1943) (Lilienthal, 1944; Clapp, 1955; Griffith, 1958), to national strategic safety (1960–64), and finally to environmental quality and the dignity of life (President's Science Advisory Committee, 1965).

As a result, conservation as a philosophy has been subject to various interpretations over time as man's appraisal of his environment has shifted and as his goals have altered. Conservation itself is not a static concept nor can it be precisely defined. In fact, it defies accurate translation into precise operational terms, and indeed suffers from being ambiguous in interpretation and shifting, inconsistent and sometimes contradictory in its perceived objectives.

Basic dichotomies in the conservation concept
Reduced to its basic meaning, conservation can be visualised as a philosophical and conceptual framework involving preferences and choice within which resources are allocated. It only becomes operationally significant when perceived supply of any given resource appears to be

Table 1.2. Tabular representation of the American conservation movement.

Period	Environmental values	Crisis	Conservationist–Scientist	President	Action
1850–1890	'laissez-faire'	no notable crises	G. P. Marsh appeals for man–nature harmony and responsibility in resource use	no sympathetic President	designation of Yosemite and Yellowstone National Parks; some concern over forestry and wildlife; Powell's survey of arid lands
1890–1920	rise of welfare economies; government intervention	end of frontier; recognition of man's destructive capability; depletion of renewable resources	McGee, Newell, Muir	T. Roosevelt sympathetic and dynamic	White House conference; beginnings of a national resource inventory; conservation becomes a political movement
1920–1933	postwar return to 'laissez-faire'	further depletion of renewable resources	no one of note	no sympathetic President	resource development agency conflict; segmented resource policy
1933–1943	government intervention; rational resources planning	Great Depression; dust bowl; widespread soil erosion	Bennett, A. Leopold, Lilienthal	F. D. Roosevelt	national resource planning; multipurpose river development; soil conservation movement
1943–1960	postwar return to 'laissez-faire'	no notable crises	no one of note	no sympathetic President	interagency rivalry; limited purpose resource development; no coordinated policies
1960–	cooperation responsibility by public and private sectors	national strategic safety; threat of environmental collapse	Udall, Carson, White, Cole, Bates	J. F Kennedy, L. B. Johnson, R. N. Nixon	search for cooperative environmental policies; regional economic improvement; rational resources planning through benefit cost, systems analysis and program budgeting; public awareness; public action groups

unable to meet existing or projected demands. Something has to be done
to increase the supply, decrease the demand, or both; that is, the
objective of conservation is to adjust the perceived future supply – demand
disparity. The nature of this adjustment may be conveniently expressed
in terms of four basic dichotomies (Figure 1.3).

1. The *amount* of adjustment (*how much*) will lie somewhere in the
preservation–development continuum: that is, some will be left and some
will be used up. In some cases where multiple uses are incompatible, the
decision may have to be far more discrete than this: for example, when
a proposed reservoir threatens a unique canyon or a priceless historical
monument.

2. The *timing* of the adjustment (*when*) (and this affects the amount of
adjustment to some extent) will be found somewhere on the present–
future continuum. Again, a decision regarding the timing of resource use
may not be mututally compatible for all component uses. It may not be
possible to develop part of a resource now and leave some for later,
particularly where present use impedes future flexibility of choice. Some
economists have based their philosophy of conservation upon this
temporal dichotomy (Ciriacy-Wantrup, 1952; Scott, 1955), and indeed
by so doing have provided an important theoretical foundation for the
discourse.

3. A third form of adjustment is related to the *location* (*where*) of the
gainers and losers (*for whom, by whom*), and involves the question of
whether conservation be initiated in the public sector or the private
sector, or some combination of the two. The question here also pivots
around the conflict between the values of personal initiative and private
enterprise, on the one hand, and social responsibility and the public
consensus, on the other hand (Milliman, 1962; Krutilla, 1966a).

4. Allied to this, and introducing a fourth dichotomous dimension to the
philosophy of conservation, is the distinction between science and
conscience, between rigorous systematic analyses and spiritual and ethical
values (Weaver, 1965).

  None of the dichotomies is exclusive of any other. For example, the
amount and timing of use is thoroughly interconnected with the locus of

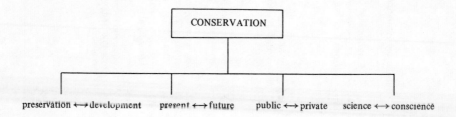

Figure 1.3. The four basic dichotomies in conservation.

decision and the nexus of facts and values that help guide final choice. Nor are any of these dichotomies simple to resolve. Indeed, the sheer difficulty of optimising adjustments between each of these four sets of extremes (in fact, this may not be possible) has largely accounted for the ambiguity and inconsistency that tends to be associated with conservation objectives

Conservation—a many-sided focus of study

Conservation cannot be fully visualised from the standpoint of any one discipline, for it really represents the coalescence of a number of interacting themes (Barnett and Morse, 1963) (Figure 1.4). Each of these themes extends into the domain of the others, and over time various combinations of approaches will emerge as being more relevant and vital according to the perceived crises in resource availability. At the broadest conceptual level is the viewpoint of the philosophical naturalists (Thoreau, 1893; Glacken, 1967; Tuan, 1967, 1968a) who viewed resources in theological, metaphysical, and psychic terms. This approach probes into the legacies of classical philosophy, where nature was visualised as the progenitor of life, and the nurturer of life-sustaining processes, where man and nature were bound by divine creation. Man and nature are entirely indivisible according to this view, for man is the guardian of the earth, and earth is the life force for man. The union is both symbolically and biologically inextricable (Kates, 1966b). An essential component of the philosophical stance is the consideration of ethics. The contribution of ethics to the philosophy of conservation has most brilliantly been

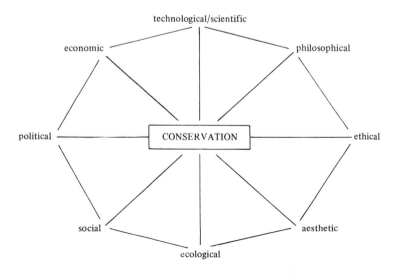

Figure 1.4. Conservation—a fusion of approaches.

discussed by Leopold (1949), who first proposed the idea of 'ecological conscience'—a framework for a man–land ethic in resource management. Ethics involve the concepts of right and wrong and of duty and obligation. The question of right and wrong is largely value-based and derives from our cultural traditions and mores. Akin to this, duties and obligations involve a sense of responsibility and due regard for the interest of other resource users and society as a whole, and towards the fundamental processes that constitute the biophysical environment.

A closely related approach is that provided by the ecological perspective. Broadly, there are three ways in which man can approach his environment: he can attempt to conquer it (for example, by constructing a dam across a river to control floods), he can succumb to it (for example, by accepting the flood and moving off the flood plain altogether), or he can cooperate with it (for example, by adjusting his flood plain occupancy to the perceived flood intensity/frequency and by protecting those structures which are still susceptible to the flood hazard). In the last case, he elects to study consciously what nature is trying to achieve (her goals) and the processes by which she is attempting to bring these about (her strategies and tactics), and adjust his own strategies and tactics to harmonise with those of nature. Failure to recognise the warning signals when man's tactics are at strife with those of nature has resulted in the past in widespread undesirable consequences involving environmental disturbances which have aroused considerable public concern.

The aesthetic viewpoint is essentially a plea for the preservation of natural beauty. Beauty is not an easy concept to define nor to evaluate, for it is fleeting, elusive, personal, and subjective, depending on the emotional, spiritual, mental, and intellectual state of the observer (Kates, 1966a). A pleasing landscape is aesthetically attractive owing to its sense of identity, relatedness, and meaning, and though it may not be functional in the sense of being directly useful, nevertheless, it does have a purpose and meaning for it is made up of carefully juxtaposed functioning parts. Discussion of the aesthetic values in conservation inevitably brings up the question of use or functionalism versus beauty and nonfunctionalism. The issue centres around the philosophy that we may wish to protect and enhance an object or a view purely for its own sake rather than for its functional (monetary) value to us. It is essentially the dichotomy of spiritualism versus materialism in our culture. There is also some argument as to whether beauty is synonymous with uniqueness or relatedness and meaning. Uniqueness cannot provide a *prima facie* case for being beautiful or worthy of preservation, for an ugly object may also be a unique one. Rather we should concentrate upon the concept of *misfits,* that is, phenomena that appear out of place or nonpurposeful with their surroundings when appraising aesthetic value (Leopold, 1969).

The aesthetic component of conservation is largely nonquantifiable, but it is of the utmost importance for it influences judgement through its role in our value schema.

The issue of conservation philosophy and the public interest has received increasing attention from political scientists and students of public administration. In the past, as Barnett and Morse (1963) have pointed out, their contribution has tended to be rather selective and empirical with few insights into the formulation of public policy, the clarification of issues, and the development of guidelines for future concerted action. However, these writings did provide important conceptual foundations as to the manner in which governments became involved in conservation and the political struggle over the control and development of natural resources. The viewpoints tended to develop along two clearly defined paths. On the one hand, resource allocation was visualised as a complex bargaining process energised by the value schema of politically-motivated groups (Wengert, 1955). This view was likened to the market process where bidding took place not in dollars but in political property (favours, political debts, election promises, and so on), and gains and losses were measured in terms of influence and prestige. Only with the resolution of competing forces will any meaningful consensus emerge as to the concept of the public interest. The other view portrays resource allocation as a quasi-monopolistic process where relatively centralised decision units control use subject to minimal constraints and separate from a broad expression of public wants (Maass, 1951; Ostrom, 1953). The criticism here was directed more at the bureaucratic process, which tended to insulate and isolate decision units from the effects of their policies and to entrench traditional concepts at the expense of maintaining flexibility. In recent years the focus has shifted towards a more probing analysis of the political decision-making process, a more conscious search for the public consensus, and the need for more penetrating policy guidelines towards the environment as an integrated resource management concept (see Chapters 5, 6, and 7).

Although it must be stressed that none of these approaches acts in isolation, the contribution of economists in developing a theory of resource allocation is probably the most comprehensive and fundamental. The economic viewpoint attempts to express the relationship between willingness to pay to satisfy wants via the willingness to sacrifice other wants, and in so doing has developed an important body of theory as to the manner and timing of resource allocation (Eckstein, 1958; Krutilla and Eckstein, 1958; McKean, 1958; Hirshleifer et al., 1960; Barnett and Morse, 1963). The economic theory of resource allocation rests upon the assumptions of efficiency and the concept of maximisation of net returns. Net returns are maximised when the marginal value of goods and services consumed just equals the marginal costs involved in producing them.

At this point any increase in resource use or shift between resource uses would be inefficient, in the sense that greater marginal costs would be expended for lesser marginal returns. Unfortunately, this premise relies upon assumptions about the knowledge of supply and demand, about the clarity and consistency of human wants, about the quantification of willingness to pay, and about the separation of resource wants into neatly packaged commodities whose value is internal to the consumer. We shall see (Chapter 2) that none of these assumptions exists in the real world, and that considerable conceptual difficulties are encountered, which are by no means simple to overcome.

The geographer has also made an important contribution to the theory and appraisal of conservation, for he can carry the analysis provided by these approaches one step further by relating cause and effect over space and time. By so doing, he is in a position to evaluate the impact of resource decisions upon the landscape (the biophysical environment), and upon groups and individuals (the sociopolitical environment) who are using and valuing elements of the landscape in relation to their own particular desires and preferences. In addition, because of his traditonal concern with the man–environment relationship, the geographer can provide valuable insights into the processes by which public attitudes towards resources are formed and expressed, and how they in turn affect public decision and behaviour in a given environmental situation. In particular, he is well qualified to recognise and assess the spatial linkages that are created when the effects of a given resource use impinge upon the activities of other individuals and groups and their evaluation of the landscape.

Apart from their interest in the man–nature theme, geographers have made a number of valuable contributions to the philosophy and practice of conservation. In fact, the first 'textbook' about conservation consisted of a number of remarkable essays edited by a geologist, Van Hise (1910), which served as a model for later contributions in this field (Parkins and Whitaker, 1939; Whitaker and Ackerman, 1951; Smith, 1951). These works were significant, not simply because they allied principle and practice in the conservation of natural resources, but, in addition, they presented a much needed inventory of resource use and misuse across the United States and pointed out the principles and processes that were involved for increasing resource availability. Whitaker and Ackerman (1951) were among the first to coin the phrase 'conservational resource management' and to clarify some of the objectives and organising concepts of this movement, particularly the need for individual responsibility, social action, and international cooperation. Geographers were also searching for a clearer philosophy of conservation, and a number of articles appeared in the years between 1930 and 1960 which help to clarify some of the confused thinking, while bearing in mind the problems of application (Innis, 1938; Whitaker, 1941; Fairchild, 1949; White, 1949; Price, 1955). More recently geographers have helped to bridge the gap between the old conservation based on emotionalism and tangible natural resources and the new conservation with its emphasis on rational allocation and amenity resources. Ullman (1954) first expounded in the latter vein, while Zobler (1962) and Duncan (1962) helped to illuminate the changes in attitudes to resource conservation that were taking place, as absolute resource scarcity becomes increasingly perceived and metropolitanisation engulfs most of the world's population.

The concept of resources in the modern age

As man's appraisal of his environment has altered, so the concept of resources has changed in meaning. Our amazing ingenuity for technological substitution, the tremendous rise in the demand for services as opposed to primary raw materials, the increasing elaboration of commodity processing (so that the intrinsic value of raw materials is dropping relative to the value added), and the recent upsurge in the public interest in environmental quality, have led to a new and much broader interpretation of resources (Ciriacy-Wantrup and Parsons, 1967). These new resources Perloff (1969) has termed 'amenity resources', and can be subsumed under the general rubric of environmental quality. As an example, Perloff (1969) lists peculiar combinations of environmental phenomena, such as climate, topography, attractive view, and open space, as being more highly valued by increasingly urban populations.

The swing in public preferences towards environmental quality management is the outcome of a number of complex factors. As income levels rise and the standard increases with it, so the demand for durable consumer goods slackens in favour of 'superior goods' (Ayres, 1969). This demand for quality tends to increase exponentially as incomes rise, reflecting the decreasing marginal utility of consumer durables in the face of increasing environmental deterioration. In other words, there is a general willingness to forgo a second colour television set in order to enjoy cleaner air, and so on. Also, environmental deterioration is becoming more obvious to the layman owing to the influence of the mass media and to tangible personal experience, so that public awareness is now much more widespread. In addition, public concern is aroused when man's unthinking acts create serious environmental crises which may lead to very undesirable long-term repercussions. Examples include the Torrey Canyon disaster off the Cornwall coast in 1967, the discovery of DDT in the fatty tissues of penguins in the Antarctic, increasing dust concentrations in the upper atmosphere, and the not unreal possibility that sea pollution may inhibit the growth of marine plankton which furnish about 75% of the world's oxygen supply. Possibly of more immediate impact is the assault made upon all senses by day-to-day living in large cities. And, along with general acceptance of the philosophy that man should attempt to live in harmony with nature, comes a very genuine fear that environmental quality may be denied to us, or at least to our children and to our children's children. As in any decreasing supply situation, so willingness to sacrifice other more available goods increases. Finally, there are some grounds to believe that many people are becoming increasingly pessimistic about the future of man and the maintenance of certain values and symbols of those values that are cherished. For example, destruction of wildlife is associated with the overthrow of the feelings of a sensitive minority. Increasing social unrest, particularly amongst young people today, is in part a reaction to the recognition that the patterns of life as it is and life as it should be are diverging. Associated with this feeling is a demand that part at least of corporate profits should be channelled into improving environmental quality.

The modern concept of resources places greater emphasis upon the intangible values, such as quality, variety, and ecological harmony, and visualises resources as 'bundles' of existing and potential uses (the multipurpose concept), where the importance and variety of the constituent functions vary over time in accord with changes in technological and organisational ability and social appraisal (the dynamic concept). The ability with which the 'old resources' can be renovated, substituted, or extracted from the most minute original concentrations has dampened the fears that natural resources are running out and quietened the demands that certain specified quantities should be preserved for the use of future generations. Indeed, promoting a contrary argument, some economists have shown that increasing scarcity has served to stimulate technological advance rather than retard it, and that, by utilising the resources of today, greater gains can be made for tomorrow (Barnett and Morse, 1963; Burton and Kates, 1964a). But it is becoming more apparent to most economists (Krutilla, 1967a, 1967b) that there is a difficulty (if not an impossibility) in providing meaningful substitutes for such socially valued phenomena as unique landscapes, historical monuments, and other artifacts of our cultural legacy. The implication is clear: as our technological society makes more demands upon environmental quality and the preservation of man's heritage, so the intangible and spiritual values embodied in these phenomena will become increasingly more important. Society's willingness to pay for environmental quality should thus increase exponentially into the future.

This newer concept of resources introduces serious management problems, since being neither tangible nor individual, nor entirely products of the biophysical environment, they cannot be owned or valued in the market place, nor can they be expropriated without creating external effects (either positive or negative) impinging upon other users or upon the biophysical environment. Nor can such resources be readily packaged and sold as individual units. Indeed, no pricing mechanism exists for the use of such resources, for no social institution of ownership and exchange exists at present which would permit the striking of an economic balance between incompatible uses through the operation of the competitive free market (Kneese and Bower, 1968; Ayres, 1969; Ayres and Kneese, 1969a). Thus the given demand situation for such resources cannot be assessed at any given point in time, nor is the available supply (in terms of quantity and quality) known. These resources come under the heading of public goods or 'common property resources' and include such commodities as air, water, and the landscape, which exist in myriads of different combinations and are employed and evaluated in myriads of different ways. Sometimes the phrase 'fleeting' or 'fugitive' resources is used to denote particular combinations of intangible factors (silence, beauty, colour, shape, and so on), which are difficult to preserve and frequently impossible to recreate. In the face of our rapid scientific and technological achievements these are the resources that count, but they are so much more difficult to define, to evaluate, and to allocate than the old ones. As such, proper management and clear social guidelines are urgently needed, and the creation and implementation of such guidelines represent the present challenge in resource management.

The 'new' conservation
Accompanying these shifts in attitudes towards resources, it is to be expected that there would be significant changes in the modern philosophy of conservation. This is indeed the case. The factors that have brought about such changes are complex and difficult to identify clearly. In essence, it is the sum of these forces acting in differing intensities at various times that has caused the new trends. These forces are isolated here only to help clarify the picture.

1. The closing of the frontier has increased speculation that many natural resources are finite and diminishing and that the costs of exploitation are increasing, as the search for new supplies requires deeper wells, less accessible deposits, and lower grade ores. Despite the optimism of some economists who feel that owing to increased productivity and accumulating knowledge "(a) limit may exist but can be neither defined nor specified in economic terms" (Barnett and Morse, 1963, p.11), most governments are now concerned that supplies of natural resources are not limitless (President's Materials Policy Commission, 1952) and that some degree of government intervention is necessary to regulate the timing and use of resource complexes.

2. Associated with this, the continuation of the cold war and the formation of major military alliances has placed renewed emphasis upon national security and the need to preserve sufficient reserves within national boundaries.

3. The recognition that environmental quality is becoming more precious as it appears to be less available has meant a need to apply management principles which aim to maximise the combination of resource outputs, while minimising the social losses associated with excessive environmental destruction (National Academy of Sciences–National Research Council, 1966a, 1968). The emphasis here is upon preserving options for future action and for identifying more clearly the time distribution of social benefits attendant on the preservation of unique environmental values (Krutilla, 1967a, 1967b; Carlin, 1968; Parker and Crutchfield, 1968).

4. The concern with public property and fugitive resources has brought with it a realisation that existing social and economic institutions are incapable of dealing adequately with the proper use and allocation of such resources. Because the market allocation process has failed, it is inevitable that greater pressures will be placed upon government intervention and financing in the management process, though this point is still under some contention by those who have proposed alternative solutions (Hirshleifer *et al.*, 1960; Milliman, 1962; Krutilla, 1966a; Dales, 1968).

5. The fact that previous efforts at resource development have failed clearly calls for a new approach. Thus, while expenditures on flood control have risen steadily, the costs of flood damage have increased at a greater rate (White, 1964); while expenditures on irrigation supplies are astronomical, drought is no less of a threat (Saarinen, 1966); while public aid in soil conservation has risen, soil erosion has not been significantly reduced (Clawson and Held, 1965), and generally the impact of environmental hazards is becoming more costly rather than less so despite efforts to reduce damages (Burton *et al.*, 1968b). New strategies are therefore called for, aimed not simply at control but at the reduction of social distress and the maximisation of social well-being (White, 1966a). Resource management which is aimed at the best combination of means and objectives has superseded resource development which merely sought to minimise tangible costs.

6. Finally, the threat to the world's resource base is significantly increased by the rapid growth of population and the increasing demands for material comfort as standards of living rise (Ackerman, 1959). The Second World War showed clearly how resources can be consumed and destroyed on an unprecedented scale: but this is trivial compared with the potential demand of nations emerging from subsistence. Few students of the problem are optimistic (Brown, 1954; Brown, Bonner, and Weir, 1957; Fisher and Potter, 1964), and most are direly pessimistic (Vogt, 1948; Osborne, 1953; Ackerman, 1959; Borgstrom, 1965). The whole question of resource availability and environmental quality hangs in the balance of future population mangement. This is the major issue facing all governments and resource managers. Because of its complexity and

scale the question of population management is not developed here, though the reader should bear in mind that all attempts toward the better management of resources will come to no avail should we fail to limit our own growth (Ohlin, 1967).

Conservation and resource management

The concept of conservation can therefore be visualised as an amalgam of interacting forces which are embodied in the viewpoints of a number of disciplines. There is no central focus to this philosophy, no concrete issue around which it coalesces and becomes operational. Rather it is an ambiguous, vaguely conceived notion which reflects great disparities in the views of its proponents (Herfindahl, 1961). Furthermore, it is subject to subtle yet important shifts in emphasis over time, which further reduce the clarity and consistency of its expression. Because of this and because conservation is still popularly misidentified with the protests of naturalists seeking to protect apparently unique associations of flowers, rocks, and wildlife, it has been felt wise to substitute the phrase 'resource management' for conservation. Resource management is a more comprehensive and positive term than conservation, and may be defined as a process of decision making whereby resources are allocated over space and time according to the needs, aspirations, and desires of man within the framework of his technological inventiveness, his political and social institutions, and his legal and administrative arrangements. Resource management should be visualised as a conscious process of decision involving judgment, preference, and commitment, whereby certain desired resource outputs are sought from certain perceived resource combinations through the choice among various managerial, technical, and administrative alternatives. Resource management should therefore be conceived as the new conservation (*Daedalus*, 1967). It tends to emphasise rationality over emotionalism, ethics over economics, and ecology over engineering. Resource management involves strategies of action involving computations of tactics and methods and a variety of objectives. The emphasis is upon flexibility and the minimisation of long-term environmental catastrophes, while maximising net social welfare over time. The allocation process is dominated neither by the market place nor by the quasi-political forum, but by a combination of social, cultural, economic, and institutional processes that strive for the best solution, but which inevitably must seek compromise.

Resource management is thus becoming increasingly concerned with the protection and enhancement of environmental quality and the establishment of new guidelines for the public use of such common property resources as air, water, and the landscape. In the search for an optimal philosophy, a number of fundamental difficulties have been encountered, each of which has led to the emergence of new research needs. In Figure 1.5 the major trends in resource management are portrayed schematically to emphasise their interdependence and common objective—the enhancement of net social welfare over a given investment period.

Chapters 2 and 3 assess the various evaluation techniques which are being used at present to aid decisions as to the manner and timing of resource management. The quantification of 'cost' and 'benefit' over time provides the central theme, and again no single systematic approach is found to be satisfactory. Chapter 4 is devoted to the question of improving the efficiency of resource use, particularly through various means of controlling demand by relating the costs of resource inputs more closely to the total costs of use, and by identifying more specifically the location, incidence, and frequency of gains and losses. Chapter 5 probes the whole concept of environment from the philosophical, ecological, and ethical viewpoints, and attempts to identify the problems faced by policy-makers in their search for an overall public policy with regard to the total environment. In addition, this chapter surveys and assesses the recent work done on the role and formation of public attitudes towards the environment and the relevance of this research for public policy. Chapter 6 follows up this discussion with an appraisal of the research aimed at understanding and interpreting the values and preferences of professional resource managers and administrators. Chapter 7 attempts to develop a general decision model for resources

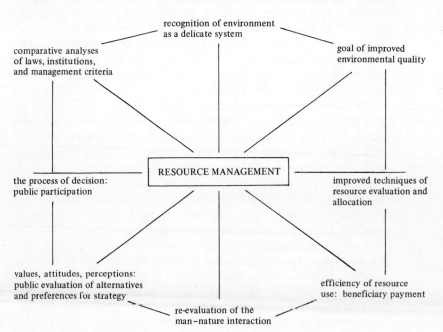

Figure 1.5. Dominant research themes in resource management.

management based upon the findings of the previous six chapters. Finally, new perspectives are reviewed in Chapter 8 and a number of interesting future lines of research are assessed. The aim of this chapter (and indeed of the monograph generally) is to stimulate the interested reader to search for useful future research possibilities in this exciting and ever changing field.

Feasibility and evaluation in resource management

From the discussion so far, it is clear that resource management is in reality a most complex phenomenon because resources are interlinked in use over space and time, yet are appraised separately by different groups according to their needs and aspirations. And, because resources play such a vital role in our economy, resource management cannot be dissociated from the wider fields of planning and regional development. We have also noted that conflicts abound not simply between the incompatible opportunities that a given resource complex offers, but even as to the very aims of the programme. And, even if we assume that a clear statement of goals is available, our problems are by no means solved since, for each set of objectives, there are a number of alternative management techniques available involving a complicated array of technical, economic, social, political, and legal parameters. So at the core of the resource management process there is the basic issue of resource allocation, how much to use, when to use it, where the use is most demanded, what quality of use is desired, who desires it (or who does not desire it), and so on. This process involves assessments as to quantity, quality, space, and time, not only with regard to the actual employment of resources, but also with consideration of repercussive side effects of the sociobiophysical environment.

This assessment procedure we can term evaluation. The concern is to devise a mechanism by which we can evaluate the benefits (desirable productive streams of goods and services) and costs (a combination of capital expenditures and undesirable side effects) of alternative resource combinations and management techniques in relation to the achievement of desired goals. In this chapter we shall deal specifically with the problem of resource allocation. A number of ingenious devices have been employed to enable better decisions to be made regarding the amount, quality, timing, and whereabouts of resource use, but each has to face up to the problem of evaluating the costs and benefits stemming from different combinations of resource use, as these are distributed over space and time and impinge upon the desires and aspirations of different social groups on the landscape.

At the same time it is important to realise that the recognition of the need for and significance of allocation techniques depend to a considerable extent upon the resource user's concern over possible resource conflicts, and his attitude towards possible resource scarcities in the future. If he considers that resources are plentiful, or that cheap technical solutions to provide more resource benefit streams are readily available, or that the development of one resource is largely independent of other resource uses, or any combination of these factors, it is doubtful whether there will be any attempt made to evaluate a proposed project in any rigorous or systematic fashion. In the past, this was generally the case. Few, if any, allocative devices were used, and resource development practice fell prey to flexible legal controls, political bargaining, and extensive opportunism.

The pattern was sadly predictable. A long period of single-purpose resource use would end abruptly with some form of crisis, usually in the form of a national catastrophe, such as drought, flood, depletion or extinction of wild game, or fish kill. The underlying causes of these crises were rarely perceived—increasing water-demanding agricultural use in the face of variability of rainfall regimes, excessive encroachment on the flood plain with limited knowledge of flood intensity and frequency, overkill in excess of natural biological replenishment, leakage or inadequate control over poisonous waste discharges. The fault was attributed to man's inability to control Nature rather than his mismanagement and limited vision. Hence expedient technological solutions—irrigation schemes, dams, canals, and such like—were demanded and were successful, for they appeased powerful voters, provided jobs and stimulated economic opportunity, while allaying fears that such crises would recur, which, of course, they inevitably did (Hart, 1957a, 1957b; White, 1969).

This vicious cycle of crisis and expedient solution began to be broken with the recognition that resources were interlinked, and thus single-purpose solutions impinged detrimentally upon other resource management programmes, and that, as both the intensity and variety of demands upon the resource base increased, so the possibility of resource scarcity threatened (White, 1969). Furthermore, it became apparent, particularly in the United States, that resource development agencies justified their vast and expensive projects with no recognisable standardised procedures, with the result that there was no effective means whereby Congress (or any other decision body) could evaluate and compare either the need or the adequacy of the various proposals placed before it (Maass, 1951).

All this led to the need to devise some procedure whereby widely differing resource programmes could be compared and evaluated on the grounds of technical feasibility and economic efficiency, to rank these diverse proposals in terms of their contribution to the national and regional economy, and generally to bring about the best combination of resources with the minimum of conflict. This emphasis on maximising output (benefits) and minimising input (costs) (that is, maximising net returns) led to the search for and development of evaluation techniques based upon the mathematical principles of optimisation.

The rationale which came to be employed rested squarely upon the constructs of economic efficiency. The theory itself depends on a number of rather critical assumptions, namely that (1) inputs and outputs are separate, (2) production and consumption functions are independent and discrete, (3) a demand for a resource or combination of resources can be identified, (4) that consumer preferences for different combinations of resource uses are known, (5) that these preferences can be compared from one consumer to another, (6) that resource use is independent of third party physical and/or economic external or internal effects, (7) that resource benefits can be conveniently packaged and quantified in economic terms, and (8) that all this takes place in a well-functioning economy, where decisions are decentralised at the consumer level (Samuelson, 1954; Krutilla and Eckstein, 1958; Musgrave, 1959).

Under such circumstances each productive resource should be used up to the point where the cost of an additional input is just equal to its contribution to the value of production. In order to obtain any unit of a resource, a user must forgo a certain number of units of other resources, either because the use of that particular resource impedes his use of another resource (for example, maximum timber output is not compatible with optimum wildlife management), or because, by releasing capital, he is denying himself the availability of spending money and other factors of production in other sectors of the economy. Thus the value (market price) of a resource represents the opportunity cost, that is, its contribution to the value of output in all alternative uses (Krutilla and Eckstein, 1958). In this way, consumers seeking maximum satisfaction from a given income will tend to allocate their expenditures so that the last dollar spent for any particular resource will yield an amount of satisfaction equal to that yielded by a marginal dollar spent on any other resource. Thus market price reflects marginal valuation and can be employed as a measure of a consumer's evaluation or want satisfaction derived from the use of that resource.

So much for the theory. We shall see that none of the above assumptions is tenable in the real world, with the result that considerable distortions from the optimum can be expected. There are a number of complex reasons for this divergence, of course, but probably the most fundamental is the fact that resources, especially amenity resources, possess certain peculiar attributes that sharply differentiate them from the concept of common market goods. These attributes are the outcome of the functional and spatial indivisibility of resources and as such are of fundamental concern to the geographer. In each case they impede the proper functioning of the market and raise serious doubts as to the validity of a purely economic approach to evaluation and allocation in resource management. It is convenient to distinguish between the spatial and economic components of these distorting attributes, though it should be realised that no factor ever acts in isolation. The spatial components include collectivity, externalities, and scale, whereas those of primarily economic interest are direct and indirect benefits and costs, intangibles, opportunity costs, interest rate, uncertainty and risk, and unemployment effects.

Collectivity

Certain benefits and costs associated with resource management are universal in character, in the sense that they cannot be individually packaged and sold but must be provided for a group of consumers regardless of individual preferences and evaluation. Included under this heading would be flood protection, pollution abatement, fishery protection, wildlife preservation, and the enhancement of aesthetic attractiveness. Since individuals cannot state their preferences or valuation in the market place through the usual procedure of willingness to pay, collective benefits and collective costs can only be distributed and paid for on a unified areal basis (for example, regional financing). One method of evaluating collective benefits on an economic basis is to calculate the least-cost alternative to provide a similar supply of goods and services. Thus an estimate of the benefits gained for the construction of a navigation canal can be related to the difference in cost between the canal and other transportation means (roads, rail, and so on) to provide a similar movement of goods (Kuiper, 1966).

Externalities

Resource uses are too closely intertwined to permit separate management of any one sector without impinging upon the production and development of at least one of the other sectors within the total complex. Such a relationship is called an externality or spillover effect or third party effect, for its impact on an unrelated third party is not reflected in the input–output calculus of the individual firm, and there is no market mechanism whereby a consumer can pay either to consume it or to avoid it (McKean, 1958; Buchanan and Stubblebine, 1962). Externalities are positive where the relationships are complementary (for example, the release of protectively stored floodwaters may be beneficial for dilution of waste discharges downstream), and negative where the outputs of one function impinge upon the inputs of another (for example, the loss of fish as a result of a poisonous waste discharge). Externalities may have a strong spatial component, for the effects of one function may be spatially removed from the management of another. Thus a reservoir provides benefits both on site (recreation, power, water supply) and downstream (flood protection, pollution dilution).

It is convenient to distinguish between technological and pecuniary spillover effects (McKean, 1958). In the case of technological spillovers the interaction between one activity and another alters the physical production possibilities of the other party or the amount of satisfaction derived by consumers of the affected resource [for example, where a power dam reduces the commerical fish catch (Crutchfield, 1962)]. Insofar as technological spillovers do affect net satisfaction (net social welfare) they should be included. Pecuniary spillovers, on the other hand, involve purely a spatial (distributional) transfer of income (for example, where a new highway bypasses a small town), and as such should not be included, since we are concerned only with incremental change as a result of investment and not with changes in sunk costs.

The classical discussion of externalities has been limited to consideration of the two-party effect (Buchanan and Stubblebine, 1962). Because of the importance of environmental quality and owing to the very real world-wide repercussions of certain actions on delicate environmental mechanisms, it is now necessary to look at multi-party effects. In fact, some economists (Ayres and Kneese, 1969b; Kneese and d'Arge, 1969) argue that such external diseconomies are now so pervasive in our economy that they should no longer be considered 'economic freaks' but should be integrated into a new body of economic theory. They conclude that the traditional input–output model of production–consumption should be modified to reflect an 'undistorted' economy, where factor prices include the costs of waste reduction, In fact, they go further and assert the need for strong public intervention to offset the effects of multi-party environmental diseconomies.

Scale
The identification and calculation of costs and benefits accruing from a project depend to some extent upon its geographical and economic scale. Thus a project large enough to bring about repercussions throughout the entire economy must be treated differently from a regional resource management project, where secondary effects, particularly the extent to which they affect the local economy (the multiplier effect), assume a greater meaning (Miller, 1961; Tolley, 1966);

Direct and indirect benefits and costs
Whether to include secondary or indirect benefits and costs in a feasibility analysis is another source of dispute. Most economists accept primary or direct benefits and costs (that is, benefits accruing directly as a result of a project) as being legitimate factors when accounting is carried out within the framework of national income gains and losses. Secondary benefits, which may be 'induced by' or may 'stem from' the completion of a project [for example, wages paid to employees working in a food-processing plant whose inputs stem purely from increased yields due to a local irrigation scheme (Sewell *et al.*, 1961)], are normally considered 'regional' or 'local' in nature and hence irrelevant in the context of national welfare (Ciriacy-Wantrup, 1964). Despite this, recent US water resource agency policy appears to favour the inclusion of secondary benefits in their accounting procedures (US, Water Resources Council, 1969). The dispute is important, for the handling of indirect benefits and costs is crucial in its impact on the choice of the project, the nature of repayment by beneficiaries, and the price of the primary goods and services generated by the project. In addition, it is difficult to dissociate

the inclusion of secondary effects from double counting and padding (Ciriacy-Wantrup, 1964).

Intangibles

In any economic allocation process some common yardstick of evaluation is necessary by which to compare production inputs and outputs. We have seen that this is commonly reflected by the consumer's marginal willingness to pay. However, some goods and services stemming from a resource management programme are essentially subjective, personal and internal in nature, and as such are difficult to identify in monetary terms. Such factors, because they cannot be evaluated in the market place, are sometimes referred to as 'extra-market goods'. These include such values as the visual beauty of a landscape, the preservation of a unique ecological habitat, or the satisfaction in preserving a nationally important landmark or historical monument. Intangible services such as these cannot easily be plugged into the quantifiable arithmetic associated with more tangible benefit streams, such as power output or increased crop yields, and in the past have tended to be overemphasised or underemphasised depending on the personal views of the decision makers, political pressures, and the nature of the proposed project.

Opportunity costs

Opportunity costs are of two kinds. One involves the value of benefits forgone in one resource sector owing to the selection of an incompatible alternative proposal, for example, the loss of productive farmland when the headwaters of a river are dammed for the purpose of floodwater retention. In such cases it is possible that the intangible costs involved may be of greater *social* value than the net *economic* worth of lost agricultural produce. The other kind of opportunity cost is fiscal in nature: under the constraint of a limited budget, expenditure in one resource sector causes the diversion of capital from other investment (Steiner, 1959, 1966).

Unemployment effects

While it is generally acknowledged that the market is an inadequate guide for the measurement of social and intangible benefits and costs, it is less widely realised that under conditions of relatively high unemployment, it is no longer acceptable to employ market prices of factor inputs as the relevant guide for tangible input costs (Haveman and Krutilla, 1968a, 1968b). For, as unemployment rates rise, the opportunity cost of employing otherwise idle labour and capital declines, so that the use of real prices of factor inputs is faulty. Recognising this deficiency, Haveman and Krutilla developed a model to improve the assessment of factor inputs in water resource investment projects. They concluded that factor prices should be adjusted downward by between 9% and 18% to account for the lowered opportunity costs when unemployment rises above 5%. The implication of their analysis is significant in the case of projects designed to alleviate severe regional unemployment, for it can render feasible a project whose nominal benefit–cost ratio is slightly less than unity.

Market imperfections

Where perfectly competitive conditions do not exist the theoretical investment decision rules are inappropriate. Unfortunately, in the real world a number of factors exist to distort the principles of pure competition. Included among these are the effects of monopolies and oligopolies (Krutilla, 1966a), the failure to achieve true marginal cost pricing (Dahl and Lindblom, 1953), and the ever present problem of risk and uncertainty. Risk is identified as the gamble that is taken in the face of unknown but probabilistic variations in supply and demand, while uncertainty includes the unpredictable occurrence of such factors as changes in the level of economic activity, technological innovations or new policy directives, which may make a project obsolete or redundant before its physical life is over. All of these issues are discussed fully by Prest and Turvey (1965).

Interest rate

The interest rate may be regarded as the opportunity cost of borrowed money on the assumption that capital investment in the present will produce increased returns in the future. The issue here centres on the timing of the cost and benefit streams. Rarely do costs and benefits accrue simultaneously over the life of a project. It is more common for costs to be lumped early in the life of the project and for benefits to extend some distance into the future. In some instances annual value of costs and benefits decreases over time to be negligible at some future point (this is usually calculated to be the economic life of the project). However, in the case of projects where environmental quality is being preserved, benefits (measured as net social value) may actually increase over time as aesthetic values increase in their desirability (Haveman, 1965; Krutilla, 1967a; Lind, 1968; Parker and Crutchfield, 1968).

But, whatever the time period, it is necessary that benefit and cost streams are adjusted to be comparable. The usual practice is to discount all future streams of both benefit and cost values to the common base of present value, namely, that value, which if invested at interest today would amount to the future payment if made at that time. The rate at which these value streams are discounted may be regarded as the interest rate (Grant and Ireson, 1964).

The interest rate at which money is borrowed to finance resource management projects is critical both in determining the economic justification of the project and in deciding upon the time distribution of expenditure. As a result much has been written concerning the meaning and significance of interest rates in resource management financing (Krutilla, 1961; Marglin, 1963; Feldstein, 1964; Lind, 1964; Haveman, 1965; Krutilla, 1966a; Marglin, 1966; Arrow, 1966). The issues revolve around six major factors.

1. To what extent should the interest rate reflect the borrowing rate in the public sector, or the private sector, or both?

2. To what extent should the interest rate be associated with a marginal social time preference function (Feldstein, 1964), and what is the role of intertemporal preference generally?

3. To what extent should the interest rate reflect the internal rate of return of the proposed investment?

4. To what extent should the interest rate in the public sector reflect the artificially depressed government rates (in the USA this means the coupon rates on Treasury Bonds) or currency yields (Krutilla, 1966a)?

5. To what extent should the interest rate reflect risk and uncertainty in the analysis of future benefits and costs?

6. Given the fact that costs and benefits occur at different times in the life of the investment, to what extent should costs be discounted at similar rates to or different rates from benefits to reflect the varying levels of uncertainty and risk for these two critical parameters (Haveman, 1965)?

The calculation of interest rate is a complicated and extremely difficult procedure in resource management, and is reflected in the tremendous variation of 'optimum rates' that are recommended by numerous experts (for a summary, see Haveman, 1965). All of the distorting economic and spatial factors outlined above are involved in the full computation of interest rate (Figure 2.1), and in the absence of clear guidelines it is clear that political forces and value judgements must play an important role. Certainly the tendency in both the USA and Britain is to rely heavily on the lower rates of the public sector cushioned by long-term loans and massive government credit, despite the fact that economists argue that such rates are artificially depressed (Fox and Herfindahl, 1964; Krutilla, 1966a).

The emergence of these major factors distorting the pure market concept of commodity valuation via willingness to pay resulted in the development of a body of economic theory designed to deal with the allocation of public goods, particularly with regard to the correct form and amount of public intervention (Krutilla, 1966a). This was first propounded by Pigou (1946), rehabilitated by Baumol (1952), and further developed by Samuelson (1954), Musgrave (1959), Margolis (1957), and Marglin (1966). It is upon the foundations of this considerable body of theory that present techniques in resource allocation are laid.

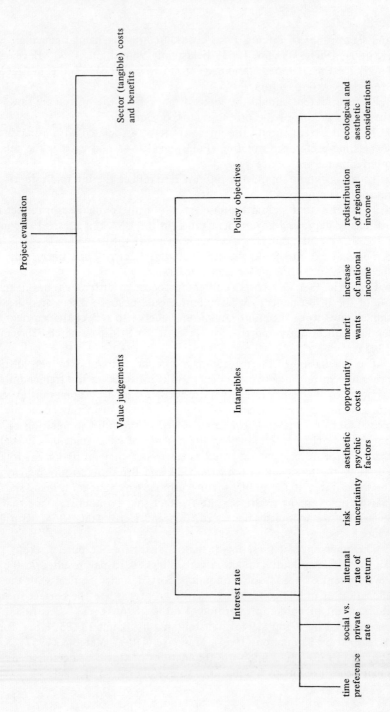

Figure 2.1. The complex process of project evaluation.

Benefit-cost analysis

The oldest and still the most commonly used resource allocation technique is benefit-cost (b-c) analysis. Although formally proposed in the USA in the early 1950's (US., Federal Interagency Committee on Water Resources, 1950), and later extended and refined (US., Federal Interagency Committee on Water Resources, 1958; Hufschmidt *et al.,* 1961; President's Water Resources Council, 1962; US, Water Resources Council, 1969), it was first employed in that country in 1908 to evaluate harbour navigation projects, and was implicitly built into the 1936 US Flood Control Act (Prest and Turvey, 1965). This Act, while conferring massive financial responsibility on the Federal Government for flood control programmes, required that economic feasibility be met when "the benefits to whomsoever they accrue must justify the costs".

Benefit-cost analysis is a technique for enumerating, evaluating, and comparing the benefits and costs that stem from the utilisation of a productive resource base. The economic theory upon which b-c analysis is based assumes that a desired objective is achieved by choosing the lowest-cost alternative of a number of alternatives designed to meet this objective, or, in the case where the quantity of resource use is specified (for example, a fiscal constraint), the appropriate choice is that alternative which maximises the desired objective at minimum cost. In terms of welfare, b-c analysis does attempt to maximise the net social benefits to that point of resource utilisation where the benefit accruing to any one set of consumers cannot be further increased without incurring further losses upon another set of consumers. This condition, where no one can be made better off by any change in the production function without making someone else worse off, thus decreasing total or net social welfare, is known as the 'Pareto optimum' and constitutes the fundamental theoretical underpinning of welfare economics (Rothenberg, 1961).

According to b-c theory, the ideal combination of resource use is that point where the present value of total net benefits (total benefits minus total costs) is maximised (Figure 2.2). At point X on Figure 2.2 the ratio between benefits and costs is at its greatest for the project, but the scale of the project is not maximised since an increase in costs (even though costs are now rising in relation to benefits) will still produce sufficient benefits to add to total net benefits. The optimal scale of development is reached when each component resource sector of the project is developed to the point of diminishing returns, that is, where the last increment of cost invested just equals the value of the benefit it produces. Theoretically, the construction of such a project makes the best use of all resources in the sense that no greater net gain could be produced elsewhere in the economy. Economic *feasibility* is justified by the condition that all discounted benefits must exceed discounted costs.

This is the well-known condition that the ratio of benefits to costs must exceed 1:1. (The criterion of economic feasibility should be distinguished from that of financial feasibility which is justified by the rate of return in investment from the project.)

B–c analysis does have merits as an allocation technique and is still widely used in evaluating the feasibility of resource management projects for the following reasons:

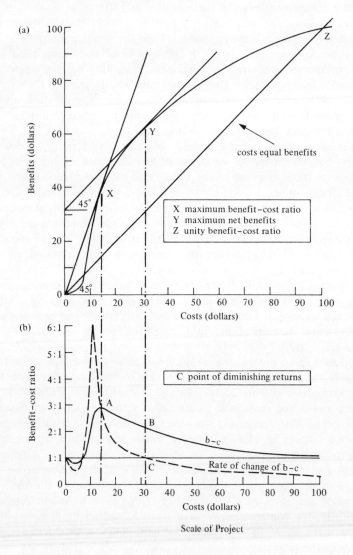

Figure 2.2. Benefit–cost relationships for various scales of development

(after Sewell *et al*, 1961).

1. It is simple to understand and relatively easy to calculate, for in essence it compares different cost and benefit streams stemming from a number of alternatives. Also, it does attempt to take the long view in the sense of analysing both short- and long-term benefits and costs, and the wide view by introducing the concepts of social costs and benefits and externalities.

2. By sifting out the uneconomic proposals (that is, where the b-c ratio is less than 1) it does provide a yardstick for measuring the relative feasibility of resource management programmes, whereby public money will achieve the most satisfying return.

3. On the assumption that a common procedure for calculation is adopted, b-c analysis does assist in establishing relative priorities among a group of alternative resource management proposals of a similar scale, and may also help in the sequence and timing of projects (Krutilla, 1960).

4. B-c analysis calls upon a detailed study and evaluation of each of the component resource uses that constitute the project and assists in identifying the location, intensity, and frequency of all benefits and costs, thereby helping to pinpoint specific beneficiaries. In other words, not only is b-c analysis concerned with what? how much? what type? and where? but also with who gains? who loses? how much? and how often?

5. While the evaluation of intangibles is difficult to reconcile within the b-c framework, such cost and benefit streams are placed in juxtaposition with more tangible ones, thereby providing at least some rationale for their inclusion in the decision-making process.

To sum up, b-c analysis is most relevant in a choice between resource management projects within one resource context, where the costs and benefits are relatively easily recognised and calculated (water resource management in preference to education or health programmes), and at a comprehensible scale (river basin as compared with national context) (Dorfman, 1965a).

The considerable complexity of economic and political issues that beset optimum resource allocation in the real world exerts severe constraints on these theoretical constructs of cost-benefit analysis where perfect knowledge of the market (no risk or uncertainty), quantifiable benefits and costs, explicit statements of individual utilities (preferences), and clear unambiguous objectives are assumed. Furthermore, the objective of maximising net social welfare relies upon equating individual marginal utilities, when clearly these will vary with income and a number of complex cultural factors and thus can neither be equated nor aggregated. In addition, there is considerable fuzziness as to the relationship between evaluation of benefits and reimbursement or compensation. The classical b-c model only requires that beneficiaries be willing to compensate losers and still be better off than when they started, but not that they actually do so (Lind, 1968).   The issue raised here is the age-old one of efficiency versus equity or social welfare, and relates to the incompatible objectives of attempting to maximise national economic growth, while adequately recognising the broader considerations of sociopolitical economic welfare (Maass, 1966).   A weakness of conventional b–c analysis is that resource management projects can be implemented to meet a variety of objectives, of which economic efficiency is only one. Maass (1966) has questioned how b–c analysis can be geared towards other objectives that would conflict with the constructs of efficiency, such as redistribution of national income, regional economic growth and increased aesthetic satisfaction, and concluded that a 'trade-off value' should be developed to indicate the discrepancy between efficiency and nonefficiency objectives.   Marglin (1963) has developed a suggestion by Dorfman (Maass *et al.*, 1962) and proposed a two-term objective function to overcome the problem of conflicting objectives.

At issue here is the consideration of the welfare implications when benefit-maximising criteria alone are applied in benefit–cost analysis, that is, when private investment dominates over possible broader-based public intervention.   This has led to the discussion that should one or more of the conditions necesary for the achievement of the Pareto optimum not be attained, then no solution, no matter how 'second best', will be satisfactory in safeguarding maximum welfare (Lipsey and Lancaster, 1956; Davis and Whinston, 1967).   This viewpoint has been criticised by Dorfman and Krutilla (Krutilla, 1961), who judge that it fails to take into account the dynamic and adjustable nature of investment, and that under certain circumstances appropriate public intervention is a sufficient condition to approximate the welfare maximum.   Kneese and d'Arge (1969) extend this point and show how the use of 'second best' can be developed to produce a model of the economy which allows for environmental externalities.

Undoubtedly the optimum will never be achieved.   But judicious use of benefit –cost analysis can point to the nature of divergence from a 'better solution' in cases where public intervention is short-circuited by private development.   For example, Krutilla and Eckstein (1958) compared the benefits and costs of two alternative proposals to develop Hell's Canyon in Idaho, one by Idaho Power Company which involved three single-purpose dams for hydroelectric power supply, and the other by the Federal Government to construct two multiple-purpose dams in conjunction with its comprehensive Columbia River development programme.   The results are summarised in Table 2.1 and show that if the Federal programme had been accepted additional benefits would have amounted to about $2.7 million annually.   This figure might be construed as an indication of the opportunity cost imposed upon the United States for permitting private development at that site.

Another difficulty is that b-c analysis often emphasises a static view of project objectives, whereas in reality the goals of any resource management programme change over time as new needs develop and as more data are collected. In other words, there is often considerable feedback (interaction) between policy making and programme design, a feedback which is not represented in the benefit-cost calculus. Also, from a mechanical point of view, b-c analysis is such a laborious and time-consuming exercise that only a limited number of alternatives can be scrutinised with the necessary care and precision, so that a step-by-step analysis through time is virtually impossible (Wildawsky, 1966).

As a result of these fundamental theoretical defects, serious questions have been raised regarding the efficacy of b-c analysis as a resource allocation technique in the world of sociopolitical reality. Haveman (1965), in particular, has shown that this technique can easily be manipulated to prove anything that is required, and that there is an alarming degree of reliance by members of the US Congress on the magic numbers representing the actual benefit-cost ratio. Of prime importance is the political suppression of the interest rate. Fox and Herfindahl (1964)

Table 2.1. A comparison of the costs and gains from two alternative schemes for developing Hells Canyon in Idaho.

Item	Scheme A Private development by Idaho Power Company involving three dams	Scheme B Public development by Federal Government involving two dams and integrated with the Columbia River project	Gains from scheme B over scheme A
average annual generation of prime power	669 000 kw	711 000 kw	42 000 kw
	$ thousand	$ thousand	$ thousand
value of prime power at $41·58 per kw	27 817	29 563	1 746
value of flood protection	1 400	1 800	400
value of navigation services	100	150	50
total average annual value of added benefits	29 317	31 513	2 196
total average annual costs	15 869	15 397	472
total average annual economic gains scheme B over scheme A			2 668

(Source, Krutilla and Eckstein, 1958, p.154.)

have reviewed water resource proposals submitted to the US Congress in 1962, and have shown that when applying interest rates of 4%, 6%, and 8% to these proposals (all of which had b-c ratios exceeding unity at the US Federal computed rate of 2.625%), 8%, 64%, and 80% of them, respectively, would fail under the assumed rates of interest. Boulding (1964, p.84) describes this more humorously:

"Around the mysteries of finance

We must perform a ritual dance

Because the long term interest rate

Determines any project's fate:

At two percent the case is clear

At three some sneaking doubts appear,

At four it draws its final breath

While five percent is certain death." †

Where it is realised that b-c analysis is only but one of a number of tools to aid in the decision-making process, this technique contains various features of sufficient importance to warrant refinement rather than rejection. It is conceded that certain difficulties common to all evaluation techniques lie outside the b-c framework, such as the appropriate interest rate, the time scale of the project, and the setting of goals and objectives.

Cost accounting. Although the calculation of real costs (construction, labour, operation, and maintenance) would appear to be the easiest aspect of the b-c calculation, costs have consistently proven to be underestimated in resource management projects, partly because of price uncertainties, but equally owing to poor accounting (Fox and Herfindahl, 1964). However, attempts are now being made to improve cost accounting in an effort to overcome the discrepancies between estimated and actual costs. In Britain, consulting engineers are being asked to prepare fairly precise critical path analyses which include constant cost re-evaluation over time (Water Resources Board, 1968).

Social costs. A major source of cost in a resource management programme is the intangible social cost associated with such factors as the loss of scenic beauty, danger to fish spawning grounds, and the concomitant effect on individuals and communities on the landscape. Such costs are virtually impossible to evaluate in monetary terms though attempts have been made to do so (see Chapter 3). The real problem here is the clearer identification of social costs and their relationships to production inputs. We shall show how the concept of the effluent charge is designed to reflect downstream social costs, and Krutilla (1966a) has extended this theoretically to the general case (see Chapter 4).

† Reprinted by permission of K. E. Boulding, "The Economist and The Engineer; Economic Dynamics of Water Resource Development", in *Economics and Public Policy in Water Resource Development,* Eds. S. C. Smith, E. N. Castle, © 1964 by the Iowa State University Press, Ames, Iowa.

However, in this discussion the whole question of compensation has been bypassed. As we have seen, the new welfare economists postulate that, although the ability of gainers to compensate losers and *still* be better off is *sufficient* condition for Pareto optimum, this does not *necessarily* create a welfare maximum, and it is of little comfort to the dispossessed to know that beneficiaries could compensate them if the appropriate means of transfer were possible. Two issues are involved here: one is whether social costs need to be imposed at all; the other whether beneficiaries can be identified and forced to compensate the losers. The first issue of social cost 'internalisation' is becoming increasingly more pressing, and such refinements as the effluent charge and regional institutional arrangements in water and air quality management are designed to reflect this (Kneese and Bower, 1968; Ayres, 1969) (see Chapter 4). The latter case (that of compensation) still requires research, so that the nature of the loss can be identified more closely and improved means of *equivalent* compensation (not simply the monetary value of property) sought. Laws relating to compensation are notoriously vague and urgently in need of review.

The goals–achievement matrix.   In an attempt to identify social costs and benefits more clearly, and in particular to permit the evaluation of resource management programmes where a number of goals and means are available, Hill (1968) has developed an ingenious model called a 'goals–achievement matrix'. His idea evolved out of the work of Lichfield (1964, 1966, 1968) who produced a cost–benefit balance sheet for alternative proposals in urban planning. Both writers recognised the futility of relating social costs and benefits to more tangible values, and sought to create meaningful surrogate values wherever possible in order to produce a representative comparison of all forms of costs and benefits in the decision process. Hill went further in that he also compared the relative importance of groups of alternatives, which he weighted according to various community goals (which in turn were also weighted). His matrix therefore represented a number of different strategies each with a different combination of outcomes, which were evaluated in turn against a number of desired goals. To clarify this a little further, a hypothetical example of such a matrix is presented in Figure 2.3. By so doing, Hill clarified much of the confused thinking that surrounds the decision process, for he pointed out the fundamental fact that there is no single unique solution, but rather a combination of means to meet a variety of objectives. Hill's modified use of the cost–benefit analysis technique does not solve the problem but at least it puts the whole concept of multiple goals and multiple strategies into clearer perspective. Figure 2.4 shows how this concept was employed to search for a combination of strategies to promote the better use of the resources of the Colorado River.

Goal description	α			β		
Relative weight	2			3		
Incidence	Relative weight	Costs	Benefits	Relative weight	Costs	Benefits
Group a	1	A	D	5	E	–
Group b	3	H		4	–	R
Group c	1	L	J	3	–	S
Group d	2	–		2	T	–
Group e	1	–	K	1		V
		Σ	Σ			

Goal description	γ			δ		
Relative weight	5			4		
Incidence	Relative weight	Costs	Benefits	Relative weight	Costs	Benefits
Group a	1		N	1	4	R
Group b	2		–	2	S	T
Group c	3	M	–	1	V	W
Group d	4		–	2	–	–
Group e	5		P	1	–	–
		Σ	Σ			

α, β, γ, δ are description of goals.
A, B... are costs and benefits in monetary or nonmonetary units.
– is no cost or benefit to group affected (groups a, b, etc.).

Figure 2.3. A hypothetical goals–achievement matrix. (Source, Hill, 1968, p.27.)

Systems analysis

With the development of the high-speed electronic computer and the improvement of sophisticated mathematical programming models, the use of systems analysis as a technique for resource allocation has gained great favour. Disregarding the complex mathematical theory for the moment, systems analysis as a tool in the allocative process has many distinct advantages, though many of the basic evaluation problems confronting b–c analysis are still evident.

It should also be stressed that systems analysis, like b–c analysis, does not *make* decisions; it simply *aids* decision making. A system may be visualised as a unit composed of interrelated parts whose functions and performance mutually impinge upon one another, and which can be expressed in mathematical terms and analysed as a whole. Though there are numerous kinds of systems ranging from physical systems to social systems, they have two basic attributes in common.

Alternative solutions[a]

Goals	do nothing	store and pump water	increase water supply[b]	change present water use	manage population & land use	save water	pricing of water	redistributed funds & taxes
National economic efficiency								
Income redistribution								
encourage regional growth								
help local communities								
rescue areas of decline								
promote family-sized farms								
Preservation—aesthetics								
preserve landscape								
Political equity								
commitment to Mexico								
allocations to basin states								
rights of Indians								
maintain regional political arrangements								
Control of the river								

[a] Not necessarily mutually exclusive. [b] Includes: importation, desalting, weather modification.

Figure 2.4. Goals and alternative solutions for water management on the Colorado river. (Source, National Academy of Sciences–National Research Council, 1968, p.73).

First, systems are capable of being expressed in mathematical terms so that a definite relationship exists between inputs and outputs. Thus, while the inner workings of a system need not necessarily be fully understood, a mathematical relationship can be derived to predict the level of output stemming from a certain combination of inputs. This is an important feature. Systems analysis is capable of predicting and measuring the effects of any input or combination of inputs on output streams, and hence is able to evaluate inputs in relation to certain desired ends.

Second, systems are capable of expressing a relationship between output and input. This relationship is known as 'feedback' and may be either positive or negative. Positive feedback takes place when the nature of the output reinforces the input, so that the system is progressively regenerating itself until a totally new system state is reached. Negative feedback occurs when the output produces dampening effects, reducing the effects of future inputs and maintaining equilibrium in the system state.

Detailed descriptions of resource management systems, particularly with regard to water management, have been produced by a number of workers at Harvard University (Maass *et al.*, 1962; Dorfman, 1965a, Hufschmidt, 1965a, 1965b, 1966; Hufschmidt and Fiering, 1966; Fiering, 1967; Dorfman, 1970), though Watt (1968) has explored the use of various systems techniques in the field of applied ecology. Briefly, systems analysis is an optimising procedure where outputs, expressed usually in the form of objective functions, are to be maximised, while inputs (in the form of cost functions and constraint functions) are to be minimised. Unlike the classic b–c approach, systems analysis can account for and incorporate a number of goals into its objective function specification, including those of a physical and socioeconomic nature, and, moreover, it can allow for changes in objectives over time and incorporate such changes in programme design (Wildawsky, 1966). An in b–c analysis, the first step is to maximise the discounted present value of net efficiency benefits, a relationship that can be expressed mathematically as follows (Hufschmidt, 1965b, p.560):

$$\sum_{t=1}^{T} \frac{E_t(y_t) - M_t(x_t)}{(1+r)^t} - K(x)$$

where $E_t(y_t)$ are the gross efficiency benefits in the tth year from the output y of the system x in that year; $M_t(x_t)$ are the operation, maintenance, and replacement costs in the year t for the constructed system; $K(x)$ are the capital costs for the constructed system; r is the discount rate; and T is the length in years of the economic time horizon.

This formula applies only to the single objective function of economic efficiency (that is, the maximisation of net benefits). The second step is to maximise each set of objective functions with respect to constraints.

Constraints may be broadly defined as attributes of the system which affect the attainment of the objective, and the constraint function is simply a mathematically definable relationship between constraints and objectives. Depending upon the complexity of the system under review, constraint functions may either be simple (physical, fiscal) or complex (institutional, legal, political, social) and capable of less precise mathematical definition. However, attempts are being made to quantify and incorporate a variety of constraint parameters into system design. Isard *et al.* (1968) have recently tried to incorporate an ecological component into a regional economic input–output system.

Once the relationships between objective and constraint functions have been defined, the next step is to search for the optimum solution. The mathematical procedures involved include three very important techniques known as linear programming, nonlinear programming, and dynamic programming. Each of these techniques involves a trial and error procedure whereby the outputs of different input combinations are tracked and assessed. In essence, systems design is part of the theory of games where different strategies are reviewed to discover the most promising. *Linear programming* is an optimisation procedure to find the maximum or minimum value of a number of linearly related variables subject to constraints on the values they may take, yet yielding the lowest cost of production. A simple example of a linear-programming model with respect to a water supply management decision may be found in Ardern and Kavanagh (1968). Where the objective function involves nonlinear expressions the method of *nonlinear programming* must be incorporated to find a solution. Here the relationships are slightly more complicated, for many of the variables may be stochastic (random) in occurrence and thus can only be expressed in terms of probability functions. (Examples of stochastic input functions include stream flow, forest fire occurrence, and the spatial diffusion of pests.)

To this point we have ignored the time dimension and the fact that different system states are dependent on the conditions imposed by previous system states. Ideally, we need a programming method that recognises the changing states of systems over time, the relationship between previous system states and present and possible future states, and the need to change system design as objectives change over time. *Dynamic programming* techniques have been developed to incorporate these features. In so doing they also simplify the selection of system variables by stepwise sampling procedures, by 'vector' statements of groups of system variables, and by simultaneous analysis of different resource management programmes. Dynamic programming thus permits optimal decisions to be made in a time-related sequential manner to allow decision inputs and systems relationships to change from one programming sequence to the next. Watt (1968) has shown how the use of dynamic programming has considerable value in the analysis of ecological effects of resource management programmes, where the initial impact created by side effects may take two or three generations to even out and cannot be anticipated in the original decision. His most important findings relate to a pest control programme in an eastern Canadian forest. He found that homeostatic mechanisms will tend to maintain pest densities if a control programme is adopted where spraying takes place only when pest densities cross a certain threshhold value. He reached the possibly surprising conclusion that in some instances no control might produce better long-term results than some control.

Where insights into the dynamic nature of system states are not easily available, *adaptive control processes* may be incorporated, whereby successive states of the system are consciously manipulated to develop deeper understanding of the processes involved. Watt (1968) has shown how this can be used to develop heuristic computer simulation models of great sensitivy.

Each one of these mathematical programming techniques involves numerous complex calculations involving many variables. The large number of variables involved, their range of characteristics (hydrological, ecological, economic, sociopolitical), and the extreme complexity of superimposed relationships and constraints makes mutual optimisation extremely difficult, if indeed possible. To overcome this, simplifying mathematical procedures are employed, usually in the form of models (Dorfman, 1965a). *Analytical models* enormously reduce system complexity by concentrating upon a small number of parameters over a low range of variance to analyse their performance more closely. *Simulation* is a more complex procedure in that it incorporates the time element. Markhov-type equations are employed, where each step is derived from the conditions existing in the preceding system state. System inputs for each new time period may be adjusted in the light of the preceding output either in a positive or negative fashion, and new system states may be added. The result is a fair approximation of real-life conditions, allowing for adjustments over time yet constantly surveying a wide range of alternative outcomes. With the use of judicious sampling of design variables, the simulation can be run again and again on the computer to approach optimisation by improving the combinations of system variables and system states as design changes over time. A fine example of simulation in the multiple-purpose water resources context is the model produced by Hufschmidt and Fiering (1966) for the Lehigh River in Pennsylvania. The model involved 42 major design variables with accommodation for up to 10 changes in investment and target output levels; yet with only 3 possible states for each of these 52 design variables 6 million billion, billion design combinations were possible.

As might be implied from the above discussion, the introduction of systems analysis techniques into the resource allocation process has tended to merge the approaches of economics, engineering, and ecology into one common mathematical focus. The result is often referred to as an 'engineering–economic system' though perhaps an 'engineering–ecologic–economic system' would be more appropriate. A recent trend is to graft a sociopolitical component onto such models, and hence to derive sophisticated design apparatus where a wide range of alternative goals, means, and constraints are scanned. Such models are yet in their early stages, but the mathematical techniques do exist to make them meaningful for future complex environmental situations. One can foresee the time when it will be possible to evaluate the social, economic, and political implications of actual decisions as they are projected into the computer, and hence to estimate more accurately the social costs and benefits incurred when nonoptimum distortions are introduced to meet different objectives (for example, efficiency versus welfare).

However, no matter how sophisticated the techniques employed the resource system model is but a handmaiden of man's ingenuity. Man must derive the relationships and select the inputs. At present serious computational difficulties arise owing to the nature of the input data. Stochastic variables have to be represented as probability functions, some input variables are simply not obtainable so 'dummy' variables have to be inserted, and the uncertainty of future states can only at best be crudely simulated by the use of contingency and *a fortiori* functions (Wildawsky, 1966). In addition, the problems of maximising multiple objective functions are enormous and involve a number of complex techniques, including the use of partial differential equations and Lagrangian multiplier functions. Dorfman (in Maass *et al.*, 1962) has attempted to develop a model to combine the objectives of efficiency with income redistribution, and in so doing has shown the power of the systems analysis technique. Resource systems will always be models and thus abstractions and simplifications of reality: they have great potential value, particularly as communication and information systems improve, but in the real world of the political–institutional decision process, that complex of vested interest, group bargaining, opportunism, public emotion, and personality clash, where the scientist is more regarded as a disturber than a saviour, the true role of such models may well be to evaluate in broad social cost and benefit terms how far 'real' decisions diverge from the 'optimum'.

Planning programming budgeting systems

To help overcome some of the shortcomings of b–c analysis and the systems approach, most public investment agencies have recently adopted the concept of planning programming budgeting systems (PPBS) (Public Administration Review, 1966). The emphasis here is upon planning and policy formulation, where goals and objectives are carefully assessed and reassessed at each stage in programme design. In addition, investment inputs are continually reappraised in the light of changing objective functions. Benefits can be achieved both through improving the efficiency of investment and through minimising duplication of interagency funding and action. Programme budgeting is undoubtedly an improvement on existing evaluation procedures in that it centres upon goals, alternative courses of action, and administrative responsibilities. However, because of this approach it is liable to pitfalls, since goals cannot easily be ranked and anyway are imperfectly perceived, and administrative jurisdictions at all levels of decision making are notoriously vague and overlapping (Millward, 1968). But the very fact that PPBS can pinpoint these inhibiting factors and hence focus critical reappraisal should be considered an improvement on existing evaluation techniques.

Engineering-economic systems in water quality management

Apart from Watt's (1968) work in applied ecology, probably the greatest contribution of engineering–economic systems has been in the field of water quality management (Bramhall and Mills, 1966; Liebman and Lynn, 1966; Loucks and Lynn, 1966; Kneese and Bower, 1968; Paulson, 1969). On the Delaware estuary the US Federal Water Pollution Control Administration (1966) developed an analytical model where stochastic measures of waste discharges were superimposed upon the biological and hydrological assimilative capacity of the receiving water, divided into sections each between two and four miles long. The objective was to raise the dissolved oxygen content either to 2 parts per million (ppm) or 3–4 ppm throughout the estuary. Three alternative strategies were employed: high-treatment solution (equivalent to regulation of effluent and imposition of stream standards), uniform effluent charge solution (uniform charge levied against all discharges over the estuary), and zone effluent charge solution, where an effluent charge was established for each of the three water quality zones (see Chapter 4). Each of these strategies was compared with a least-cost solution, where mathematical programming techniques were developed to arrive at the minimum cost distribution for maximum waste removal. (The least-cost solution was designed more as a control than a practical alternative, as it assumed considerable changes in existing arrangements for waste distribution and disposal.)

The conclusions appear in Table 2.2. Though the least-cost solution appears to be optimal at both quality levels, at the lower quality level (a final water quality of 2 ppm) both the uniform effluent charge and the zone effluent charge solution would cost half as much as the uniform-treatment solution to implement, regardless of the considerations of equity. At the higher-treatment level the zone effluent charge solution comes very close to the least-cost solution, for this strategy tends to favour upstream dischargers who can rely on a greater assimilative capacity of the receiving waters. In fact, by charging 10 cents per 1lb of

Biochemical Oxygen Demand discharged it has been estimated that the total costs (effluent charge plus treatment) would be similar to those involved in a uniform treatment programme, except that the effluent charge would generate considerable revenue (Kneese and Bower, 1968).

A similar analysis was developed for the Potomac by Davis (1968). In 1963 a US Federal dam construction agency, the Corps of Engineers, recommended that low-flow augmentation was necessary to improve downstream water quality, and proposed a plan to construct 16 mainstream multi-purpose reservoirs and more than 400 upstream detention structures. The stated aim was to reduce floods, provide industrial and municipal water supplies, and enhance recreational values, in addition to diluting downstream waste discharges. Davis reviewed this programme by comparing the costs of the single-purpose low-flow augmentation proposal with a number of alternative means for achieving similar levels of water quality, namely varying combinations of reoxygenation and waste load reductions. His conclusions are summarised on Tables 2.3 and 2.4. It is obvious that at higher-quality levels the low-flow augmentation alternative diverges seriously from the least-cost system model. Indeed, at little extra cost a combination of reoxygenation and load reduction could bring about higher levels of stream quality which could only be met at prohibited cost using the low-flow augmentation alternative proposed by the Corps of Engineers.

In England, a similar engineering–economic model for regional water quality management is being developed for the River Trent (Collinge, 1967). At present the waters of this river are not considered potable, but forecasts for future water needs in the Midlands show that demands will exceed existing water supplies by as much as 300 million gallons per day (mgd) [1371 million litres per day (mld)] in 1985 and 600 mgd (2742 mld) in 2000 (present supplies are 318 mgd (1453 mld), and it is expected that up to 100 mgd (454 mld) may have to be provided by the

Table 2.2. Summary of total costs of achieving two water quality objectives in the Delaware Estuary by various means (in $ millions per year).

Objective	Least-cost solution	Uniform-treatment solution	Single effluent charge	Zone effluent charge
(dissolved oxygen content)				
2 ppm	1·6	5·0	2·4	2·4
3–4 ppm	7·0	20·0	12·0	8·6

(Source, Kneese and Bower, 1968, p.162).

Trent. The objective of the model is to survey a number of alternative proposals (singly and in combination) in a search for the least-cost solution that satisfies the criteria of both efficiency (minimum total cost) and equity (optimum distribution of costs and benefits).

Table 2.3. Costs of some alternative systems for meeting the dissolved oxygen objective of 4 ppm in the Potomac Estuary.

System	Cost (in $ millions per annum)
Single-process solutions	
(1) reoxygenation	29
(2) effluent distribution	85
(3) low-flow augmentation	115
Multiple-process solutions	
(1) various combinations of low-flow augmentation, reoxygenation, polymer precipitation, step aeration	22–35
(2) combinations using effluent distribution or microstaining or step aeration with low-flow augmentation and/or reoxygenation	35–47
(3) combinations using lime–alum coagulation and higher degrees of low-flow augmentation or effluent distribution	48–78
Systems using powdered carbon adsorption	79
Systems using granular carbon adsorption	127
Complete range of system costs	22–146

(Source, Kneese and Bower, 1968, p.222.)

Table 2.4. Costs of alternative systems for achieving alternative water quality goals on the Potomac (in $ millions).

Dissolved oxygen content (ppm)	Cost of flow augmentation	Cost of least-cost alternative
2	8	8
3	27	18
4	115	22
5	–	27

(Source, Davis, 1968, p.95.)

The evaluation of social costs and benefits

A feature common to all resource allocation techniques is the conceptual difficulty of evaluating the social benefits and costs involved in the management of publicly-owned resources such as water, air, and the landscape. The increasing public concern with environmental quality as a legitimate and important goal, and the greater significance of amenity resources in the allocation calculus has created a crucial research front in the field of resource management, namely, the clearer identification of the social value of environmental quality. Economists have long realised that, owing to the existence of externalities, intangibles, and collectivities, the normal market mechanism whereby resources are valued and allocated, namely, willingness to pay as reflected in price, fails. Accordingly, economists have begun to search for surrogate values to act as an approximate measure of such cost and benefit streams. Kneese (1968) has outlined the state of recent research.

There are two aspects of this problem. One is the measurement of costs imposed collectively and individually upon society, and the other society's willingness to avoid these, or its evaluation of the benefits derived by not suffering such costs in the first place. Because the market mechanism fails there is no direct method of evaluating social costs and benefits. Common property resources possess certain attributes that render them incapable of traditonal supply–demand analysis [Herfindahl and Kneese (1965) outline the theory most clearly]. Firstly, with regard to supply, neither the total quantity, nor the location, nor the timing of the availability of such resources is known. The availability over time is particularly difficult to estimate, as the supply functions are usually stochastic (probabilistic) in occurrence (for example, the assimilative capacity of environmental media such as air and water). Secondly, the demand for the use of such goods cannot be assessed accurately owing to the indivisibilities and collectivities mentioned earlier. (For reviews of attempts to improve recreation demand analysis see Clawson and Knetsch, 1966; Daiute, 1966; Boyer and Tolley, 1966; Pearse, 1968b.) Thirdly, the future trends of supply and demand for these resources are highly uncertain, but likely to become even more critical. Fourthly, in the case of amenity resources the demand function is further complicated by the existence of a 'merit want' or 'option value' (Hufschmidt et al., 1961; Kahn, 1966; Krutilla, 1967a), which simply means that some individuals are willing to pay for the psychic pleasure (benefit) of knowing that a unique landscape is preserved or that a particular object (or objects— paintings, sculptures, buildings for example) is protected from, let us say, air pollution, even though they may never see the object of their concern. Though the option value is virtually impossible to measure, it is becoming increasingly relevant in evaluation problems since it relates to resources that are unique and whose loss may prove irredeemable. Fifthly, predictive models of future recreation demands are made hazardous by the problem of 'learning-by-doing' (Clawson and Knetsch, 1966). As recreational pursuits become more generally available, so demand will increase owing to more widespread participation. For example, it is only recently that owing to the increase of disposable income pleasure boating and skiing have become available to middle-income levels. Thus a potential demand is now fast becoming an actual demand, but its prediction is exceedingly difficult (Knetsch, 1969).

When evaluating the social costs in any resource management problem, there are three kinds to be considered, (1) the costs of cleaning up environmental damage after it has occurred, (2) the costs of preventing such damage before it occurs, and (3) the costs of the disutility to the public of environmental deterioration (Dales, 1968; Ayres, 1969). Of these, the first two are rather less difficult to calculate than the third. For example, it has been estimated that the damages attributed to air pollution cost the American taxpayer $60 per capita per year, though this obviously varies between country and city and between city and megalopolis (Goldman, 1967). The British counterpart pays between £3 and £15 per capita per year (Smith, 1966). However, actual estimates of damage are not easy to establish partly because it is so widespread and partly because its repercussions may be delayed or may build up over time. For example, the health costs due to air pollution can be calculated as in Table 3.1, but long-term health effects, particularly synergistic effects (that is, the combined effects of separate emissions interacting harmfully), have simply not been established and make the setting of standards exceedingly difficult and frustrating (*Law and Contemporary Problems,* 1968; UN, World Health Organisation, 1969).

Table 3.1. Annual costs of diseases possibly associated with air pollution.

Disease	$ million
cancer of the respiratory system	680·0
pneumonia	490·0
common cold	331·0
asthma	259·0
chronic bronchitis	159·7
emphysema	64·0
acute bronchitis	6·2
Total	1989·9

(Based on four categories of cost: premature death, morbidity, treatment, and prevention. Capitalised for 1958 at 5% interest.) (Source, Ridker, 1966a, 1966b, quoted in Kneese, 1968, p.173.)

The costs of prevention include the costs incurred in research and in the production of control equipment, while the benefits include the resources saved in not having to clean up the damage. Again, figures can be found, but their reliability is now always beyond question (Gehardt, 1968).

The third kind of cost, namely the social welfare costs (or malefits) associated with the ethical and aesthetic dissatisfaction stemming from decreasing environmental quality, is by far the most difficult to evaluate, yet possibly the most powerful reason for improving existing conditions. In the absence of true market prices surrogate values or simulated market prices must be applied. A number of ingenious attempts have been made to produce satisfactory surrogate values, but none has been entirely satisfactory. One method has been to assess the impact of a deteriorating environment on property values. Ridker (1966a, 1966b) places great faith in this approach, for he postulates that property values integrate the sum total of positive and negative discounted value streams, and since they are fixed in relation to air pollution it is unlikely that the air pollution malefits can be shifted onto other markets. He found that a relationship existed between property values and the intensity of sulphur dioxide in the ambient air as measured in eight zones, and that the decline in property value was about $250 per lot per zone. In other words, the marginal disutility of air pollution was $15–20 per lot per year discounted at 6% over 20 years.

While the results of this study and similar studies appear encouraging in helping to assess the economic impact of environmental costs (Kneese, 1968), there are many pitfalls to be overcome, particularly those of data collection, isolation of the relevant variables, and the presentation of data so as to reflect the stochastic variations of emission and environmental assimilability.

In addition, it is doubtful whether a purely economic approach, no matter how sophisticated, will ever truly represent the social costs of environmental deterioration. Analyses of market surrogates and even observation of human behaviour (see Chapter 5) fail to account adequately for the nature and the intensity of impact on a way of life. For example, Gregory (1965) vividly described the gradual social deterioration in a public housing scheme accompanying the increase of air pollution from a nearby chemical plant. Not only did property values drop and maintenance costs rise, but any feeling of respect for the neighbourhood soon waned and signs of social pathology (high tenant mobility, rent arrears, and high unemployment) began to appear.

Similarly, in the case of flood damage reduction, the accepted approach is to compute the expected loss from a given flood intensity through the market value of the protected property for various flood frequencies (Krutilla, 1966b). This calculation is repeated for various alternatives of flood damage reduction, and the measure of benefit is assumed to be the avoidance of loss (Sewell *et al.*, 1961). However, this approach bypasses the issue of the economic impact of the loss of life (for a discussion see Prest and Turvey, 1965; Headley and Lewis, 1967) and the social disruption wrought on the local community. Many flood control engineers consider this impact all but priceless (Nixon, 1966; Lloyd, 1968), though some work is now being done to assess more rationally the social effects of this impact in an attempt to discover the willingness to pay to avoid such environmental hazards (see Chapter 5). Nevertheless, society does appear to place a very high value on the social costs of community disruption, as evidenced by the large amounts of public relief offered to disaster-struck communities (Bates, 1963).

Recreation

One of the most important phenomena that has stimulated interest in evaluating environmental quality has been the recent upsurge in demands for outdoor recreation. The statistics are well documented (Outdoor Recreation Resources Review Commission, 1962; Burton and Wibberley, 1965; Clawson and Knetsch, 1966). At present there appears to be no sign of abatement to a growth pattern in recreation demand that is twice the rate of population increase, though presumably this will drop off in the future as there simply are not enough man-hours of leisure to accommodate projected demands if these continue to rise unabated.

The growth in demand for outdoor recreation activities had added an interesting dimension to the field of resource management, for it has created new values for reservoirs, scenic areas, and forest which previously had not been included in management strategy. Thus, in a very short space of time, the benfits of outdoor recreation have become a major factor in the project feasibility analyses of a number of resource management agencies (Schiff, 1966a). At the same time the inclusion of recreation has brought about much greater consideration of social intangible costs, as it is a function whose needs are frequently incompatible with traditional uses of resources. Examples include the preservation of certain stands of trees for campsites, the careful mixing of hardwoods within conifer stands to improve landscape amenity (Whyte, 1968) (both of which affect sustained yield policy in timber management), the preservation of certain standards of water quality, and the stability of lake levels at the expense of waste discharge abatement and flood control programmes.

Traditionally, public outdoor recreation is not subject to an entrance fee, so no convenient means exists for calculating consumer willingness to pay. By the same token it is not possible to generate a demand curve to predict various levels of user attendance under differing prices. In recent years a number of economists have made significant contributions toward a more rigorous methodology for the evaluation of recreation

benefits and the prediction of recreation demand. These attempts fall
into six categories:

1. *Recreation expenditure methods*
The first crude attempts at recreation benefit estimation assumed that
the recreationist's total expenditure (equipment, accommodation, travel,
and so on) reflected his willingness to pay, and that by summing all such
expenditures for all users an estimate of total user value could be reached
(Clawson, 1959). Apart from the difficulties of calculating total user
expenditures the method is conceptually unsound, for it simply indicates
costs and thus provides no basis for marginal willingness to pay for
additional increments of recreation.

A slightly more sophisticated version of the expenditure method was
developed by Hotelling (1949), who employed the concept of consumer
surplus to travel costs. On the assumption that each consumer valued
his recreation experience to the same extent (that is, their marginal
valuations of recreation were equal), he believed that the marginal
willingness to pay for any recreation experience would be reflected in the
travel cost of the most distant user. All other users would be enjoying
a consumer surplus by paying less for the same experience. Thus he
divided the recreation 'hinterland' into zones, derived the average travel
cost per zone, and developed a demand curve based upon the proportion
of users in the zone-base population and the difference between furthest
travel cost and average travel cost. The gross value of the recreation
resource would therefore be the area under the demand curve.

The Hotelling method was adopted by Trice and Wood (1958), but
sharply criticised on the grounds that interpersonal recreation utilities
could not be equated nor aggregated, that travel costs failed to account
for intervening-opportunity, joint-purpose trips and time-convenience
function, and that travel costs saved in recreation might be offset by
additional travel costs for other (nonrecreational) pursuits. Nevertheless,
despite these reservations, modifications of this method have been used
by Ullman and Volk (1962) and Burton and Wibberley (1965).

2. *Recreation-experience method*
Clawson (1959, 1963, 1969) has developed an interesting extension of
the travel-cost method by viewing the total recreation experience as a
package deal involving five distinct phases (Figure 3.1): (a) anticipation
and planning, where recreationists make decisions and commit expenditures
on the nature of the activity, the location of the experience, and the
length of time available; (b) travel to the site; (c) on-site experience;
(d) travel home (which psychologically at least, will differ from travel to);
(e) recollection, where selected images of the recreation experience play
a major role. Clawson visualised this total experience as a combination
of different kinds of costs (or sacrifices), namely money, time,
convenience, satisfaction, and energy. He recognised that each of these

would be assessed differently by every individual, but postulated that by stratifying groups visiting any particular recreation site on a travel-time-cost basis an empirical demand curve could be generated.   His procedure involved establishing concentric zones of equal distance from the recreation site, deriving the number of recreationists per thousand of base population and calculating the average travel cost (including a parameter for time) for each zone.   The result is a fairly neat demand curve, where recreation participation is a function of travel cost and time (the surrogate for willingness to pay).

Clawson's model was used empirically by Knetsch (1965) in the United States, while Kavanagh (1968b) developed it to estimate the value of a trout fishery in Graffham Water, in England (Smith and Kavanagh, 1969). In an interesting and valuable analysis Kavanagh found that 69% of the variation in visitation rate by trout fishermen could be explained by distance, and calculated the distance elasticity to be $-2 \cdot 29\%$ and the cost elasticity to be $-2 \cdot 39\%$.   In other words, a 1% increase in distance and travel cost would lower attendance figures by about $2\frac{1}{4}\%$ and $2\frac{2}{5}\%$, respectively.

Clawson, Knetsch, and Kavanagh justify this approach on the basis that recreation is a commodity which like food or automobiles is used in a manner that is dependent upon (a) the characteristics of the consumer (income, leisure time, mobility, socioeconomic factors, personal taste), (b) the availability of commodity choice (access to and knowledge of different kinds of recreation experience), (c) his valuation of the quality of the commodity (a sports car costing the same price will be purchased by different people for different reasons—performance, style, colour, comfort, sex appeal, and so on), and (d) the willingness to sacrifice certain personally available resources (time, money, convenience, energy)

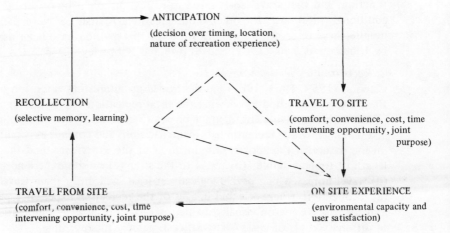

Figure 3.1. The five-stage recreational experience 'package'. (after Clawson, 1959).

to enjoy a particular quantity and quality of the recreation experience. In other words, these economists believe that recreationists like any consumers possess rational and consistent preferences and values towards recreation, and that their behaviour in the event of a price change will be predictable (see also Davis, 1963; Wennergren, 1964; Merewitz, 1966, 1968; Seckler, 1966; Robinson, 1967; Pearse, 1968a, 1968b).

However, there are a number of peculiar features associated with recreation that raise some doubts when considering travel cost and time as a major basis for the evaluation of recreation benefits.

a. Attitudes towards time are difficult to quantify in any meaningful measurement terms. Indeed, time valuation deserves much greater attention in recreation demand analysis, for it may be traded off in terms of cost (for example, travel by air rather than by road), or convenience (joint-purpose trips and intervening opportunity). Smith and Kavanagh (1969), in particular, have expressed some difficulty in relating the time component to the travel cost data.

b. Reliance on travel cost as a basis for valuation tends to skim over some important considerations in recreation travel patterns, namely joint-purpose trips, intervening opportunity, knowledge of alternative recreation experiences, and method of travel.

c. Certain factors that are quite independent of travel time and cost should be included in the evaluation of recreation quality and quantity. These include the exponential rise in the valuation of environmental quality in the future as it becomes relatively scarce in relation to other substitutable resources, and the concepts of 'merit want' or 'option value' and 'learning-by-doing', discussed earlier.

d. Perhaps the most fundamental criticism is that the Clawson model only develops a correlation and does not reveal the underlying *causes* of recreation valuation influencing visitation patterns. The issue here is that of quality. Clawson dismisses the suggestions raised by many that recreation is 'different' because it is a personal, aesthetic, and possibly a psychic experience (Farina, 1961; Mack and Meyers, 1965; Meyersohn, 1969). It may well be the case, for example, that a recreationist would be willing to sacrifice more than his neighbour to enjoy a less crowded site or a particular experience. Indeed, it is quite possible that he may visit a particular site (and hence be recorded in the demand schedule), yet experience considerable dissatisfaction at the lack of facilities, overcrowding, or other environmental disamenities. Though the question of recreation quality or 'environmental capacity' (that is, the ability of a recreation site to provide maximum user satisfaction) is not directly related to demand curve simulation, it does have relevance in the evaluation of the recreation experience and in the formation of recreation management policy (T.O'Riordan, 1969a) (see Chapter 5).

3. *Questionnaire surveys*

Attempts have been made to understand more clearly the factors that affect the demand for recreation by asking the users themselves how they value their recreation experience. Two methods of approach have been tried—questionnaire surveys of recreationists both on-site and off-site, and on-site interviews.

Off-site interviews. Davidson, *et al.* (1966) used the responses from 1352 households in Michigan to derive an empirical multi-regression analysis with which to estimate the probability of participation in swimming, boating, and fishing. The independent variables were stratified along two lines, socioeconomic (for example, age, income, race) and locational (for example, region, variety, and quality of facilities, urban–nonurban). Their results are only partly conclusive, possibly owing to the inadequacy of their data, and because they did not include children in their sample. However, they did find that both swimming and fishing participation were more affected by socioeconomic factors (particularly age, income, education, and race) than by locational/geographical ones, while participation in boating was more dependent on the existence of good quality facilities available close by. The major finding of their study, however, related to recreation quality, for they found that the availability and quality of existing facilities, where poor in relation to potential demand, became a significant factor in the analysis of future participation rates.

On-site surveys. Davis and Knetsch (1966) reported on an interesting technique of measuring willingness to pay in recreation by offering a series of bids to recreationists, where each bid represented successively increased entrance charges. The break-off point would reflect the user's evaluation of his recreation experience in monetary terms. Although doubts have been expressed over the use of hypothetical questions to indicate consumer preference and behaviour, Davis's results produced a demand schedule remarkably similar to one derived by the travel-cost method. Willingness to pay was primarily affected by income, length of stay, and the number of previous recreational visits to the area, and willingness to travel additional distance was significantly correlated with length of stay and distance already travelled. Both these findings are intuitively sound, but the fact that their estimates of total recreation valuation based on user surveys correlated so closely to the classical travel cost demand schedule is possibly questionable. Further probing is needed, for during interview respondents did not consider travel costs a significant determining factor. Certainly, a major research drive is needed to improve interview techniques and to sophisticate the computerisation of interview data.

4. *Water quality and recreation evaluation.*

A further refinement of the efforts to estimate recreation evaluation was developed by Davidson *et al.* (1966) and Stevens (1966) to determine the benefits of a water quality improvement programme in terms of increased recreation participation. Their findings, though empirical, are important, for Frankel (1967a, 1967b) has reported that industrial and municipal costs appear to be surprisingly insensitive to changes in intake water quality over comparatively large ranges, and hence that water pollution control cannot be justified solely on the basis of benefits to industrial and municipal users. The prime benefits derived from a water quality control programme appear to lie in the aesthetic and ethical satisfactions of preserving living waters and the enhancement of recreational opportunity. Davidson *et al.* (1966) attempted to estimate future recreational participation rates in the Delaware estuary for various levels of improved water quality, and concluded that, if a willingness to pay $2·55 per boating day was imputed, this alone would pay for the costs required to raise the dissolved oxygen content in the Delaware estuary from about 1 ppm to 3 ppm (about $200 million).

In a similar vein, Stevens (1966) attempted to identify the relationship between deteriorating water quality and resulting recreational losses, as measured by decreased satisfaction from river fishing (represented by reductions of angling success per unit of effort) in the State of Washington. His study is rather novel and experimental, but it does provide some interesting conceptual guidelines as to the evaluation of water quality and outdoor recreation and contains some useful ideas about the management of simultaneous incompatible resources where the costs and benefits are largely intangible.

Stevens' analysis is based upon the classic problem of incompatibility in resource management. If we wish to increase the probability of angler success (a surrogate value for recreation benefit), we cannot have deteriorating water quality. The biological relationship which exists between these two is represented by the function AB on Figure 3.2, where 0A represents the total quantity of fish available should the water be pure, and 0B represents that threshold in water deterioration (measured in units of B.O.D.) where no fish survive. Any point on this function, which is known as the technical possibilities curve (for an example, see Pearse, 1968b), represents a biologically attainable combination of fish and water quality. The optimal combination is at X, where the social marginal substitution function MN reflects the marginal value of exchange between an additional quantity of fish and an improvement in water quality (that is, the relative social value of an increment of fish to the costs of an increment of water purification). In other words, point X represents the most socially desirable combination of fish survival and water quality. Any change in either of these factors would result in gains to one that would not be offset by losses in the other, and hence would be inefficient (points X', X''). How we decide what is socially 'desirable' is a critical question of course, and this will be discussed in Chapter 5.

Stevens found that, even if the point B were reached (that is, no fish left in the river), the loss which, would equal the loss of consumer surplus or total willingsness to pay, would amount to $22747 annually or over half a million dollars if discounted at 6% over 20 years. This is less than the cost of a moderate-size sewage treatment plant for a small community. However, his analysis is valuable in that it also measured environmental losses to the sports fishery with gradually deteriorating water quality (points X' and X''), a function which, because it reflects gains and losses at the margin, in practice would be a valuable management tool. His analysis is unrealistic, however, in that it is static and does not allow for growth in recreational demand over time; nor does it consider any other form of recreational or environmental benefit in the area. However, this valuable empirical study is worthy of refinement rather than rejection.

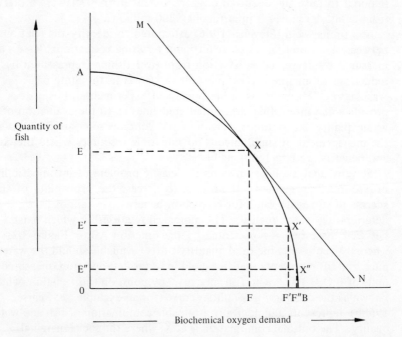

Figure 3.2. Optimum combination of output for two incompatible resource uses.

5. Recreation unit day.
So far we have looked at the results of various empirical studies which have tried to estimate the willingness to pay for one day or outdoor recreation. Though no hard conclusions emerge, it is obvious that there is great variation in the prices that people are prepared to pay for a day

of outdoor recreation, and one of the determining factors was the nature of the particular activity under consideration. To devise an easy method of estimating total recreation benefits for project feasibility analyses, the US, Ad Hoc Water Resources Council (1964) adopted the concept of the recreation day, where a standard price is imputed for different kinds of recreation activity per user per day. To derive total benefits, this average value is multiplied by the number of actual or potential users. Two basic categories are employed: a *general recreation day* ($0·50–1·50 per day), where the activity is popular, involves extensive public sector expenditures, and low personal costs (swimming, boating, camping), and a *specialised recreation day* ($2–6 per day) for activities such as hunting, bird-watching, and wilderness hiking), where private expenditures are high and public expenditures low, and demand is relatively small. These prices are assumed to reflect a user's willingness to pay for a day of recreation should he be forced to pay an entrance charge. Thus they are designed to simulate a market value for various kinds of outdoor recreation activities net of all associated costs. However, the apparent simplicity of this approach belies its conceptual failings, for the prices imputed are necessarily arbitrary and only partly take into account regional availability of recreational facilities. In addition, there is the ever present danger of manipulation by interest groups to justify a local project.

6. *Indirect methods.*
All the methods described above have been aimed at measuring the primary benefits from recreation in terms of the real value to the consumer via his willingness to sacrifice other resources for an increment of recreation. However, some studies have been directed toward the impact of a recreation site on the local economy, particularly as it stimulates a regional multiplier effect through increased employment, food and accommodation, manufacture of equipment, and so on. In the USA the recreation industry is worth over $40 billion annually and should rise to $50 billion annually by 1975 (Outdoor Recreation Resources Review Commission, 1962). These studies have developed along the lines of economic impact analyses, using such techniques as comparative impact (comparing similar areas with and without recreation facilities) and input–output analyses (Jewett, 1968). For example, Beyers and Sommarstrom (1968) have embarked upon an extensive investigation of the economic impact of a new US National Park (North Cascades National Park) upon a local community. The aim is to measure the amount, location, and source of expenditures in recreational, commercial, and capital development, and public agency operational activities. However, the authors admit to the considerable practical difficulties involved, including the identification of 'tourists' and 'recreationists', the delimitation of the 'zone of influence'. and the usual problems of

predicting recreation demands with any certainty, particularly as there
are a number of other National Parks in the vicinity.

Another method of assessing the local impact due to a recreation
project is to measure the increase in land values as a result of enhancing
local recreation facilities (for example, the construction of a reservoir).
This approach was first devised by Knetsch (1964) and by Knetsch and
Parrott (1964), and later extended by David (1968), who developed a
fairly refined model where land value increase was based upon proximity
to urban centres, median regional income, and the landscape characteristics
of the project in question. Considerable refinement of these approaches
is necessary before they become really meaningful as an evaluation
technique, but because the burgeoning recreation industry does have
considerable impact on the regional economy, more detailed analyses of
the methods involved warrant attention by the geographer.

The quantification of intangibles

A number of writers have recently devoted their attention to the question
of quantifying the attributes of landscapes in an effort to represent more
fairly the aesthetic impact of resource development projects in the
cost–benefit calculus. The intention is to derive some objective function
of landscape value that is independent of subjective emotionalism
(Leopold and Marchand, 1968; Leopold, 1969). Whether subjectivity
can ever be divorced successfully from objectivity is doubtful. For
example, Leopold (1969) does attempt to produce objective ratings of
riverscapes on the basis of uniqueness (by assessing a combination of
physical and chemical characteristics, biological parameters, and human
use and interest functions), only to discover that the most beautiful and
the most polluted river valleys rank very closely for they are both
'unique'. The problem here is that site uniqueness cannot be separated
from the values and the preferences of the observer (see Chapter 5).
However, he does try to get round this problem by employing the
concepts developed by Kates (1966b) and Wohwill (1966) of 'misfits' or
negative stimuli that are produced by landscape uniqueness characteristics
which appear out of place. He did so by factorising his uniqueness
characteristics into components representing valley character (width,
height of valley sides, landscape interest, view, degree of urbanisation,
existence of 'misfits') and river character (speed, variety, waterfalls, and
so on), and substantially improved his ranking procedure.

Similar attempts to quantify landscapes have been presented in Great
Britain from the point of view of a physical geographer (Walton, 1968),
an agricultural geographer (Coppock, 1968), and a landscape geographer
(Linton, 1968). Linton developed the work of Fines (1967) (who, with
the aid of helpers, divided landscapes into six graded categories ranging
from unsightly to spectacular) to produce a map of the scenic attributes
of Scotland based upon land form (relative relief, degree of dissection and

erosion, amount of surface water) and land use (urbanisation, forest, treeless farmland, moorland, wilderness). This work deserves refinement for it has some considerable potential in the management of tourism, since it points to the areas of positive scenic value and negative scenic ugliness (and hence areas likely to be either attractive or unattractive to tourists) and provides guidelines for the enhancement and protection of landscapes in the future in relation to expected demands and environmental capacity. An excellent case study of this approach was produced for Donegal (An Foras Forbartha, 1967) (see also Chapter 8).

Efficiency in resource use

The purpose of this chapter is to survey recent attempts aimed at improving the efficiency of resource use. Various approaches to this problem are analysed, including the appraisal of the demand function, the efforts to relate the total costs of resource use more closely to those who are benefitting from such usage, and the adoption of a number of technological, managerial, and economic alternatives for improving the manner of resource use in such a way as to maximise output, yet minimise throughput (wastage) per unit of resource consumed. The implications of this work are significant for it is designed to sharpen management tools, broaden management strategy, and reduce undesirable and unwanted environmental deterioration.

The need to control the demand function

We can now accept that a 'resource' in a socioeconomic sense is an element of the natural environment appraised by man to be of value, but whose supply falls short of demand. The supply–demand relationship becomes important when anticipated needs appear to be in excess of future perceived supplies, and where due recognition is given to the undesirable effects of single-purpose demands upon a multiple-use resource base. Until the turn of the century, few limitations were imposed upon resource demands, other than those of an economic nature, owing to a prevailing belief that resources were plentiful and/or that in the unlikely event of a shortage man's technological ingenuity would prevail. In the case of amenity resources, the linkages between multiple demands were imperfectly perceived and the ecological implications of certain needs rarely understood. Despite the efforts at government intervention in the private use of traditional natural resources (such as oil, forests, ores), attention was mostly directed at the control of supply rather than at limitations of demand. The assumptions upon which demand projections were made were rarely seriously questioned and seldom tested, with the result that linear or exponential extrapolations of demand were accepted at their face value. Still rarer were analyses of the factors that influenced the nature of demand, so that at best only hazy consideration was given to the conditions that might give rise to changes in demand. In short, demand projection ruled and supplies were managed accordingly.

However, during the past ten years, in view of the disturbing effects of uncontrolled demands upon multiple-resource complexes, serious questions have been raised about the manner in which demand projections are calculated, especially regarding the assumptions upon which demand behaviour is predicted. At the very core of this concern lies doubts as to the validity of society's value priorities. Galbraith (1958a, 1958b) has questioned whether present material wants should take precedence over

future spiritual and health needs. In a penetrating article (Galbraith, 1958b) he argued against the implicit assumption that economic growth is sacrosanct and posed some very interesting questions about the concept of waste, namely that waste is a by-product of inflated consumption standards and that it is encouraged by a mythical phobia of economic insecurity, an antipathy toward restrictions on consumer 'liberty', and a complex persuasive power exerted by the advertising media that enables us to consume more than we really want. Demand, he argued, is not a function of true wants in relation to hierarchical social values, but the product of an age promoting consumer hardware and planned obsolescence. The significance of Galbraith's contribution lay not so much in its economic implications as in triggering off a number of thoughtful essays dealing with the crucial relationship between man's needs and the orientation of his values in favour of environmental quality (Barnett and Morse, 1963; Boulding, 1966; Christian, 1966; Arvill, 1967; Dubos, 1968b).
Arvill (1967, p.277), in particular, expresses this viewpoint very clearly,
  "People must know the implications of their tastes and preferences: for example, that consuming vast quantities of newspapers and magazines imperils the forests; that veneering furniture requires the chopping down of certain trees; that growing speck-free fruit and vegetables needs the use of chemicals; that using certain types of indestructible plastic involves special methods of refuse disposal; that an open coal fire leads to air pollution; and so on. People cannot both demand a product and oppose the means of getting it and the the damage it may cause. Knowing what lies behind a chosen product is not, in itself, enough. People must be helped to develop some criteria so that they can demand alternatives and can judge what shortcomings may be due to plain mismanagement."
Because all resources appear to be becoming absolutely more scarce, there is a growing need to reassess not simply the demand function for all resource uses but to reappraise critically the assumptions upon which predicted resource use needs are based. The point here is that excessive and inefficient resource use at present will become increasingly more costly, since by limiting the availability of multiple-use resources options are closed and flexibility is reduced.

Analysis of demand

A recent and probably one of the most comprehensive attempts to analyse the nature of the demand function has been prepared by Sewell and Bower (1968) to enable improved forecasting of Canada's future water needs. They identify demand as that amount of water or water-related services for which individuals are willing to sacrifice other resources rather than go without, and relate it to price (willingness to pay), opportunity cost (willingness to forgo other opportunities), technology, public policy, social tastes, and the nature of the physical system. They point out that many of these variables are unknown or uncertain and that detailed analyses of the assumptions upon which some of these (for example, public policy and social tastes) are based have not yet been made. They also stress the importance of the time horizon in demand projection, since this relates partly to the life expectancy of a specific project and partly to the degree of interaction between planned resource use and the institutional setting of the planning process. The important conclusion made by the two authors is in line with Galbraith's thesis, namely that pricing controls in themselves are not enough, particularly where issues of environmental quality are concerned, and that an array of probable assumptions and alternative forecasts should be presented together with specific recommendations as to the appropriate public policies needed to relate demand more closely to its total social costs.

While Sewell and Bower's framework provides an important overview of the complexity of interacting factors affecting demand analyses, the most comprehensive theoretical statement relating to resource demand was presented a number of years earlier by Hirshleifer *et al.* (1960). Their classical analysis was based upon the theoretical constructs of economic efficiency, and is broadly the model developed by several other economists in their discussions of optimal resource allocation (see Chapter 2).

Conceptually, the Hirshleifer model is relatively simple to follow. As increasing qualities of a given resource are consumed, the value of an additional increment to the resource user falls relative to the increasing opportunity costs of sacrificing benefits from other potential resources. Eventually there will be a point where the willingness to pay (or willingness to sacrifice) for an additional increment of the resource just equals its utility (benefit) to the consumer. Any further use of that resource would cost more than it would be worth. In other words, demand would rise until the marginal cost of production would just equal the marginal value in use. Under ideal conditions resources would thus be allocated amongst users, so that the marginal value in use would everywhere be equal. The essence of Hirshleifer's model was to show that, where marginal productivity becomes equalised, each user has adjusted his demands in such a way that should he need more of that resource it would be worth his while to search for alternative ways of satisfying his need: for example, he could reuse, improve his production process, or seek lower-quality supplies of the resource, rather than seek additional increments of that resource. Consequently, resource use throughout all sectors of consumption would be maximised, and a broad range of alternative methods to promote increased efficiency in use (that is, maximum output per unit of input) would be canvassed in order to find the optimum combination of management techniques to meet desired goals.

If the relevant incremental cost and demand functions are known, it is easy to determine output (demand) by setting a price which reflects the consumer's marginal valuation in use (or willingness to pay at the margin). This procedure is known as marginal cost pricing, and, if followed, should lead to optimum allocation in resource use (Scitovsky, 1951).

Though the emphasis is upon questions of economic efficiency and pricing (namely, *how much* a user is willing to pay), we should not lose sight of the fact that the distributional issue of economic equity (namely, *who* should pay) also arises. This involves the principle of *beneficiary payment*, where the aim is to relate the costs more closely to those who benefit in proportion to their demands upon the total resource base. Though this would appear to be a basic tenet of economic morality, we shall find that the principle of beneficiary payment is rarely carried out and is by no means simple to administer.

But, despite the emphasis on economic efficiencies in this chapter, it is important to realise that considerable efficiencies in resource use can also be brought about through technological and managerial innovations. *Technological innovations* involve largely physical or process improvements, including such things as the better distribution of water-transfer systems, the various aspects of recycling, renovation and reuse of water and other factors of production, the increased efficiency of waste-disposal systems (discharging into air, water, and onto land), product substitution, and so on (Bower, 1966). Research in this area is largely highly specialised and technical in nature, but a number of publications are available to enable the interested social scientist to keep abreast (see Appendix).

Managerial innovations are aimed primarily at multiple use. The intention here is to devise new administrative techniques [which may well involve changes in existing legal and institutional arrangements (see Chapter 8)], which will enable a greater variety of resource functions to be derived from a given resource complex, while minimising the conflicts of incompatible use (National Academy of Sciences–National Research Council, 1966a). The emphasis here is upon improving the range of choice of various managerial and institutional approaches and upon zoning in space and time. A broad research front confronts the interested reader here, as much of the basic methodology awaits to be developed. Good empirical studies are few and more are urgently needed (Hills, 1961; Schiff, 1962; Nature Conservancy, 1965; T.O'Riordan, 1969a).

The topics selected for discussion below are suggestive rather than exhaustive. To date the focus of this new approach has concentrated on creating a policy (particularly a pricing policy) that encourages a broad search for technical, managerial, institutional, and legal innovations to achieve maximum resource output at least cost to the resource user and to society at large. The emphasis has principally been directed toward improving water-use efficiencies.

Domestic water use

Probably the most classic case of unquestioned assumptions leading to linear demand projections lies in the realm of forecasting and providing for future domestic water supplies. The reasons for this are principally institutional, in that public water supply undertakings have for long been responsible for their own supply and distribution systems, which in turn have been legally safeguarded in both quality and quantity in the interests of public health and hygiene.

However, the recent upsurge of interest in water-based recreation has created an interesting pattern of user and institutional conflict over the protection or development of public water supply reservoirs both in Britain and in the United States (Institution of Water Engineers, 1965; UK, Ministry of Land and Natural Resources, 1966; Bauman, 1969). In most cases the inclusion of controlled recreational use of public water supply reservoirs represents an efficient multiple-use management strategy. However, whether such a strategy is adopted appears to depend more upon historical and attitudinal factors than environmental ones. Bauman (1969) found that, in areas where surface water sources were developed early for public water supplies, there was considerable resistance on the part of water managers and the public alike to the idea of recreational use of public water supply reservoirs. However, in areas where surface sources for public water supplies were developed more recently, this prejudice did not seem to appear, nor did there seem to be many state or local regulations restricting the multiple use of such reservoirs. Bauman called these two major kinds of regions 'geo-behavioural' regions to underline the influence of tradition and habitual use in determining social attitudes and reinforcing unquestioned assumptions about untested public opinion. His findings also seem to apply in Britain where resistance to the public use of surface water supply reservoirs has traditionally been strong and upheld by Parliamentary legislation. But the tremendous pressure for water-based recreation has caused a change of heart on the part of water managers and the government alike, and supervised public access through membership of a club is now permitted (Institution of Water Engineers, 1965; UK, Ministry of Land and Natural Resources, 1966; Water Resources Board, 1968).

Public policy has usually directed that domestic water is priced on a *pro rata* basis measured by meter (which at best is related only to average cost and usually is a function of the cost of the supply and not of the value of demand), or upon an annual tax based upon some proportion of the property value. In neither case is there any price incentive to use water efficiently and in the latter case there is no marginal cost at all. It is no wonder then that domestic water supply has always been considered by the public and politician alike as cheap and plentiful, and has held precedence over the demands of other water needs or water-related services. Moreover, there is still some scepticism on the part of water supply managers that pricing would affect domestic demands to any significant degree. In other words, there is a prevailing belief that the demand for domestic water supply is virtually inelastic. The result is that domestic water demand is at present largely unaffected by price and that future needs are conveniently calculated by multiplying *per capita* consumption by future population. (For examples, see Water Resources Board, 1966; Sharp, 1967; for discussion and criticism, see Milliman, 1963; Northeastern Illinois Planning Commission, 1966.)

Serious questions have been raised about this procedure on both sides of the Atlantic. Probably the most comprehensive econometric analysis of domestic water demand patterns was undertaken by Howe and Linaweaver (1967) in a detailed investigation of metered and flat-rate supplies for both domestic and lawn-sprinkling requirements in the United States. The authors showed that, far from being a simple matter, residential water use was a function of the type of dwelling, lot size, property value, number of persons per dwelling, waste-disposal methods, socioeconomic characteristics of the user, climate, source of supply, and the pricing mechanism, and that a marginal pricing policy, while theoretically sound, failed in practice owing to the problems of daily and seasonal peaking and a general unwillingness to tolerate temporary water shortages. Howe and Linaweaver found that domestic water use was remarkably insensitive to price (price elasticity of -0.23), and noted that, by raising prices slightly, considerable increases in revenue could be obtained without substantially reducing domestic water use. This finding also revealed some discrepancy in the setting of domestic water rates, possibly as a result of attitudes discussed earlier, and pointed out the potential power of pricing as a resource management tool. Nonessential domestic water needs such as summer sprinkling use were found to be far more sensitive to price (price elasticity of -0.93), so that demand could be sharply curtailed simply by raising prices without incurring a major loss in revenue. The appropriate price theoretically should reflect the real costs of reservoir construction and water distribution, plus the social costs (if any) stemming from the resources forgone owing to the construction of the reservoir (scenery, fish, wildlife, and so on), both discounted over a relevant time period and measured at the margin. If such were the case, the domestic consumer would be forced to re-evaluate his *true* desire for a well-watered lawn or frequently washed car, for it is these price-elastic, nonessential, consumptive categories that place such a considerable strain on public water supplies. From Table 4.1 it will be seen that, in areas where water is served at a flat rate, lawn-sprinkling demands represent about 61% of total daily use per dwelling but drop to only 40% when supplies are metered, while total use per dwelling is reduced by one third. Thus, faced by water priced somewhere near its marginal value in use, the domestic consumer seeks to reduce wastage and

to limit unnecessary use in his own way. Likewise the authors concluded
that daily and seasonal peaking could be reduced to some extent by
judicious use of pricing. Conley (1967) substantiated these findings in a
regional context, but Bonhem (1968) recommended a water supply
pricing policy that recognises the positive social externalities of well-watered
lawns, especially in water-short neighbourhoods, so that water rates are set
lower than the marginal cost function by an amount that reflects
enhanced neighbourhood amenity.

Turnovsky (1969) developed the Howe and Linaweaver model further
by developing an index of per capita housing space (based on the number
of rooms per occupant) and including age characteristics and an index of
industrialisation for the community in question. He also found a very
low price elasticity for domestic water (−0·3), but a higher sensitivity to
price fluctuation by industrial users (price elasticity of −0·5). He further

Table 4.1. Water use in metered and flat-rate areas in the Western U.S.
(October 1963 to September 1965).

	10 Metered areas	8 Flat-rate areas
	(in gal per day per dwelling unit)	
Annual Average		
Leakage and waste	25	36
Household	247	236
Sprinkling	186	420
Total	458	692
Maximum day	979	2354
Peak hour	2481	5170
Annual	(inches of water)	
Sprinkling	12·2	38·7
Potential evapotranspiration	29·7	25·7
Summer		
Sprinkling	7·4	27·3
Potential evapotranspiration	11·7	15·1
Precipitation	0·15	4·18

(Source, Howe and Linaweaver, 1967, p.14.)

discovered that a relationship existed between the uncertainty of water supply and consumer behaviour. Consumers with no experience of water shortage tended to consume large amounts when faced with a possible curtailment of supply, while those who were more adjusted to drought conditions were more willing to conserve.

The impact of metering in promoting the efficiency of residential water use has also been discussed in Britain (Jackson and Bird, 1966; Warford, 1966; Kavanagh, 1967, 1968a). Much interst has centred on the case of Malvern, Worcs., where metering of domestic water supplies has been in operation for over 30 years. While no sophisticated econometric studies have been undertaken, it has been shown that average per capita consumption in Malvern is reduced by a third compared with unmetered per capita consumption in surrounding towns (Jackson and Bird, 1966). Despite the thorough theoretical foundations of these analyses and the sympathetic interest shown by water management undertakings, no further pilot metering schemes are proposed in Britain owing to concern over the cost of installing meters and the prevalence of 'cheap water' philosophy.

An editorial in the influential magazine *Water and Water Engineering* (1967, p.348) stated "(the) only reason now put forward for not metering domestic supplies is that metering would not reduce consumption sufficiently to pay for the cost of the metering. But with consumption continually rising (encouraged by the lack of restraint which payment by water rate produces)... it is inevitable that the time will come when metering will become an economic necessity." Despite this statement by the water managers, the government has stated that there will be no change in charging practice so as not to put an 'undue hardship' upon householders in view of the general restraint upon prices. This latter view is supported by the Water Resources Board (1968, p.46) in its Annual Report. "Although the cost of water from new sources of supply will generally exceed the cost from existing sources, we do not expect the rate of increase to be such that, if it should be brought to bear on the consumer, it would noticeably affect his demands upon the public water supply, nor is there any practical pricing system which would enable this cost to be brought to bear on him." The point here is that, though econometrically sound, the establishment of a pricing policy that encourages increased efficiencies in domestic water use can be impeded by more powerful managerial, social, and political considerations (see Chapter 7).

Geographers have also made some notable contributions to the analysis of domestic water supply use in various countries (Van Burkalow, 1959; D. J. Fox, 1965; White, 1968; Lee, 1969; White *et al.,* forthcoming). Their concern has been mainly with the locational aspects of urban water supplies, though the studies by Lee, A. White, G. F. White, and others

have also turned to the social and cultural aspects of domestic water use
and the manner in which this affects demand in underdeveloped countries.
White (1968), for example, pointed out the influence of distance, quantity
and quality, and ease of withdrawal on the choice of water supply source,
and the effect of cost (money, time, and energy) and social custom on
the nature of water demand. She found that as much as 8% of income,
30% time, and 20% energy was consumed in obtaining water in Uganda
(though there was considerable variation) compared with less than 1% of
income for the average US consumer with no significant time or energy
expenditures. Lee (1969) found that Western attitudes towards domestic
water use (namely that water is 'plentiful and cheap') prevailed in India,
but he did establish a relationship between the nature of water use and
the stage in economic development, income, household characteristics,
and water-using habits for various socioeconomic groups in Indian cities.
His most important findings were that, owing to current, depressed living
standards, actual water use was far below the potential water demands
should income levels rise. In other words, unlike the case in most
Western countries the income elasticity of water demand is still rather
high in many less developed countries. Lee also advocated a policy of
building a skeletal water supply system to cover the whole urban
population, rather than one of providing massive supplies for the fortunate
few (as is the present practice). For, as living standards rise and social
customs change, water supply officials will be faced with the costly
problem of distributing water throughout large sections of the city over a
short time period.

Irrigation water use
In Western North America, irrigation needs account for about 90% of
total water demand (US, Senate Select Committee, 1960; Ruttan, 1965;
US, Water Resources Council, 1968). Political demands for increased
irrigation water have resulted in large-scale water transfers in the Western
United States (Quinn, 1968), and concern over future projected needs
has led to proposals to dam part of the Grand Canyon in Colorado
(National Academy of Sciences–National Research Council, 1968;
Carlin, 1968) and to construct a continental water-transfer project to
convey water from Alaska to Mexico (Sewell, 1967). Both these latter
proposals involve tremendous social costs in terms of damaged scenic
beauty and community disruption, which, many have accused, have not
adequately been treated in the calculations of project feasibility. A
serious question of equity enters here. At present irrigators pay back
only a small proportion of the total cost of water supply via water-use
charges, while the rest is made up by taxes at the expense of the general
public (Renshaw, 1958). Generally, water in irrigation is undervalued in
relation to the other factors of production, thereby creating little incentive
for the adoption of water-saving practices. Studies by Wollman (1962),

Young and Martin (1967), and Martin and Young (1969) have shown that, not only are the costs of irrigation water undervalued in relation to its value in use, but that its productivity per acre foot is but a small fraction of the value added by the same volume of water in industrial or domestic use (Table 4.2). In fact, as Landsberg *et al.* (1963) pointed out, a transfer to municipal and domestic use of 10% of projected irrigation requirements to the year 2000 could nearly double the projected water allocation for these two higher uses and add as much as 90% to the total economic product (Fox, 1966a, 1966c).

Research is now being undertaken across a broad front to increase the efficiency of water use in agriculture. In terms of the physical component, considerable research has been directed into the mechanisms of the soil–plant–atmosphere system to identify more closely the factors that control transpiration. With this knowledge a deeper understanding is being gained as to the appropriate timing and quantity of application to produce optimum yields (J. O'Riordan, 1969). Recent experiments show that it may be possible to alter part of the physiology of certain crops and thus reduce the basic transpiration requirements (Waggoner and Bravdo, 1967).

Changes in the method of application can also bring about considerable savings in irrigation water use. Seckler (1969) has shown that the introduction of automatic sprinkler systems to replace the old furrow irrigation method in the western USA has increased irrigation flexibility in rough terrain, decreased labour costs by 20%, raised yields by up to 15%, and improved the efficiency of water use from between 20% and 400%. He cautions against the validity of some of his figures, however, owing to the tremendous variation in operation from farm to farm. In addition, improvements in distribution will lead to reduction in unnecessary water

Table 4.2. Personal income per acre foot of water intake in Arizona, and rank of each sector 1958.

Sector	Dollars of personal income per acre foot	Rank of sector
manufacturing	82301	1
trade, transportation, and services	60761	2
agricultural processing industries	15332	3
mining	3248	4
utilities	2886	5
livestock and poultry	1953	6
primary metals	1685	7
high-value intensive crops	80	8
forage crops	18	9
food and feed grains	14	10

(Source, National Academy of Sciences–National Research Council, 1968, p.72.)

losses: in British Columbia, Willcox and Ferries (1955) showed that savings of up to 20% are made by eliminating leakage and excessive evaporation.

Again, it is evident that a pricing policy that goes some way toward marginal cost pricing might drastically alter the demand for irrigation water in the future. At present the costs of irrigation water are deliberately suppressed below their marginal value in use for political, institutional, and legal reasons (Wollman, 1962), but it is evident that, in view of recent advances in plant genetics research plus improved application techniques, few incentives are being offered the irrigator to search for improved efficiencies in water use. Ruttan (1965) has illustrated this point most effectively. By developing an 'elasticity' framework for the projection of irrigation needs, he departed from the traditional approaches which simply assessed water 'requirements' and 'physical potential' and derived a model which enabled him to look at alternative means of increasing crop output in the United States. He showed clearly that many publicly-financed irrigation projects were inefficient in the sense that net economic returns failed to exceed the total costs to society, and that irrigators were also subsidised in an inefficient manner; he also cautioned against hasty decisions to construct more large-scale irrigation schemes in the Western United States, when improved management of land and water in the sub-humid east could produce more economically efficient returns at less cost to society at large.

In Britain, though much work has been done on the technical aspects of irrigation-use efficiencies (Penman, 1963), little attempt has been made to predict future demands for irrigation in view of the present policy of charging all abstractors for water (UK, *Water Resources Act,* 1963; Lloyd, 1968). It is evident that water management officials foresee a gradual decline in irrigation demands relatively unaffected by the charging scheme imposed by the *Water Resources Act* (1963) (Sharp, 1967), while the author (O'Riordan, 1970) has questioned these calculations and has forecast that future demands for irrigation water will probably drop off sharply as irrigators are required to price water more closely to its marginal value in use. This effect should be most noticeable in the case of low-value crops (grass, cerals) and in regions where irrigation needs are low.

Industrial water use

An analysis of industrial water use efficiencies is rather more complicated than is the case for domestic and irrigation use efficiencies, since industries use water for a tremendous variety of purposes. All in all, industrial demands account for about 40% and 70%, respectively, of total US and Canadian water abstractions annually (Bower, 1968). Approximately 72% of total water abstractions in England and Wales is due to industry, of which 56% is used primarily for cooling by the Central Electricity

Generating Board (Water Resources Board, 1968). The emphasis on
water-use efficiencies in industry is technological rather than economic,
for Bower (1966, 1968) has reported that water costs rarely exceed 5%
of total cost of factor inputs, and indeed may be as low as 0·1%. In
fact, many industries set their own water price as a large proportion of
industrial water sources are privately owned. For example, Wong (1969)
discovered that 90% of all industrial water withdrawals in the Chicago
area were privately owned. However, where industries do draw water
from public supplies, they appear to be more sensitive to price
fluctuations than do domestic water consumers (Turnovsky, 1969).
    Wong (1969) has clearly described the various methods of increasing
the physical efficiencies of industrial water use. These include recycling,
reuse, elimination of losses by such techniques as mechanical control
and evaporation suppression, substitution of nonaqueous materials in
place of fresh water, and process changes where adjustments are made in
the process design. Bower (1966, 1968) has shown that industrial water
demands are a function of three major factors: (1) the nature of the
production process, which includes the nature of the raw materials used,
the product output mix and the rate of operation, (2) the physical
layout of the plant (which affects the cost and physical possibilities of
recirculation and other internal conservation measures), and (3) the
controls and costs (if any) on waste discharge.
    The principle of increased efficiency is to increase output per unit of
water abstracted. However, despite major attempts to improve physical
efficiencies (Ackerman and Löf, 1959; Cootner and Löf, 1966; Löf and
Kneese, 1968), industrial use is still remarkably inefficient. For example,
Wong (1969) found that the estimated physical efficiency of water use
for all sources of water supply for 35 case studies in the Chicago
Metropolitan area was only 21%. He attributed this neither to poor
technology nor to weak economic incentives but to the failure on the
part of industrial water managers to perceive a wide range of water-saving
adjustments and to adopt the most promising. Part of this failure was
apparently due to inadequate information and part to inadequate controls
over water use and, more particularly, waste disposal.
    Nevertheless, it is evident that various technological efficiencies are
available, and most of these do result in economic efficiencies for the
firm. For example, recirculated water costs only one fifth of fresh-intake
water in the mineral industry (Bower, 1968). It is also evident that some
industries are using water more efficiently for, though pulp and paper
production increased by 26% between 1954 and 1959, water intake for
this industry rose by only 8·5%, while in the oil-refining industry
capacity increased by 51% during the period 1949–1959 when water
intake rose by only 5% (Bower, 1966). Subsequent analysis in the latter
case showed that, while water intake decreased, gross water applied per

ton of output increased, an indication of improved internal efficiencies in
water utilisation.

In summary, it appears that, though changes in the price of intake
water will force industrial water managers to seek in-use efficiencies
within the physical constraints of the production-process/product mix
(Fair *et al.*, 1966; Institution of Public Health Engineers, 1968; Institute of
Water Pollution Control, 1968), the major incentive to industrial water
managers to seek water-use efficiencies lies in the imposition of effluent
controls. Since little water is actually consumed, waste-water generation
is large in most industrial processes, so strict controls over effluent
discharges seem to be the best method of curtailing water intake, while
at the same time reducing water pollution (Ayres and Kneese, 1969a).

Charging for water use

An interesting policy innovation in promoting the efficiency of use across
a broad spectrum of water abstractors is that of the charging scheme as
laid down in the Water Resources Act for England and Wales (1963).
The objective of the charging scheme is to levy on all abstractors a
precept (tax) roughly in proportion to the effects of their abstraction on
the total water resource, and to use this revenue for the augmentation of
future water needs. The charge itself is based upon four relevant
characteristics: namely, the nature of the source, the time of year during
which abstraction takes place, the purpose for which the water is to be
used, and the location, quantity, and quality of disposal. In point of
fact, it is doubtful whether the charge will induce major efficiencies in
water use, since it is designed merely to offset the cost of future water
supply projects rather than to reflect marginal value in use. In addition
it is assessed against a broad category of use (that is, industry, irrigation,
and so on) rather than against individual abstractors, and hence incentives
for individual water-use efficiencies are lacking.

But the charging scheme is designed more as a practical measure than
to meet theoretical expectations. The very fact that abstractors have to
pay for water at all when it has always been considered a free good
should reduce consumption to some extent. The scheme does penalise
abstractions that take place directly from rivers during the summer and
thus should cause irrigators to search for alternative sources and timing of
supply (O'Riordan, 1970). In addition, it penalises abstractors who use
high-quality supplies for low-quality uses (for example, cooling or gravel
washing) and should encourage them to search for alternative low-quality
sources (brackish water, tidal water, or reused water). Furthermore, it
does penalise abstractors who dispose of their water in places far
removed from the source of supply (the sea or another river) and whose
discharges are undesirable in quality. Thus, in the sense that the
charging scheme will provide incentives for all classes of water abstractors
to search for more suitable sources and more suitable qualities of supply,

the charging scheme is a very valuable management tool, for it allows the consumers themselves to search for and adopt the most desirable use of water at minimum social cost. It is an excellent example of the promotion of efficiency in resource use and deserves further study in the future (Lloyd, 1968; Craine, 1969).

Water and air quality management

It might appear at first sight that in each of the cases described above improvements in water use efficiency are internal to the cost–benefit calculus of the particular economic unit investigated. However, this is not the case. In some instances increased efficiencies can lead to serious social costs external to the production process and reflected in terms of diminished social welfare. For example, improved in-plant recycling may result in deteriorating effluent quality; irrigation reuse increases salinity in the runoff which accumulates downstream. We come then to the problem of identifying the social costs of effluent discharge (water, air, and onto the land), and of devising the best means of relating this cost to the discharger (Ayres and Kneese, 1969a).

Kneese and Bower (1968), Dales (1968), and Hagevik (1968) have made important theoretical contributions towards this end. They begin by surveying the three principal means of controlling effluent discharges, namely (1) *regulation and enforcement* through the establishment of stream quality standards and/or of effluent quality standards, (2) *subsidies of payments* either as grants or tax incentives to install pollution-control equipment, and (3) *charges* through the assessment and levying of effluent fees. Enforcement of stream standards is regarded as an inefficient mechanism for promoting optimum water quality, since the parameters upon which such standards are based are difficult to define and there is no incentive for the individual discharger to improve his effluent quality above the general standard. Inevitably, some dischargers will find it more costly to conform than others, and overall waste discharge reduction costs will not be minimised. Stream standards are not without some value, since they may be necessary to safeguard public health and welfare. Thus the maintenance of a certain minimum level of dissolved oxygen or suitably low levels of toxic substances (arsenic, cyanide) may be necessary in the public interest (Kneese, 1965). In fact, as we shall see later, the identification of stream and lake water quality standards may provide the focus around which to assess broad public preferences for certain levels of water quality.

These authors also present clearly the case for the regional control of air and water quality management rather than uniform (nationwide) controls. The theoretical argument here hinges on the concept of separable facilities (Mishan, 1967), where the management technique of zoning is enforced to safeguard relatively unpolluted areas from serious deterioration and to permit some degree of effluent discharge where the environment is already seriously degraded.

The regulation of effluent standards suffers from the same defects as enforcement of stream standards, since, unless they are established for each individual discharge (an arduous and expensive administrative procedure), they are likely to be unfair and inefficient if established across the board. Yet, because effluent standards can be set on a regional basis to reflect the assimilative capacity of receiving waters throughout a river basin, and since they are relatively simple to administer, monitor, and enforce, adoption of the effluent discharge standards forms the primary basis of pollution-control legislation at the present time, despite criticism by experts as to their adequacy (McGauhey, 1965; Lyon, 1966).

So, despite its limitations and the failure of adequate enforcement, regulation via standards is the most common method of pollution control today, mainly because it is administratively more practicable than either of the two alternative management approaches and because it is politically and socially more acceptable to polluters (industries and public).

Subsidies, in the form of payments not to pollute, or tax incentives for the purchase of pollution-control equipment are becoming increasingly popular as water and air quality management tools under the influence of political pressures (Gehardt, 1968). The principal advantage of subsidies would appear to be as a short-term measure to avoid undue financial hardship in the case of firms which have been permitted to pollute in the past and which dominate the economy of a locality (Kneese and Bower, 1968). However, the administrative problems are immense and the opportunities for dischargers to generate excessive wastes in order to receive higher subsidies too tempting (Dales, 1968). Also, the dividing line between pollution-control equipment and process-improvement equipment (which, in fact, is a vastly superior method of reducing waste discharges) is a tenuous one; yet in the latter case the taxpayer would directly be subsidising the industry. Actually, the provision of pollution-control equipment is a very inefficient and uneconomic means of controlling pollution, since its purpose is negative (it contributes nothing to the productive process) and funds would be far better allocated in encouraging waste dischargers to search for process efficiencies (Bower, 1966; Ayres and Kneese, 1969a). In addition, this method searches for a solution through a single means, namely pollution-abatement equipment, when there may be a variety of alternative measures whereby waste generation could be reduced. Finally, the principle of subsidies violates the basic tenets of economic morality and benficiary payment, since the public is paying the would-be polluter not to pollute.

Most economists now favour the technique of effluent charge as the means best suited to achieving efficiencies in waste generation reduction (Kamien *et al.*, 1966; Whipple, 1966; Johnson, 1967; Brown and Mar, 1968; Crocker, 1968; Dales, 1968; Kneese and Bower, 1968; Ayres,

1969; Wright, 1969). The charge to be set against any given effluent would theoretically be equivalent to the marginal cost of improving an additional increment of waste discharge. This in turn should be equal to the incremental change in external damages, and thus should reflect the assimilative capacity of the receiving waters and the social 'illfare' imposed upon other users in the stream. In essence, then, the proposed system of charges would be equivalent to the social-opportunity cost brought about by the waste discharger who normally escapes this when standards only are imposed. Kneese and Bower (1968) point out the advantages:

1. The charge offers an incentive to every individual discharger to minimise the level of his waste generation, for it encourages him to seek constantly for the most economical means of diminishing his waste, including such techniques as pollution-control technology, product substitution, improved processing methods and by-product renovation. The proper mix would be the one that minimised the costs of waste generation and discharge (that is, the combination of costs of waste generation control and the effluent fee paid).

2. Under this system, resource managers rather than government officials would bear much of the burden of investigation and decision making. Management is probably much more suited to evaluate the advantages and disadvantages of different discharge reduction processes and to adopt the most desirable combination (Hagevik, 1968).

3. The charging scheme, if properly calculated and imposed, would tend to equilibrate around the optimal stream (or air) assimilative capacity, as the objective is to minimise downstream damages to other users. Optimal stream assimilative capacity would therefore form the water (or air) quality standard, which ideally would be the result of rational cost–benefit appraisal. This would bring the problem into perspective and might restrain the pure water and air enthusiasts who tend to ignore economic realities in favour of a pure environment at all costs.

4. It is possible to establish charges so as to reflect the stochastic nature of stream-receiving flows (an advantage not found either in the setting of standards nor in the provision of subsidies). For example, the effluent charge would encourage the waste discharger to seek temporary storage during periods of low stream flow rather than to pay the additional charge.

5. An effluent charging scheme would have to be administed in a basin-wide context and thus could be fitted into an integrated regional water (or air) quality management policy.

6. The burden of payment falls upon the polluter not the taxpayer, though some of this would undoubtedly be passed on. The revenue could be used as a valuable water-management tool, for example, to provide subsidies where needed, or to construct regional water quality treatment plants, such as those found on the River Emscher in the Ruhr Valley (Kneese, 1967).

At present, the only major effluent charging scheme in operation is that
being successfully implemented in the Ruhr Valley in West Germany
(Fair, 1961; Kneese, 1967; Kneese and Bower, 1968). Because of this
it has been subject to intensive scrutiny in Britain, the USA, and France
(Kneese, 1967). Meanwhile the USA is becoming increasingly sympathetic
to the concept of effluent charges (Kneese and Bower, 1968; Cleary,
1967) in the face of mounting evidence favouring their reliability as a
resource management tool. Kneese and Bower (1968) cite two examples
where the imposition of sewer charges levied against waste generation led
to a sharp and rapid decrease of effluent loading, and some former
polluters even began to reclaim valuable by-products from their waste.
A rather significant side effect of the effluent charge was the reduction in
basic intake water requirements, reflecting improved process efficiencies.
The clear implication here is that present public policy towards waste
generation control tends to be inefficient and permissive and that a
reassessment of management strategy is urgently required.

However, the effluent charging technique does contain a number of
drawbacks, the most serious of which is the evaluation of downstream
damages, particularly where these are decentralised over a number of
users and difficult to quantify (for example, the effects of water quality
deterioration on swimming participation in a lake). It is possible that
charges could be set to create a surrogate value which would indicate
how much the damage *at least* is worth, though this method does not
indicate its true value. Ideally, this value should be the maximum
amount which all users of the lake would be willing to pay to avoid the
effects of the polluting discharge (Krutilla, 1967b), but of course there is
no economic or social mechanism by which this information can be
obtained. Secondly, there is the problem, of equating damages from
various kinds of waste discharge. Dales (1968) has suggested the concept
of an 'equivalent ton of waste', which, if looked at critically, implies
rating discharges in terms of 'damage equivalents'. Apart from the
overriding question of damage evaluation, this would require a double
'correction', one to allow for the varying assimilative capacities of the
receiving water into which a particular discharge is released, and a second
for equating different forms of damage resulting from different
compositions of discharge. This latter correction is particularly hazardous
to assess since (1) knowledge about the cause and effect relationship
between discharges and damage is at best hazy and frequently unknown
for many forms of polluting effluents, (2) predictions as to the probable
future effects (long-term exposure) of various polluting emissions with
which to estimate a discounted damage function are presently extremely
difficult to determine, and (3) waste discharges rarely occur in isolation:
accurate estimation of equivalent damage effects is thus seriously impeded
by the combined (synergistic) effects of waste discharges.

Additional difficulties in administering the effluent charge for air quality management have been pointed out by Hagevik (1968). He notes the tremendous dearth of reliable data, the frequent and large-scale variations in airshed assimilability, the theoretical problems encountered when allocating damages to specific polluters when synergistic (multiplier) effects occur, the complication of deciding who benefits from the enhancement of the air resource, and the possible legal repercussions stemming from the 'taking' of a long-enjoyed private property right without due compensation.

In an intriguing effort to overcome some of these difficulties, yet keeping in line with the concept of effluent charges, Dales (1968) explored the interface between the management of free goods, such as air and water, and property rights. He showed clearly that unrestricted access to the use of a publicly-owned good (be it air, water, open space, or wildlife) can only bring about gross mismanagement since "everybody's property is nobody's property", in other words, there is no incentive for the individual to conserve in the face of a neighbour's selfish exploitation. Dales proposed the ingenious solution that governments should create a system of air and water property rights which would then be sold to potential polluters on the open market. He envisaged a scheme where the pollution control agency would 'sell' a certain number of 'Pollution Rights', each Right permitting the holder to discharge one equivalent ton of waste over a given period of time (say five years). The number of Rights sold could be regulated to meet desired levels of waste generation by region. As population and industry increase, the price of each Pollution Right would rise to reflect the growing demand for the right to pollute. With rising price each individual polluter would search for the least costly means, or combination of means, to minimise waste generation and discharge costs.

Though this solution does not completely overcome the difficulties mentioned earlier (damage estimation, damage equivalents, and the need for rigorous monitoring), it does provide a framework for analysis by developing a mechanism whereby the legal dimension can be integrated with the political, social, and economic aspects of pollution abatement. It would appear that the best solution for efficient air and water quality management would have to involve a multiple strategy employing each of the three techniques described above (regulation, subsidy, and charging) on a regional basis. For, as we have shown, regulation is necessary to provide certain minimum safeguards to public health and is administratively relatively simple, subsidies provide a convenient short-term solution to polluters facing a massive clean-up campaign, particularly where they dominate the local economy, while charges are technically and economically efficient and provide valuable revenues for regional management controls. The appropriate combination of strategies will obviously vary, depending upon the nature and amount of wast generation, the receiving water/air assimilative capacity and the socioeconomic political framework within which the management policy is to be formulated.

In practice, water and air quality management strategy consists of a process of bargaining between the affected public officials, on the one hand, and the polluters, on the other. Gains are made incrementally and are realised only very slowly. The basic theory underlying this bargaining process is that applying to the theory of games (Luce and Raiffa, 1957) and the theory of conflict (Coser, 1956). Holden (1966), Chevalier and Cartwright (1966), and Hagevik (1968) have developed both of these theories with respect to pollution control. Game theory involves common interest, uncertainty of each other's actions in any given situation, and tremendous dependence upon precedent. The process of bargaining to resolve conflict means that both sides must give ground to gain ground. This whole procedure is clothed in ritual, opening with threats (bombastic statements) by the pollution-control agency, followed by a period of withdrawal when behind the scenes bargaining takes place, and ending in some form of compromise, either as to the amount or timing of pollution-control measures or both. The emphasis is upon incrementalism (major institutional changes do not occur rapidly), ritual, and continuing negotiation to achieve what is desirable rather than optimal by searching for common ground amongst all interested parties. In some instances the recognition of the need for cooperation and the establishment of a common purpose is a notable achievement (Chevalier and Cartwright, 1966). This entire process centres around some focal point, be it air or water quality standards for specific kinds of emission, or individual effluent controls, since bargaining cannot take place in the abstract or across a wide range of issues. (For a case study, see Cleary, 1967.)

In an important exploratory analysis of the bargaining process in pollution abatement, Holden (1966) pointed out that politics is a process of conflict which permits the orderly distribution of advantages and disadvantages amongst competing interest groups, and that policy making is a procedure which depends upon 'enough' of the 'right' people complying with the rules or suffering some kind of loss. In a game situation, the pollution abatement agency must choose air and water quality standards (or effluent standards, or even an effluent charging scheme) which require some form of compliance, but yet are not impossible to achieve. In so doing, the agency must placate the various antipollution interest and wield sufficient power to ensure respect by the waste discharger(s) and the public. The decision as to the *nature* of the standard, the *timing* of the enforcement, and the *tolerance* of deviation from expected compliance will depend upon (1) the economic importance of the waste discharger(s) to the community, (2) the technological feasibility of waste-reduction methods (for example, a 'clean' automobile engine), (3) the social values and popular myths associated with different kinds of pollution, (4) the amount of adjustment which the waste discharger(s) must make to achieve minimum reasonable compliance, and (5) the amount and nature of potential contact between the pollution abatement agency and the waste discharger(s) in question.

The development of this body of theory is still relatively recent, but its inclusion in resource management research is vital, for it aids immeasurably in the understanding of the real-world processes by which environmental management policy is formulated and subsequently implemented.

Environmental management

In the introductory chapter we discussed the changing concepts behind the philosophy of conservation. We showed how it has meant different things to different people at different times, how it is a conglomerate of conflicting aims and a repository for various forms of social morality, and how it has waxed and waned in the political spotlight as crises came and went and were forgotten in the mists of the past. In this chapter we shall review and assess the role of individual and group attitudes towards the environment in which we live and act, attitudes which are beginning to coalesce into the 'new conservation' of environmental quality management.

The emphasis throughout will focus on the man—environment interface—that complex boundary where biophysical systems and cultural systems interact, and which has been traditionally at the core of the geographical discipline.

A number of lines of approach have been followed with regard to the man—nature relationship, as it is of direct relevance to resource management analysis. The first, which might be classified as the cultural—historical approach, deals with the broad sweep of man's attitudes, and the expression of these attitudes as they are reflected on the landscape and in his institutions. A second approach views the man—environment interaction from the biomedical standpoint, and is concerned with the effects of environmental extremes upon man's physiological and psychological makeup. A third field of study is devoted particularly to the manner in which man responds to the stochastic occurrence of extreme natural hazards, such as floods, drought, hurricanes, and to the analysis of man's technical solutions and institutional means which he has adapted to overcome these. A fourth approach deals more directly with the formation and role of public attitudes to various environmental situations and seeks to develop a methodology whereby these can be canvassed, evaluated, and related to the decision-making process.

Each of the latter three lines of research analyses the impact of differing kinds and degrees of environmental stress upon man in terms of the effects upon his body, his mind, his decisions, his actions, and his institutions. The emphasis of this research is upon the factors affecting *response* (or perception) of the stress, and nature and degree of subsequent *adjustment* (if any) as a result of the perception process. Adjustment may be physiological, psychological, or behavioural, or it may involve managerial and institutional changes, or any combination of these.

Cultural-historical studies

The major contribution in this field can be attributed to the writings of Glacken (1956, 1965, 1966, 1967), Lowenthal (1961, 1962, 1967), and Tuan (1961, 1967, 1968a, 1968b). Each of these scholars has explored the man-environment relationship through lengthy literary excursions based upon a broad historical perspective. The approaches taken can broadly be classified into two kinds. The first is an extensive analysis of the attitudes of a nation towards its landscape or towards particular phenomena on the landscape. The source of research material used is very wide, including art, fiction, nonfiction, drama, poetry, and folklore. Lowenthal and Prince (1964, 1965) made use of this approach in their survey of the English landscape, and Lowenthal (1968) later used the same technique when he somewhat humorously described the American scene as interpreted by its artists, scholars, and citizens. No 'hard' conclusions emerge from either study, but the message is clear. Landscapes are not seen as physical realities, rather they evoke images and register symbols in the minds and the hearts of men according to their desires and imaginations, and the cultural setting within which they act.

The other line of approach adopted by cultural-historical geographers focuses upon particular landscape phenomena or environmental processes and compares the evolution of response toward these features as expressed throught the writings, maps, and behaviour of various cultures. For example, Lowenthal (1962) has shown that the concept of landscape itself conjures up different images in the minds of Americans and Europeans at different periods in their cultural evolution. To the American the landscape is wild and nonhuman, while to the European it is gentle and secure, reflecting the longer period of integration between cultural and biophysical environments in Europe. The concept of wilderness has held a particular fascination. Lowenthal (1962), Williams (1962), and Nash (1967) have each described changing American attitudes to wilderness, resulting in differing responses to the use and management of wilderness areas. In early America, the wilderness was feared and thence had to be overcome and destroyed, but today the vanishing wilderness is cherished and protected partly for its scientific and recreational value, but equally for its role in American heritage (Simmons, 1966).

A superb essay which makes use of this technique is that by Tuan (1968a), which describes various cultural appraisals of the hydrologic cycle. Apart from its scholarly excellence, his study is noteworthy for its findings, since Tuan shows clearly how long-established beliefs endure even in the face of contrary scientific evidence. Because of a faith in the concept of a 'well-watered earth', the idea of deserts and the recognition of dry climates was delayed. It appears that fanciful and unrealistic images of our environment and unvisited areas are deeply ingrained in our cultural psyche and influence our attitudes and actions regardless of scientific 'fact'.

Although such studies appear to be essentially a literary activity and can be criticised on the grounds that they are highly selective and biased in favour of extant research sources, the writings of a literary minority and the interpretations of the authors|concerned, they do provide valuable insights into the nature of landscape development and the manner in which the spatial dimensions of cultural associations with the landscape are derived. Above all, these studies have presented an important perspective into the formation and nature of cultural attitudes towards the landscape. The relevance of this work in aiding the understanding of public attitudes to particular environmental phenomena, such as air and water quality or the preservation of trees and wildlife, is fundamental, particularly as it affects future environmental management strategies.

Throughout their analyses, all of these authors have pointed to a distinct dichotomy within man's attitudes to the landscape, depending upon whether the dominance in the association lies with man or with nature. The work of nature is seen as wise, purposeful, ordered, teleological, beautiful and serene, while the results of man's activities are usually considered foolish, aimless, ugly, and shortsighted. Man, the destroyer, nature, the healer: with nature harmony, with man discord. Through their rigorous historical perspective these studies have provided valuable supporting evidence for the currently developing attitude of harmony between man and nature and to a growing concern over man's potential ability to destroy large segments of the environment. Glacken (1967), in particular, has emphasised the 'stewardship' concept: that man was created by God to observe and to protect his own heritage, and, though the manner in which we visualise and behave in our surroundings is anthropocentric, men's actions are to some extent constrained by teleological and theological obligations.

A number of writers have developed this line of approach, particularly the emphasis upon man–nature harmony, from a variety of viewpoints. Of particular relevance are the writings of Leopold (1949), Dasmann (1966b, 1968), and Sears (1966) in stressing the ethical aspects of the man–environment relationship, and in creating a frame of reference which is fundamental to much of the present-day philosophy towards environmental quality management. In addition, much of their work has a distinct ecological bias which should provide a refreshingly new perspective to geographers interested in resources management. The interested reader is also recommended to read the works by Jennings and Murphy (1966), Ewald (1967), Shepard (1967), White (1967), and Shepard and McKinley (1969).

Biomedical studies

Studies of the physical and psychological stresses imposed upon man by an unfriendly environment are still in their infancy, but are yielding some disturbing results. As in all man–milieu studies, a distinction must be made between the actual external stress and the human interpretation and response to it (Van Arsdol *et. al.,* 1964). Lee (1966) sought to devise some measurement for environmental stress tolerance and to account for the various factors by which attitudes to environmental stress are formed and judged. He concluded that training, previous experience, and intensity of stress are important in developing psycho-physiological adaptations to various forms of environmental stress. His work is important because it extends beyond that of the purely medical approach, which concentrates upon the various biomedical homeostatic adjustments of which the human body is capable under extreme conditions. By adding the psychosocial component he moved into the field of reaction and behaviour when confronted with stress. For example, he showed that where stress is moderate the role played by psychological and behavioural adjustment is critical.

In conjunction with the analysis of man's interaction with extreme stress in his physical environment are studies concentrating on the effects of severe social stress upon man's psychophysiological makeup. In particular, some work has been directed at the effects of dense urban environments on social tensions and group interactions. The preliminary results are not encouraging. Significant correlations have been made between overcrowding and the peculiar nature of modern urban life styles, and the increase of mental disorders, physical diseases, and such pathological symptoms as crime and civil strife (Parr, 1966). Farber (1966) has commented on biomedical analyses of stress amongst urban residents, and noted that certain forms of neurological diseases are caused by the patient being 'out of step with his environment'. The biggest danger he felt was boredom and a lack of creativity. Much of the recent thinking relating to the need for increased civic participation in urban affairs is aimed at reducing the citizen's sense of isolation and alienation from the planning process, and creating in him a sense of identity and purpose with his environment (Regional Plan Association, 1967; *Public Administration Review,* 1969; Reynolds, 1969; UK, Skeffington Committee, 1969).

A number of ecologists have compared the urban condition to similar effects which take place when animal populations become overcrowded. It may be useful to develop some concept of 'density balance', beyond which man's psychological and emotional evolution has not prepared him (Osborn, 1962; Leyhausen, 1965). Much of the recent emphasis in city design is upon the creation of fairly dense urban environments, within which open space is maximised and integrated, where undesirable human interaction is minimised, and where the accent is upon variety and stimulation in the urban landscape to develop spiritual recreation and to provide release from tension, monotony, boredom, and frustration and even a sense of futility (Whyte, 1968). Similarly, part of the drive for outdoor recreation is undoubtedly in response to unpleasant and unattractive urban environments (*Countryside in 1970,* 1963, 1965).

Perhaps the one scientist who has explored most comprehensively the biomedical relationship between man and his environment is Dubos (1965, 1968a, 1968b). Armed with his expert knowledge in microbiology and experimental pathology, and guided by his humanistic philosophy, Dubos has systematically and lucidly analysed the changing relationship between man and his surroundings as the human race moved from a primitive to a highly-urbanised culture. In particular, he has demonstrated how man has developed a number of complex adaptive mechanisms (social, cultural, genetic, physiological, psychological, and behavioural) to enable him to adapt to changing conditions and events. But he warns that in the complex and ever-changing urban environment such devices may not continue to protect us, as our technological prowess tends to buffer us from that degree of environmental stress necessary to promote and maintain these critical adaptive processes.

Adjustment to natural hazard

One element of the man–environment relationship that has received much attention recently is the interaction between man and the occurrence of natural hazards over space and time (Burton and Kates, 1964b). It has been estimated (Burton *et al.,* 1968b) that losses resulting from impacts of extreme geophysical events amount to between $2 and 3 billion each year in the USA alone (see also Sheehan and Hewitt, 1969). The list of natural hazards embraces a wide range of phenomena, though particular attention has been directed at floods (White, 1966a), coastal storms and hurricanes (Burton and Kates, 1964c; Kates, 1967; Burton *et al.,* 1968b; Hartman *et al.,* 1969), urban snowfalls (Rooney, 1967; Relph *et al.,* 1968), and humid and semiarid drought (Saarinen, 1966; Russell *et al.,* in preparation). Yet the field for additional research is still vast. The Natural Hazards Research Program operating through the Geography Departments at the Universities of Toronto, Clark, and Chicago (until January 1970) is sponsoring studies of such hazards as frost, fire, earthquake, volcano, hail, tsunami, tornado, and landslide (Natural Hazard Research, 1969). Each of these events can be identified by a number of characteristic features, such as (1) occurrences which are probabilistic in frequency distribution yet uncertain in specific timing, (2) variability of intensity ranging from minor to catastrophic, (3) rapidity and suddenness of impact, and (4) impact which is fairly localised over space. But the scope of this kind of approach is almost limitless. Some interest is now being generated in the area of man's interaction with anthroponatural phenomena that build up slowly and steadily and are more widespread in their impact, such as air and water pollution (Hewings, 1968).

The questions which this kind of research hopes to answer are as follows:

a. Why does man continue to live in areas subject to destruction by natural hazards, particularly when these hazards continue to recur?

b. What is known about the likelihood of hazard occurrence, and how is this information diffused and interpreted by hazard-prone resource users?

c. Do resource users adjust to rare, yet extreme, events in a different or similar manner compared with frequently-occurring, yet less extreme, events?

d. What means (technological and institutional) has man developed to combat the destructive forces associated with these events?

e. Are these means sufficient either in their effectiveness or in their variety?

f. How does the hazard-prone resource user respond to improvements and potential innovations in technology?

g. In any given location, what is the optimum combination of adjustments in terms of anticipated social consequences that could be adopted to minimise the threat caused by the hazard, yet maximise the use of the threatened resource use?

h. If all the possible adjustments are not adopted, either singly or in combination, why is this the case?

i. What is the spatial distribution of the various possible adjustments available to hazard-prone resource users, and why do spatial variations in adjustments occur?

j. Is there any difference in man's attitude to natural hazard risk as compared with social or physical stresses?

k. How does the recognition, interpretation, and adaptation of adjustments to each of physical, social, and natural risks vary from one cultural group to another?

The basic theory behind this approach stems from the work by Barrows on human ecology. Barrows (1923) postulated that man is able to insulate himself from any environmental threat that is stochastic and discontinuous by a variety of culturally derived and individual psychological processes, while at the same time organising himself into complex social and institutional forms which reduce his personal identification with the threat. Barrows' contribution is important, for he showed how man can both restructure and adjust to his environment to some degree. The Hazard Research Programme has developed this idea and is concentrating upon the range of choice of such adjustments, the factors that limit the perception of such choice, and the processes by which specific adjustments are chosen. Russell (1969) has clarified much of the confused thinking about hazard damages by showing that losses should not so much be considered the sum total of damages resulting from a specific catastrophe, but a measure of the relative success of human adjustment to variable nature. In other words, the benefits of the Hazards Research Programme can be attributed to the losses saved in the future by adopting one or a number of adjustments in the present. The ultimate objective is to optimise all forms of adjustment so as to minimise the discounted total hazard loss.

The major impact of this work has stemmed from the analysis of human adjustments to floods, as developed by Gilbert White and his associates at the University of Chicago (White, 1960, 1964, 1966a; Sheaffer, 1960; Kates, 1962, 1965; Sewell, 1965; Burton, 1967). For example, the likely range of solutions to reduce flood damage are presented in Figure 5.1. It will be seen that there are two major categories of adjustment: those which regulate the cause (that is, the flood), and which may be termed technological adjustments, and those which reduce the effect of floodwaters, which may be termed structural or behavioural in nature. White (1964) has shown that adjustment to the flood hazard is dependent upon the flood-plain manager's knowledge of the various possible adjustments available, his perception of possible flood frequency and related flood intensity, his interpretation of technological and economic efficiencies of the various possible alternatives open to him, the social and institutional framework in which information is presented to him and through which his actions are guided, and his attitude to the various spatial repercussions of whatever adjustment he adopts. Essentially, the White model deals with decision making in the face of uncertainty, and he concludes that the flood-plain dweller's adoption of various flood hazard reduction adjustments will relate closely to his perception of the likelihood of threat (which in turn is influenced by the frequency and intensity of flooding, and by the existence of river management projects such as dams or levées), his faith in public relief, his previous experience of flooding and flood losses, and his willingness to transfer responsibility to the community or a government agency.

However, owing to the immense difficulty of obtaining meaningful data from interviews with hazard-prone resource users, the processes by which one or a variety of damage-reducing adjustments are evaluated and adopted are still little understood. Only weak relationships have been found between the adoption of flood damage reduction adjustments and age, education, and even previous experience, and it seems that the most promising correlation is with actual and perceived frequency of hazard. But human response and adjustment are neither consistent nor incremental. It appears that, until environmental stress (in the form of increasing frequency of hazard) builds up to a point where there is some certainty of recurrence, little or no adjustment takes place and the processes of adoption-diffusion are dampened. But where there is a high degree of certainty of hazard recurrence damage-reducing adjustment

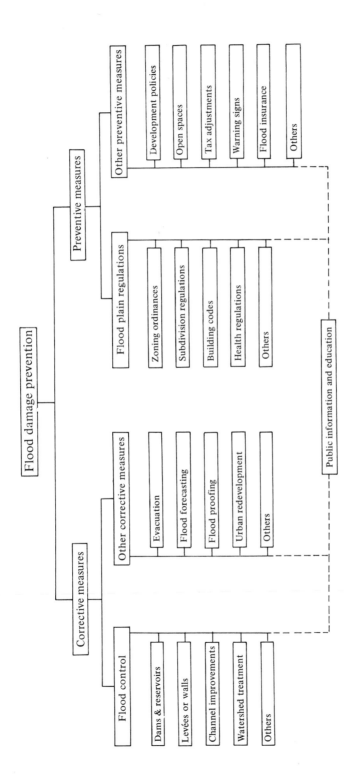

Figure 5.1. Diagram of altenative measures for reducing flood losses. (Source, Burton *et al.*, 1968, p.13).

is widespread and the diffusion processes are active. This finding
appears to be in line with Porter's (1965) concept of environmental
gradients. In the case of floods, Kates (1962) found that significant
'sensitivity points' (White, 1961) occur at recurrence intervals of 1-2 years
and 4-5 years (Figure 5.2).

The flood hazard studies have exerted a considerable impact on public
policy towards flood damage reduction. Traditionally, the structural
flood-control measure (dam, levée) was favoured as a single-purpose
adjustment, since under US Federal legislation all construction costs
were borne not by the protected flood plain user but by the government
(that is, the taxpayer at large). Where severe floods occurred the typical
pattern was massive public relief followed by political clamour for an
upstream dam or levée (Hart, 1957a). Three adjustments were favoured:
namely, bearing the loss, public relief, and structural control (Sewell,
1969). The flood hazard analyses showed conclusively that structural
controls alone were not only very costly but frequently unjustified, and
that a number of structural and behavioural alternatives had not been
fully considered. A careful integration of a combination of alternative
adjustments would maximise flood damage reduction at minimum cost,
while preserving a degree of economic equity (beneficiary payment)
(Krutilla, 1966b; James, 1967; Lind, 1967; Whipple, 1969). Since
1966, US Federal policy has incorporated the flood-plain zoning studies,
flood proofing, and flood insurance analyses into its flood-control
programme and in addition, has improved its flood-forecasting capabilities
(White, 1969). These changes represent a significant improvement in
the resource management of flood-prone areas, and indicate the value of
the geographical contribution in developing sound public policy.

Another finding evolving from the hazard-adjustment studies is that
the more the resource user is potentially affected by a natural hazard,
the greater is his awareness of the hazard and consideration of the
possible adjustments to it. For instance, Saarinen (1966) has discovered
that wheat farmers on the Great Plains were far more aware of the
possibilities of drought than were cattle ranchers. He also reached
another general conclusion, namely that resource users faced with the
uncertain occurrence of a potentially destructive event tend to play down
the threat and be unduly optimistic about its potential effects. Symptoms
include transferring potential hazard danger to other people and places
('it will never happen here; it is far worse at place X'), conveniently
forgetting and suppressing past experience, overemphasising the hazard-
free periods, and, in the wake of a catastrophe, de-emphasising its
possible recurrence in the future. Saarinen also explored some rather
interesting psychological factors affecting attitudes to the environment
amongst the wheat growers on the Great Plains. He noted that they
lived under conditions of stress and conflict, and that the more perceptive
were generally more attuned to the fluctuating environmental response

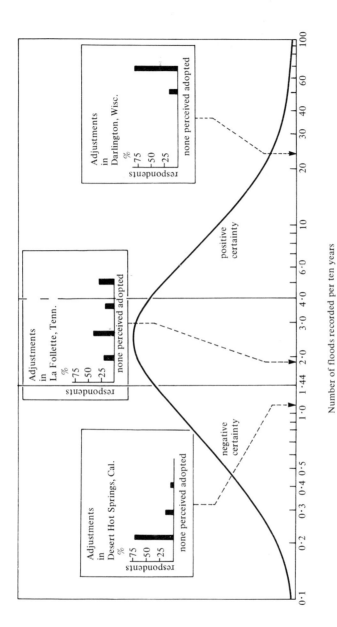

Figure 5.2. Relationship between adjustment to floods and recorded flood frequency. (Source, Burton *et al.*, 1968, p.21).

and to the danger of failure if vigilance was ever lowered. In addition, he found a general feeling of daredevilry and opportunism in the social personality of the farmers, encouraging them to gamble with drought, trusting that they would win through to the tacit approval of their neighbours.

Certainly, the role of personality in the process of environmental stress adjustment needs to be investigated further. One dilemma that needs to be resolved is that of the resource user, who in spite of his previous experience of hazard returns to the hazard-prone site. Saarinen's (1966) findings may prove most valuable here, for, despite the promise of public relief in the event of disaster and the possibility of some technological safeguard, it seems probable that a person who relishes the environmental risk of hazard-zone occupancy is more likely to return than the cautious fellow who has checked out all his options more thoroughly. Perhaps, if we could find a personality index for the gambling type, we could search for a more meaningful correlation!

Subsequently, attention in the field of hazard adjustment has been directed toward the factors affecting individual's differences in response to their hazardous environments, especially the role played by uncertainty, crisis, and technology in the adjustment process, and towards approaches that promise to be of value in cross-cultural situations. A number of students have dipped into the psychological literature to develop new methodologies with which to assess and account for individual response to various forms of environmental stress (including social and physical stresses, in addition to purely natural hazards). For example, Barker (1968) has adapted the Rozenzweig picture-frustration test, where the subject is confronted with a cartoon depicting two characters involved in some situation of stress. One of the persons is saying something to the other, and the subject is expected to identify himself with the other person and devise his own appropriate reply. Results are very tentative owing to numerous difficulties associated with the method, but there is evidence that it can solicit deep-felt responses to different kinds of environmental stress and these responses can then be subjected to rigorous statistical scrutiny. Tentative findings suggest that there is a greater tendency to search for solution to socially-derived stresses (for example, racial riots) than to environmental hazards, especially extreme natural hazards where the dominance of the source of frustration is more readily accepted. In a similar vein, Golant has experimented with such techniques as avoidance response (Golant and Burton, 1968) and semantic differential (Golant and Burton, 1969) to assess individual attitudes to different forms of social, physical, and natural stresses. Again, more questions are being asked than are being answered, but studies such as these help to provide more meaningful insights as to the cultural, social, and psychological processes that condition our response to given environmental situations.

The problems associated with these studies are enormous. For one thing, it is difficult to compare varying intensities of different kinds of environmental stress, and, for another, it is doubtful whether a subject can distinguish clearly between such phenomena when he may have actually experienced a few or none of them. More valuable findings are possible from cross-cultural experimental situations which compare the varying adjustments that have been developed by different cultural groups to similar kinds of environmental phenomena (Sonnenfeld, 1966). Certainly the whole question of choice, both at the individual and community levels, needs to be investigated further from the standpoint of theory and empirical analysis (see Chapter 7).

The role and formation of public attitudes

Parallel with, and supplementary to, these approaches dealing with the behavioural outcome of the man–environment interface have been a number of studies probing into the manner in which individual and group attitudes concerning the environment are formed, and how these in turn are expressed on the landscape through the decision process (White, 1966b). The processes through which the surrounding milieu is perceived, interpreted, and acted upon are both complex and imperfectly understood. However, we are becoming more confident that, despite the intimate and subjective nature of the individual's milieu, there must be fundamental similarities in the direction and intensity of some of these forces, otherwise we would be unable to communicate and survive. But there is evidence to suggest that, though interpersonal milieux can be broadly compared within any one cultural group, significant differences do appear when individual and group attitudes to the environment are compared cross-culturally (Sonnenfeld 1966, 1967, 1969).

We have already noted the contribution by Barrows (1923), who recognised the need to view geography as the scientific analysis of the relationships and adjustments between man and his environment. His views were supported by Sprout and Sprout (1965), who visualised man as a socioecological organism living and interacting in a bioecological milieu. Because man is possessed with psychosocial mechanisms whereby he can develop internal adjustments to external stimuli, they postulated that by isolating himself from many aspects of the natural world he is able to construct his own 'psycho-milieu' that is in some respects independent of the natural forces that operate around him. The development of this concept has led to the use of the term 'cognitive behaviouralism', as the logical outcome of the old 'determinist–possibilist–probabilist' controversy in geography (Saarinen, 1966; Pred, 1968; Harvey, 1969).

Geographers have made a notable contribution to this debate. Wright (1947) expounded upon the lack of knowledge regarding what went on in men's minds and hearts, and pointed out how anthropocentric we are. He divided the subjective and selective processes by which men relate to their surroundings into three forms, promotional imagining (where one's own desires or conceptions are built into what we see rather than what is there), intuitive imagining (where facts are selected to suit one's own impressions), and aesthetic imagining (where selectively derived 'facts' are further distorted in presentation to suit our preferences. Kirk (1963 developed the distinction between the phenomenal external (real world) and behavioral internal (distorted by cultural setting) environments, and showed that the geographical environment includes both in the sense that the facts from one enter the other "in so far as they are perceived by human beings with motives, preferences, modes of thinking and traditions drawn from their social cultural context" (*loco cit.*, p.366). Thus social cultural processes mediate between external stimuli and internal response and adjustment. In a piece of consummate scholarship, Lowenthal (1961) integrated these ideas and successfully bridged the conceptual and empirical approaches.

Blaut *et al.* (1959) and Fonaroff (1963) have produced excellent empirical analyses of human response to varying environmental conditions in specific resource management situations. Blaut especially showed how cultural and technological ignorance contributed to excessive soil erosion in Jamaica. Porter (1965) pointed out that where environmental gradients were sharp human adjustment was harmonious and discernible, but where changes in environmental opportunities and resistances were gradual maladjustments were frequent.

Later, Lowenthal (1967) extended Barrow's idea by formally recognising the interaction between the processes through which man perceives his environment and his resulting preferences for certain lines of action which subsequently alter his milieu. In Lowenthal's schema (Figures 5.3a and 5.3b) the real world lies beyond our complete understanding because everything we recognise in our environment is the result of a complex selective process based partly on cultural, partly on social, and partly on personal factors. The end result of this selective process is reflected in our behaviour, which in turn alters the real environment in some way. Whether this alteration is considered good or bad, positive or negative is dependent once again upon our values and standards which are part of the selective process. Depending upon this judgment, we may seek to reinforce (positive feedback) or to dampen (negative feedback) the forces which we set in motion. This idea was also developed rather well by Deutsch (1966), in the context of the political decision process.

The cornerstone of this interpretation of the man–environment interaction is the analysis of the selective process through which judgments are made. The phrase commonly associated with this process is 'cognitive perception', and has been defined as the process by which people select, organise, and interpret sensory stimulation into a meaningful and coherent picture of the world (Vernon, 1962). Perception is not simply a function of immediate sensory stimulus, but is the product of the cultural milieu of the sensor, his previous experience and training, his motivations at the time, and the social framework in which he acts.

The concept of perception and its relevance to behaviouristic models of decision making is not new to geography, and indeed many important contributions have been made from the standpoint of a number of disciplines (Parsons, 1949; F. H. Allport, 1955; G. W. Allport, 1955; Osgood *et al.*, 1957; Bevan, 1958; Lynch, 1960; Lowenthal, 1961; Barker, 1963, 1965; Hall, 1966; Appleyard *et al.,* 1964; Beck, 1967; Campbell, 1968; Craik, 1968; Sommer, 1969). Saarinen (1969) has recently summarised the contribution of this work for the geographer in a masterly manner.

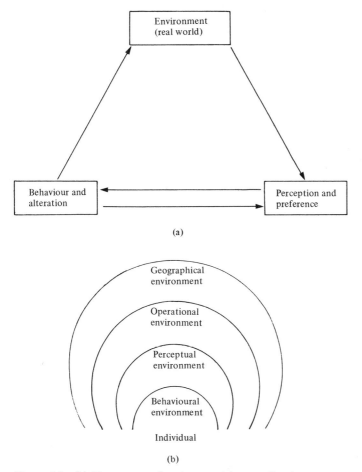

Figure 5.3. (a) The process of environmental perception in resource management (after Lowenthal, 1967). (b) The various environments which impinge upon an individual (after Sonnenfeld, quoted in Saarinen, 1969).

However, when surveying the literature it is evident that precisely because numerous workers have approached this topic from the selective stance of their own training, there is some confusion as to the correct use of various terms and meanings. Value, attitude, perception, and meaning are frequently used interchangibly, and very often no definition of any kind is supplied at all.

It is convenient to visualise the man–environment relationship as a stimulus–organism-response behaviouristic model (Harvey, 1969). A stimulus is presented in one or a number of forms (natural, physical, social stresses that may occur rapidly, slowly, or catastrophically), and this produces a response, the intensity of which is measurable. We shall see later that it is the spatial and social distribution of response intensities which are of the greatest importance to the resource manager when making decisions about environmental quality.) What we are concerned with initially is the process by which the stimulus is transformed into response by an individual. It is now recognised that this transformation is composed of two forms of reaction, habitual reaction and cognitive reaction. It is convenient to visualise these habitual and cognitive components at two levels of abstraction.

The habitual reaction is essentially an unconscious reflex which is directed by the underlying behavioural patterns expected of an individual by a society as a result of deep subconscious drives to conform to culturally-established mores. F. H. Allport (1955), and G. W. Allport (1955) have shown that these deeply-felt drives are not produced simply by a desire to eliminate disequilibrium, but are more the result of propiate striving towards end states which in themselves are unattainable but enhance stress, permit judgments, and set commitments. These distant goals may be regarded as values and play a highly significant role in the development of conscious personality, for they guide individual judgment as to what is desirable and thus create a new level of conscience—the self-conscious 'ought' as opposed to the tribal 'must'.

Values possess the fundamental characteristics of futurity and orientation and provide an essential guide through which a person can consciously and deliberately judge his actions and the actions of others (Rockeach 1968a, 1968b).

Kluckhohn and Strodtbeck (1961) have clarified these concepts further by isolating and identifying a number of 'value orientations', which they claim will affect the sensitivity of individuals to needs which arise in life. The orientations they discuss relate to the concepts of change through time, willingness to have contact with others, sense of ambition, and the man–nature relationship. The last deals with the willingness and ability of a given cultural group to adapt to and develop their environment, their sensitivity towards possible environmental change, and their degree of fatalism adopted in the face of environmental adversity and challenge. Kluckhohn and Strodtbeck believed that, by identifying the degree to which the group (1) considered nature dominant, (2) considered man dominant, or (3) believed in a harmonious relationship between man and nature, significant interpretations in this particular value orientation could be made.

Any propensity to act following the reception of a stimulus will be guided by the value framework. But, while values help to guide judgment at the highest level, the intensity with which any specific stimulus is received and the manner in which it directs action in the form of some behavioural pattern or decision is determined by attitude. Attitudes therefore tend to act as a framework within which environmental stimuli are evaluated and acted upon in specific situations. They are derived and clarified by the storage and retrieval of past experience and knowledge, and tend to be reinforced by repetition of occurrence. However, attitudes are not entirely habitual for they depend upon cognitive perception to trigger the learning–feedback process.

Like values, but in a more immediate sense, attitudes help to guide norms against which judgments can be made and the course of action set by some established yet propriate standards of acceptability. Attitudes are posed partly by values and partly by a number of social and personal guides such as code of ethics, professional standards, conforming behaviour patterns, and so on. Attitude change like value change at best is slow, and how it can be brought about is still uncertain. It is believed that the manner in which information (stimulus) is presented, the nature of the environmental stimulus (particularly its complexity), the actor's ability to make judgments and the conditions surrounding the decision situation (that is, his role in the decision-making team) are all important.

As attitudes are somewhat conditioned by values, so perception is influenced by attitudes. Perception involves a conscious, cognitive interpretation of a stimulus and represents an amalgam of a number of specific sensory stimuli. Because the nature and intensity of sensory interpretation varies with the kind of stimulus and the specific circumstances under which the act of perceiving takes place, perception is a highly subjective and fluctuating phenomenon. However, it is necessary to understand the processes underlying the perceptive act, for it may well be the summation of perceptive experiences that identify an individual's response to an environmental stimulus, direct his behaviour, and guide his participation in group action.

To sum up: the boundaries which separate values, attitudes, and perceptions are blurred and wandering. Perhaps it does not matter how precisely these phenomena are defined. But it is important to realise that these factors, acting either singly or in combination, do set the levels of acceptability by which each one of us defines such culturally anthropocentric terms as 'congestion','pollution', 'hazard', 'overcrowded',

'noisy', and the like (Atkisson and Robinson, 1969). Most important
of all, they guide us into preferences of outcome and commitments for
action when confronted with decisions involving environmental quality.
Thus, by knowing the reasons for and the intensity of such preferences,
we can begin to devise standards of public acceptability, against which
decisions regarding environmental quality can be judged.

The need to understand public preferences

Why do we need to know the nature and intensity of public preferences
for certain levels of environmental quality? Because environmental
quality is a resource (albeit a different kind of resource), increasing
amounts of which can only be derived at a cost measured in terms of
other resources forgone. So, theoretically, we should return to the basic
principles of resource allocation: how much at the margin are we willing
to sacrifice in order to enjoy an additional increment of environmental
quality? This is not a meaningless question, for decision makers are
increasingly confronted with judgments which involve the allocation of
the incompatible alternative of quality resource services versus tangible
resource goods. For example, whether to construct a reservoir that would
back up into the Grand Canyon of Colorado and alter a unique scenic
landscape, yet which would provide power, water supply, and irrigation;
or whether to control the outlet of a natural lake to increase future
water supply, yet damage the lakeshore ecosystem and the general
recreational amenity. Despite the Herculean efforts of welfare economists
to arrive at surrogate prices with which to evaluate environmental quality,
at best such indices only provide an estimate of the *least* (rather than the
most) which people would be willing to pay to maintain environmental
quality or to avoid environmental deterioration (Herfindahl and Kneese,
1965; Krutilla, 1967b; Kneese, 1968).

But what is the public's marginal preference for additional increments
of environmental quality? Research into how public attitudes towards
environmental quality are formed and expressed is fundamental, for it
represents a more positive approach towards the public valuation of the
environmental resource. When any decision body is confronted with a
choice that affects environmental quality it must use some guidelines by
which to evaluate the efficiency of various alternatives. These guidelines
we may call goals, and it is vitally important to identify these goals in
operational terms. We have shown that, in the past, such judgments were
usually evaluated in terms of increased community welfare, where welfare
was treated as some distributional function of aggregate wealth. However,
now we are realising that improved environmental quality is a legitimate goal
in itself, so we need to know the public preferences for specific levels of
environmental quality in relation to the costs involved, for the expression of
such preferences should indicate the public's willingness to pay for certain
levels of quality. We shall see in Chapter 7 that any decision faced by a

political body is subject to pressures by affected groups. The current concern for environmental quality has led to the emergence of numerous articulate citizens' groups, either demanding improved quality or affected by faulty decisions which have imperfectly solved an environmental quality problem (Patterson, 1967). Thus analyses of the intensities of public preferences over space and time with regard to the expected outcomes of each of a number of proposed alternatives is a necessary guideline, against which political decision bodies may have to make judgments.

A futher reason for the analysis of public attitudes and preferences is the need to establish meaningful operational standards for environmental quality. Present standards are based upon technical criteria established by experts primarily upon health grounds. These have been derived from a curious mixture of faith, intuition, experience, and technical knowledge, and usually emerge in the form of minimum acceptable levels of certain parameters. For example, water quality standards are often couched in such technical criteria as Biochemical Oxygen Demand, Suspended Solids, Dissolved Oxygen Content, and Coliform Counts. While it is readily accepted that in the final analysis technical criteria have to be used to operate an air and water quality management programme, it is not so evident that the standards to which these criteria are related need to be established purely by a political–technical body. Indeed, there is even some question in technical circles as to whether the traditional measurements for evaluating water quality are either sufficient or accurate (McGauhey, 1965). It is now apparent that the evaluation of environmental quality parameters, such as air and water pollution, depends upon human use at a given time and is based to some extent upon human judgment, rather than simply upon the statements of experts (White, 1969). This is not to say that experts should be ignored. But their views should be integrated with the preferences as expressed by citizens' groups, and only then translated into meaningful technical criteria. After all, the framework of goals within which environmental quality standards are to be set surely relates to public judgments of the desirability of the environment surrounding them.

However, the identification of public attitudes and preferences is no easy task. The decision maker when confronted with a number of alternative courses of action affecting environmental quality seldom receives clear signals as to public preferences, for their expression is notoriously vague, conflicting, shifting, and segmented. Rarely are public policies explicitly defined, and even more rare is the emergence of a broad public forum where such policies are discussed (Caldwell, 1964, 1966, 1967). A major difficulty arises owing to the fact that the various components of an individual's value schema are inconsistent (Rockeach, 1968a). We have shown the importance of the value schema in guiding decision and committing action, but when some of these propriate guides conflict, there may be a 'dilemma of conscience' which can prove difficult to resolve. For example, in order to reduce environmental pollution there must inevitably be a conflict between the value of profit making, individualism, and the right to use public goods, and those of health, welfare, and better environmental quality. There is a fine line here which divides the means of resource use and social obligation, but its actual location is obviously extremely difficult to determine. Indeed, it will fluctuate over time for each individual, depending upon his awareness and the specific situation with which he is faced, and will likewise vary from one individual to another.

In essence, the public preference is the sum total of individual preferences. We have already shown that the manner in which an individual interprets and responds to environmental stimuli is a highly complicated process. Figure 5.4 attempts to summarise the recent thinking in this matter. The figure shows that the individual's preference for a particular kind and amount of environmental resource use is the result of a selective process where incoming information (stimuli) is received, interpreted, and assessed, and choices as to possible alternative solutions are narrowed and listed in order of preference. The information relating to any environmental issue is selectively presented to him, depending upon existing social, legal, and institutional guides. Then his selected information is further refined, depending upon his interpretation of the problem. This process is affected by the cultural values that he holds, his education and learning, the technology he is able to utilise or invent, and the nature of the problem at hand (particularly its complexity and his degree of contact with it, his previous experience with the problem or of his knowledge of previous occurrences, and his individual personality). His actual behaviour will be affected by his expectation of the outcome, his evaluation of the desirability of the outcome (both for himself and for society as a whole), the nature of the decision situation itself, and his own assessment of his competence to make the decision.

A number of studies substantiate these points. M. L. Barker (1968) found that people tended to identify water pollution on the basis of direct sensory stimulation (particularly sight and smell) rather than to rely on the technical reports of experts. She also found that the words 'polluted water' were identified with a danger to public health, while 'dirty water' was interpreted as murky or mucky due to the addition of natural factors (silt, debris, vegetable matter). Dirty water was not considered unhealthy, though it was thought undesirable. Degree of contact was important in that swimmers were keenly aware of changes in water quality but did not consider the water polluted, while nonswimmers on the same beaches were more critical of water quality. Previous experience was also significant, for after a certain threshhold number of visits (eight in the case of this study) perception of pollution became markedly heightened. In addition, Barker found that there was a significant relationship between those who saw man as dominant over nature and their critical evaluation of water quality.

Lucas (1964) in an analysis of recreation patterns in a wilderness area in northern Michigan noted that attitudes to wilderness differed amongst the various kinds of users. Canoeists found only in the more inaccessible areas were highly sensitive to other users and defined wilderness in narrow terms covering a limited area. Motorboaters, on the other hand, tended to hold much broader views in their interpretation of wilderness, and drew its boundaries to include a greater variety of uses and

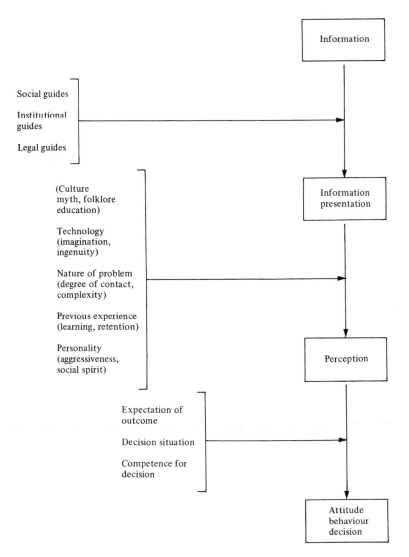

Figure 5.4. Factors affecting attitude and behaviour in the process of resource management appraisal.

biophysical characteristics. Catton (1969) substantiated these findings when he probed the psychological motivations of wilderness users and found that recreational behaviour and attitudes towards the landscape and other users differed markedly with the length of stay and the nature of the wilderness experience. Bultena and Taves (1961) have related public images of wilderness to forest management policy. In a similar study, the author (T. O'Riordan, 1969a) interviewed a variety of recreationists in Broadland (Norfolk, England) and discovered that their evaluation of the recreational environment was dependent on previous experience, the nature of their recreation experience (whether sailing or motor boating), the degree of congestion and crowding, the location, nature, and amount of the various facilities provided, and the ability to take action to avoid unpleasant environmental situations. Shafer (1969), and Shafer *et al.* (1969) have attempted to quantify the factors that constitute pleasant recreational environments by correlating these with stated preferences for particular campsites. Their results are encouraging, though not conclusive.

Other studies have probed deep into the complex psychological processes that impinge upon attitudes and public reaction. For instance, a correlation has been established between a dislike of aircraft noise and an inbuilt fear of air crashes (see White, 1966b). Paul *et al.* (1961) showed that voting patterns for and against fluoridation of the public water supply were correlated with a sense of political and social alienation. People with limited education and who expressed a wish to be left alone by society tended to vote against fluoridation, while the better educated and more affluent voted in the affirmative. However, Sapolsky (1969) found contrary evidence. He postulated that public opinion is favourable towards fluoridation until the issues are raised prior to referenda. Sufficient confusion is then created in the minds of the less well-educated during the fluoridation campaign to force the majority to play safe (especially when public health interests are involved) and vote for the *status quo.*

The real problem surrounds the question: can individual preferences be interpreted and expressed as meaningful operational guidelines? And this in turn raises some rather fundamental moral and ethical questions that cannot easily be answered:
a. What is the degree of variance in interpersonal response to similar environmental stimuli?
b. Is this variance more a personal or a cultural phenomenon?
c. If there is a 'sensitive minority' who do care, to what extent should their wishes be granted against the possible broad indifference of the majority?
d. Does the public really know what is good for it and who decides whether it does or does not?
Each of these questions involves issues of value and political judgments

that always must be made when contending groups desire conflicting uses out of a multiple resource. They are questions that cannot be answered easily nor considered lightly (see Chapters 7 and 8).

Difficulties in canvassing public preferences

We do know that there are extreme difficulties involved in gauging public preferences. For example, intensity of public feeling about an environmental quality problem, such as air and water pollution, depends partly on the severity of pollution and to a large extent upon pressures created by other community issues. For instance, Frederickson and Magnas (1968) discovered that water pollution in a lake near Syracuse, New York, was only a middle-level problem and that greater concern was expressed for schools and housing. However, suburban residents (generally white, affluent, and educated) were far more concerned about the quality of the lake which they used for swimming and boating than were the city dwellers (predominantly black, poor, and ill-educated), who put far more emphasis on local community problems and who rarely used the lake. Other studies have found that people are remarkably optimistic when confronted with environmental stress and readily rationalise their judgments. For example, M. L. Barker (1968) found that respondents interviewed on a polluted beach invariably stated that pollution was far worse elsewhere, and that even whole communities would 'trade-off' their criticisms of their own deteriorating environment by exaggerating pollution conditions existing elsewhere.

The bulk of the population appears to remain apathetic and indifferent toward an environmental stress until it has actually reached crisis proportions, despite the repeated warnings of experts or the vicarious lessons learnt from crises elsewhere. The reasons for this can be found simply in human nature. People rarely act until they are directly affected. People rarely help each other unless bound by a common cause. People become tolerant of gradually worsening situations and develop a number of adjusting mechanisms which help them to avoid the worst frustrations. People are environmental gamblers: they are prepared to do nothing in the optimism that the worst will never happen to them (Landsberg, 1967). People are schizophrenic with regard to the environment because usually they are unaware of the delicate interactions that interlink the various environmental subsystems, and will pollute, on the one hand, yet demand increased environmental quality, on the other. People always delay the difficult decisions, hoping that when they have to be faced solutions will be easier to find and decisions easier to make. People tend to leave complex issues to the politicians and experts, yet are surprised when they do not always come up with the answers in the absence of a clear expression of public desires. People play a variety of roles in their economic, social, and political lives, and frequently a number of these roles conflict simultaneously. This tends to distort the rational reasoning process and may lead to an inconsistency of attitude toward a specific environmental phenomenon. For example, the president of a large paper mill polluting a river may also be a director of a local community organisation pressing for an off-river swimming pool to protect his children from a possible health hazard. We see here clearly the conflict of values and resulting inconsistent actions of an individual who is playing simultaneous roles as a private *entrepreneur* and as a socially-concerned *citizen*. This is the basic dichotomy of freedom and obligation mentioned earlier (Chapter 1), and may contribute to lessen the competence for decision making over environmental quality.

But the faults do not rest entirely with human nature. Many of the meta-problems with which society is at present grappling are immensely complex. Most of the relevant issues are not widely known, facts are few and frequently in contention as 'experts' disagree publicly over their individual interpretations of what appears to be the same problem. Thus there is no 'expert' consensus as to solution. In addition, there is little in the way of the leadership and clear guidance that is so vital, either by public officials or by academics, and in its absence the public become confused, resentful, and hostile.

Thus the formulation of a clear public policy for environmental quality is a hazardous enterprise because the public tends to respond largely to crisis, and to perceive the environment as a rather simple set of symbols and images shifting in form and intensity and conveniently acting in isolation (Firey, 1945; Kates, 1966b). To add to the complexity, individual preferences will shift over time as knowledge and environmental conditions change. All this impedes the implementation of anticipatory action, which is so urgently necessary in a programme of environmental management, and inhibits the recognition of a spatial social cost/benefit function, as groups preferring different kinds and varying levels of environmental quality compete and conflict with one another over time and space.

Despite these difficulties, there is an urgent need to improve the methodology of attitude response, to assess more accurately how people react to stochastic variations in environmental stress, to distinguish between statement (opinion, mood) and behaviour (action), to measure better the intensity of feeling towards various environmental stimuli (Osgood *et al.*, 1957; Saarinen, 1966), and to clarify the role played by the individual decision maker, depending upon whether he is acting on his own or in a group. It is to this last important aspect that we now turn.

The role of attitudes of professional resource managers

Though the understanding, analysis, and expression of individual and group attitudes towards resource appraisal and use are vital for the better management of all resources, particularly where issues of environmental quality are involved, nevertheless, decision making is generally most influenced by a technical elite of professional resource managers— engineers, public health inspectors, medical health officers, foresters, wildlife biologists, and the like. These professionals play various roles, such as consultants, advisors, planners, supervisors of management programmes, technical staff, administrators, and politicians. They may be employed in private concerns, public agencies, or in a personal consultative capacity; they may have direct responsibility or play only a minor role in the overall decision-making apparatus; they may act in two or more capacities in any of a number of resource management situations. But whatever their role, whatever their training, whatever their decision environment, their attitudes and their preferences are of considerable interest to the resource geographer owing to the influence they have on the decision maker's interpretation of the problem, his choice of relevant alternatives, his preferences for outcome, and, in general, his views as to the ways in which resources should be managed.

A number of important questions are relevant here.
1. What is the influence of the professional resource manager in the decision-making process?
2. Do the attitudes of technical personnel and administrators differ, even though they have the same training?
3. To what extent does the professional code of ethics influence resource management appraisal?
4. What part does the decision setting play in influencing attitudes and directing preferences?
5. How are innovations (both managerial and technological) diffused to the professional resource manager, and what factors influence his interpretation and adoption of new ideas?
6. How does the professional resource manager perceive his role in the decision-making process, and how does he view his public image?
7. To what extent is the professional resource manager influenced by his own opinion of what others (particularly his colleagues) think, and his opinion of what the public want or what he thinks is good for them?
8. What role does personality play in influencing the attitudes of the professional resource manager?
A number of approaches are being adopted to answer these questions, using techniques from psychology, sociology, economics, geography, and political science. However, as the tools are still being sharpened, the answers to date are empirical and patchy.

The approaches adopted have been directed along two lines: (1) the study of individuals as members of a particular profession engaged in various resource management activities, and (2) the analysis of group attitudes in relation to the decision hierarchy of various management agencies. Let us look at the latter approach first.

The adminstrative structure of resource management

Analysis of the political and administrative structure of the resource management process has been extensive, both through academic research and through public enquiry. Much attention has been focused on the manner in which goals are set, strategies identified and alternative solutions scanned. Maass (1951) and White (1966b) in two very different studies have pointed out how the goals and strategies of resource management agencies are rarely identified clearly, and frequently conflict and overlap because of inconsistent aims. "There is not a single programme or single policy in recent United States resource management that displays a unitary unambiguous aim. Several aims are fused, and the most ardent administrators revel in the flexibility afforded by the resultant ambiguity: flood control is to save lives and protect economically efficient development; highway beautification is to enhance the landscape and make it more accessible by concrete expressways; waste treatment is to reduce health hazards and to render streams more useful for a variety of purposes." (White, 1966b, p.112).

Thus, because the environment has not been visualised as a complex system of fundamentally interlinked and interacting processes, and because resource issues generally become public policy only through crisis and 'muddling through' (Lindblom, 1959), agency operations are segmented and often seriously in conflict. In the United States the duplication between Federal resource management agencies is notorious, and has been subject to intensive Congressional scrutiny (Felser, 1965). But even within Congress the bureaucratic machinery is segmental and cumbersome and it is not impossible to find evidence of contradictory policy (Resources for the Future, 1961; Munger and Houghton, 1965; Henning, 1968). Shad and Boswell (1968) reported that of 24000 proposed legislative measures placed before Congress in 1967, about 1300 dealt with water resources and were handled by 13 committees in the House of Representatives and 11 committees in the Senate. This picture of bureaucratic segmentation is somewhat the same in Canada (Canadian Council of Resource Ministers, 1966a, 1966b) both at the Federal and provincial levels.

Management studies within agencies have shown that many of these external factors are mirrored internally (Calef, 1960; Schiff, 1962, 1966a; Martin, 1969). Communication between departments is scanty unless programmes are clearly closely related. Terms of reference and areas of operation are jealously protected and stalwartly defended. Departmental budgets and appropriations are carefully calculated to maintain viability. The use of benefit–cost analysis is manipulated to promote specific ends by exaggerating benefits and playing down costs. Annual appropriations for each agency must be met and enlarged: benefit–cost analysis, far from being a guide to economic feasibility, is frequently a tool for hazy justification. For example, a recent report by the US Federal Water Resources Council Task Force on Project Evaluation (US, Water Resources Council, 1969) supports the dubious practice of agencies providing their own feasibility studies, and suggests the inclusion of secondary benefits despite the impressive counter arguments put forward by economists (Margolis, 1957; Ciriacy-Wantrup, 1964). Marshall (1966) has pointed out that a universal characteristic of most organisations is the desire to survive and grow, for growth adds prestige, power, and income to its members, and survival means economic and psychological security. Without appropriate funds, agency growth is impossible: without programme success appropriative funds would be curtailed.

Attitudes of agency personnel
Further probing into the very attitudes and aspirations of agency personnel has unearthed some interesting findings. Marshall (1965, 1966) has reported that there is a powerful personal identification on the part of the employee with the agency's goals and its established resource management strategies, a commitment to furthering the traditional work of the agency, an absolving of direct responsibility of agency decisions, a loyalty to the point of conformity, and a resistance to innovation and to proposed solutions that radically depart from traditional practice. All of these factors, of course, tend to reinforce established practice, and increase bureaucratic insulation. The result is that agency personnel, buffered by a bureaucratic hierarchy and absolved from direct responsibility, tend to become immune and impregnable to public criticism and persist in advocating nonoptimal policies and strategies of resource use, despite clear evidence that more efficient solutions could be employed (Gore, 1964; Caldwell, 1966). White (1969) has presented an excellent case study where bureaucratic intransigence stifled the opportunity for innovative and more flexible strategies of water resource management in the Metropolitan Chicago area. The result was a policy that moved little from established norms (see Chapter 8).

Evidence suggests that many resource management agencies, especially those in the water field, are dominated by engineers, who, owing to their training and the ethics of their profession, tend to canvass alternative solutions along the somewhat restricted lines of the structural monument. Dams, levées, canals, large-scale water transfers, and the like are simple, obvious, expedient, and tangible outcomes of a resource management project: they are easily identified in the popular mind with the work of the engineering profession, and carry power, prestige, and symbolic significance. Moreover, structural solutions are supported by powerful vested interests and provide important local employment opportunities. Indeed, the dam-constructing period in the late twenties and thirties in the United States (during which time such massive schemes as the Bonneville Dam, Hoover Dam, and the Tennessee Valley Authority dams were built) was a function of the need to employ the vast amount of idle labour brought about by the Depression (Lilienthal, 1944; McKinley, 1952; Clapp, 1955) and provided a symbolic integrating focus for the New Deal.

The result has been an extraordinary emphasis on the single-purpose approach of the construction solution. Other alternatives, such as improving the efficiency of use, sharpening the liaison between potentially conflicting programmes, or clarifying the complicated legal and institutional tangles were rarely perceived, and anyway time consuming and difficult to implement. Moreover, the nonstructural solution engenders little political appeal, for it is intangible and unseen and frequently detrimental to previous patterns of resource use enjoyed by powerful vested interests at the public expense. Often, too, the choice of a construction alternative has been hastened and reinforced as a viable solution following the impact of some environmental catastrophe or political stress. Construction agency personnel therefore tend to become identified in the minds of the professionals, the politicians, and the public alike as saviours and protectors with a clearly delineated role in resource management. The fact that injudicious use of this alternative has narrowed the range of choice, crystallised inflexibility in decision structures, and foreclosed options for the future has only recently been realised as detrimental, as the increasing burden imposed on social and environmental costs becomes better recognised in the decision schema (National Academy of Sciences–National Research Council, 1966a; White, 1969).

In an exploratory analysis of a relatively small sample of water management engineers in British Columbia, Canada, Sewell (1968) noted that their identification of their role in resource management and their interpretation of their public image helped to strengthen certain attitudes. In particular, his analysis has helped to shed some light on the tripartite opinion 'complex' that confronts every decision maker, namely, opinions that he personally holds, the opinions he thinks the public holds, and the opinions he thinks the public should hold (White, 1966b). Sewell found that the expert considered the public dependent upon his opinion, particularly where the water problems involved technical or organisational complexities, and that the expert often relied on his own judgment as to what people prefer and what is good for them rather than actively seeking public opinion on the matter. He also discovered that the engineers he interviewed strongly identified their advice with the final decision and that they considered their work constructive and creative in the public interest. However, responsibility for the initial action and the final decision, they felt, always rested with the government. To his surprise,

Sewell found that the engineers he interviewed were not man-dominant in value orientation to nature, but tended, in fact, to see nature as being dominant. He tentatively concluded that this is due to the sensitivity of many engineers to public criticism that their profession is 'interfering with nature'. Generally, he found a relationship between role, experience, and responsibility: engineers in the upper echelons of the organisational hierarchy displayed a broader perspective and tended to be more sensitive to the wider repercussions of management decisions.

Sewell's findings tend to substantiate the more general conclusions of Marshall (1966) concerning attitudes of professionals. Marshall noted that professionals are bound by a mutual respect and a code of ethics that tends to isolate them somewhat from 'lay' opinion and makes them most responsive to criticism from within their own ranks. This creates a powerful, partly insulated attitudinal environment which encourages conformity to accepted codes of behaviour and established problem-solving techniques. Moreover, the hierarchical nature of the bureaucracy often favours separation of technical advice from the management and political decision-making apparatus, with the result that the professional is further sheltered from the complex sociopolitical forces of the real world, and from any expression of public preferences (Merton, 1957). These findings are well substantiated in a study of public health administrators by Romain (1967).

MacIver (1969) in a valuable empirical study has also shown how the attitudes of the professional resource manager and the choice of preferred alternative were closely related to his familiarity with the resource, his technical competence [the 'prison of experience' (Kates, 1962, p.140)], and to goals and operating procedures of the agency for which he worked. In analysing the various solutions preferred by a number of professionals for increasing the water supplies for a metropolitan area, MacIver noted remarkable differences in the analyses of the problem, the recognition of the various possible alternatives (only a few of which were considered by any single individual, and some of which, mainly those dealing with improving the efficiency of water use, were not considered by any), and the preferences for outcome, so that even in a relatively simple resource management situation concensus by the experts was simply not possible, and the decision process by no means open-ended and rational.

To date, research into the attitudes of professional resource managers has virtually by-passed the complex problem of the effect of personality on attitude formation. This is touched upon by White (1966b), and developed a little by Saarinen (1966) in his use of the thematic apperception test. This test and similar techniques derived from psychology [for example, the Rosenzweig picture test (Barker and Burton, 1968) and the Objective–Analytic Personality Battery test (Cattell and Warburton, 1967)] need to be developed further to gain a clearer picture of the influence

of personality on opinion and behaviour, though considerable difficulties
of methodology and measurement must first be overcome. But there should
be adequate rewards. We have already noted the influence of personality
in affecting hazard-zone occupancy, and there is no doubt that differences
in personality do influence the opinion and action of the individual either
on his own or as a member of a decision-making unit. Indeed Cattell
(1965), who is one of the foremost workers in this field, believes that the
nature of personality is a fundamental variable in guiding the nature of
response to external stimuli.

Appraisal

Research into the formation and role of attitudes and preferences of
professional resource managers and agency personnel is at an early stage.
The difficulties of obtaining interviews and receiving reliable data are
enormous, yet such analyses are vital in furthering the understanding of
the *process* by which resource management decisions are made and are
reflected on the landscape. It is unlikely that professionals will expose
the inner secrets of their organisations or of the decision apparatus in
which they play a part. Indeed they may become suspicious or resentful
of the intrusions of the researcher. Research techniques in this area will
therefore require unusual amounts of discretion and diplomacy. Constant
improvement of interview procedures will be necessary. However, the
researcher cannot rely simply upon what professionals and administrators
say, either in interview or as reported in the mass communications media:
he must also be prepared to analyse and interpret the *actions* and
behaviour of the expert, as expressed through the decision process and
the subsequent implementation of resource management strategy. It is
to this culminating issue in resource management that we now turn.

Decision making in resource management

Each one of the new lines of research that we have been investigating is directed towards improving the processes by which judgments are formed, and choices are made with regard to the amount, nature, and timing of resource use as it affects groups and individuals on the landscape. Resource management in the final analysis is a decision-making process where optimal solutions regarding the manner, timing, and allocation of resource use are sought within the economic, political, social, and institutional framework afforded by any given culture at any particular time. By the very nature of things, in a world of rapid scientific and technological advance, of equally rapid social and economic appraisal and reappraisal of resources, increasingly complex choices have to be made, and must be made fairly promptly. At the same time, the cost of faulty decisions weighs more and more heavily as society becomes increasingly concerned with the broader environmental side effects, especially where some of these effects may be irreversible (Hamill, 1968).

Thus it is in the nature of a summary that we review the major themes of this monograph—the recent efforts to sharpen the tools of cost and benefit evaluation, to improve the efficiency and productivity of resource use, to clarify the understanding of the man–environment interaction, and to probe into the values, attitudes, and perceptions that we hold according to the various roles we play—in the context of resource management decision making.

It will probably never be possible to make optimal decisions. For one thing there is no clear consensus as to what constitutes the 'optimal'. Theoretically, optimal allocation would be that combination of adjustments which yields the largest net social benefits over a given investment period. Yet it has been shown that there are no clearly-defined goals against which to assess the adequacy and efficacy of any programme, and that the 'public interest' cannot be gauged by any consistent means, but is multifaceted, conflicting, and shifting. It has also been pointed out that the identification of social costs and benefits is difficult and evaluation even more hazardous, and that uncertainty of future outcomes and hesitation of judgment in the face of possible technological innovations at best promotes caution, and at worst narrows focus and eliminates imaginative alternatives. These and other distortions encountered in the real world have led most students of the decision process to by-pass the search for the optimum in favour of 'second best', 'satisfying' or 'sub-optimal' solutions (Lipsey and Lancaster, 1956; Simon, 1957a, 1957b, 1960; Snyder, 1958; Davis and Whinston, 1967; Beasley, 1967; Hamill, 1968).

The resource decision maker is therefore placed in an extremely unfortunate position. The traditional, seemingly reliable, 'quick fix' technological solutions of the past are increasingly being called into question by a broadening base of sincere public opinion, both informed and uninformed. Yet the complex demands which a modern society makes upon its resources require speedy, accurate judgment with the minimum of undesirable side effects.

The logical trend, therefore, is to analyse the decision process itself. We need to focus upon the forces and resistances acting upon the decision makers when questions of resource management are judged, so as to understand more completely the factors that contribute to decisions which are ultimately reflected as changes in the landscape, and which affect future public use and enjoyment of the environment.

Formation of goals

The decision process is essentially a choice among alternatives. But judgment as to the desirability or undesirability of any given alternative or combination of alternatives relies heavily upon some implicit statement of goals. The first consideration therefore is the understanding of how goals are formulated and how they are expressed as operational guidelines and embodied in public policy. (For an up-to-date and comprehensive discussion and bibliographic review, see Mitchell and Mitchell, 1969.)

A major contribution to this end can be found in the two reports issued by the Committee on Water of the National Academy of Sciences– National Research Council (National Academy of Sciences–National Research Council, 1966a, 1968). In their second report in particular (*loco cit.*, 1968), where they scrutinised the various alternatives for developing the Colorado River Basin, the Committee showed that goals were never clearly defined nor precisely formulated, but were multiple, ambiguous, and changing, and differed between nation, state, and region and from agency to agency as a result of complex forces propelled by vested interests. "When the aims are confused and intermixed, as when a nation and a state have different and not clearly defined reasons for wanting the same project, there is a tendency to avoid rigorous examination of alternative ways of seeking any of the aims. And as aims change, investigations that earlier seemed relevant to the project prove inadequate, and new questions are raised" (*loco cit.*, p.42). The Committee outlined five specific, yet alternative, goals in the context of their study and revealed the various forces that promoted each of these goals. These five goals were (1) national economic efficiency, (2) income redistribution, (3) political equity, (4) control over the natural environment, and (5) ethical and aesthetic considerations. It summarised its position by drawing up a chart which listed a number of possible alternative solutions for meeting each goal (see Figure 2.4). The most important issue raised by this exercise was that, though judgment as to the appropriate goals is basically a political one, many of the alternatives canvased had never been considered, as these did not rely on agricultural water supply as an essential reason for project implementation. In other words, in the absence of clear articulation of goals and alternatives a number of political forces were exerting vociferous pressures which distorted resource management decisions in their favour. G. Brown Jr. (1968) in a similar kind of analysis has questioned the efficacy of water management *per se* as the most appropriate tool to promote regional economic development, and has supported the arguments of Hirshleifer *et al.* (1960) in criticising the California Water Plan (Bain *et al.*, 1966) on the grounds of false assumptions (see Chapter 8).

It would appear then that goals are not formulated by clear, rational, logical debate involving all groups concerned, but rather evolve from a complex history of vaguely-expressed public opinion, faulty interpretations, and political opportunism (Hill, 1968; Lindblom, 1968). Fox (1966a) has developed this theme extensively. He showed, for instance, that the objectives of settlement in the Western United States were derived not so much from rational economic reasoning, but as a result of "a variety of forces such as the concept of political leaders that settlement of the West was in the national interest, and a general feeling that making the desert bloom is intrinsically good. In part, because of these drives, individuals saw the opportunity for private gain or political advancement and added to the pressures for action" (*loco cit.*, p.272). Fox goes on to postulate that this view has tended to give credence to the attitude that water is the key to economic growth in the West and to increasing pressures for large-scale transfers of fresh water at public expense regardless of the wastage generated and social cost involved. Quinn (1968) has supported this evidence.

Turning to water quality, White (1966) noted that the public is assumed to prefer fresh water (as opposed to reused water) for their water supply and that this attitude is translated into the decision criteria of water supply officials. For example, when the City of New York was confronted with a water shortage, the prevalence of this attitude prompted a search for increased municipal supplies, not from the nearby (polluted) Hudson River, but from the distant (cleaner) Delaware River whose lower reaches were already threatened by shortage of upstream flows (Martin, 1960). Johnson (forthcoming) has presented similar evidence with respect to untested official assumptions about the public attitude toward reused waste water for urban domestic water supplies. Despite his findings that the public have faith in modern water-treatment techniques and will accept reused water for domestic use (American Institute for Chemical Engineers, 1967; Institution of Public Health Engineers, 1968), officials are unlikely to choose this as a solution. The point here is that political and technical judgments in resource management are not infrequently based on flimsy assumptions as to what the public wants and should get. It is no wonder that in situations where aims are vague and ambiguous political expediency and economic opportunism is rife.

We have already shown that public attitudes shift very slowly. Certainly change is not encouraged when the 'public interest' is so vaguely interpreted

by politicians and resource management agency personnel. There is a need
to establish a forum where various resource management goals (and the
various alternatives for attaining each of these) are evaluated with the
broadest possible consideration, so that the losses attendant on the solution
of any one course of action can be presented in the calculus. Caldwell
(1963, 1966, 1967) has presented a most persuasive case for the better
public administration of the environment. In particular, he urged that
public policy be made more flexible to keep options open, yet become more
clear and consistent to permit sound and stable decision making for all
aspects of environmental management. Public policy plays a similar role
for governments as does the value schema for the individual. Without some
committed public consensus as to what constitutes a desirable environment
it is impossible to develop the necessary guidelines against which to weigh
incoming proposals for the use of air, land, and water, and within which to
evaluate future strategy. It is probably safe to say that a major reason why
governments have failed to halt environmental deterioration is the lack of
clear and consistent policies for environmental management. Absence of,
or weakness, in policy formulation permits opportunism, and inevitably
results in political embarrassment.

Having somehow weighted the desirability of various goals (Hill, 1968),
the decision maker is next faced with the choice of the best available means
of achieving these goals. White (1969) has termed this process the adoption
of *strategy*, where a strategy can be defined as a combination of goals,
means, and decision criteria. He emphasises the need to adopt multiple
strategies where differing combinations of managerial and technical
adjustments are employed, both in the private and in the public sector.
The essence of his argument is the need to maintain flexibility in final
choice, and thus to hedge against uncertainty, so that, wherever possible,
opportunities be left open in the future for the adoption of new solutions
(both technical and managerial). Thus the aim would be to minimise the
possible foreclosure of future courses of action, by forestalling, whenever
possible, the onset of irreversible processes, and by avoiding the adoption
of single-purpose solutions. The emphasis should be upon a continuous
assessment and reassessment of a maximum variety of alternative
adjustments to satisfy broadly acceptable outcomes (Krutilla, 1967a,
1967b; National Academy of Sciences–National Research Council,
1966a; Water Resources Board, 1968).

White (1964, 1966a, 1969) has developed this theme, particularly with
regard to flood-loss reduction. Is the aim (1) to reduce floods, (2) to
reduce flood damage, (3) to save lives, or (4) to save property? Are the
best means (1) to build downstream dams, (2) to construct upstream
retention structures, (3) to employ some combination of both, (4) to
develop and improve flood warning devices, (5) to control future flood
plain development, (6) to remove existing flood plain development,
(7) to encourage flood plain users to protect their property, (8) to

provide a flood insurance programme, or (9) to accept a certain amount of loss? Obviously some combination of these goals and means would be most desirable: the problem is to develop this into some general decision model which would be relevant for all resource management situations.

The model that is proposed here is deliberately simple and is based on the work of White (1961, 1963) and his associates at the University of Chicago (Kates, 1962; White, 1964, 1969; Schmoyer, 1967; Wong, 1969, MacIver, 1969), and that of Snyder (1958). The model visualises the decision making process as a learning process composed of four principal stages, each of which is interconnected by feedback loops (Figure 7.1). (Figure 5.4 is also relevant here.) We shall assume that some statement of alternative goals has been formulated. Briefly, a resource is first identified via a number of signals transmitted to the decision maker in the form of information, and alternative strategies are canvased. Then choice is made based upon evaluation of the perceived outcomes of various strategies in terms of recognised social goals, and, finally, the decision is evaluated by comparing the actual outcome with the expected outcome. It should be noted that decision making is an

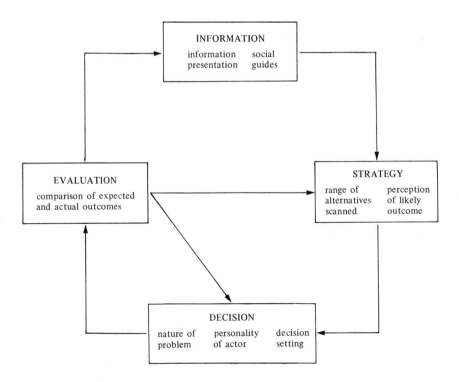

Figure 7.1. A model of decision making in resource management.

on-going process, where decisions of the past are usually reflected in decisions of the present, and where the outcomes of any present decision affect the basis for any future choice.

Of particular importance here are the factors that enter in between each of these four major stages, which not only influence the nature of each stage, but condition the very nature of the decision process and the degree of interstage feedback.

Information strategy

The range of alternatives which will be considered depends to a considerable extent upon the manner in which the decision maker receives information about the problem, the source of this information, (whether directive or inducive) and his own interpretation of this information, that is, the use to which he will put this information when making his choice. The manner in which information is presented is influenced by what White (1961) calls social guides. These are of two forms. One is the influence of existing laws, policies, directives, and standards which guide action along more or less clearly defined paths, depending upon the clarity of such guides. The other is the apparently confused and frequently contradictory emanation of statements by agencies, professionals, citizens' groups, and individuals, each distorting the information in favour of their respective preference of outcome. Thus in the absence of personal investigation (which often is impossible), the decision maker is confronted by a selectively directed form of information presentation, which tends to distort his interpretation of the problem and encourages the selection of certain strategies at the expense and even possible exclusion of others. We have already shown the need to consider a broader range of strategy in the decision process, and there is no doubt that the influence of forces which either inhibit or promote a wider evaluation of alternatives is vital in determining the outcome of the final decision (see Chapter 6).

Strategy choice

Basically, the actor makes his choice according to his opinion of the utility of the expected outcomes stemming from each of the alternative strategies under consideration. Expectation is a highly subjective process when dealing with uncertainty, though a number of models based on sound mathematical theory have been developed (Luce and Raiffa, 1957, Simon, 1960; Churchman, 1961; Altouney, 1965; Conrath, 1967). White (1961, 1963) has developed this strategy-choice linkage a stage further by assessing the actor's evaluation of each of the various strategies with respect to the relative technological and economic feasibilities, and the perceived effects of each strategy upon space and over time in relation to individuals, groups, and the landscape (spatial and temporal linkages).

Though actual choice relates closely to the values and attitudes of the actor, it can also be closely identified with the nature of the problem, which in turn relates to his appraisal of the opportunities provided by the resource, and with the decision setting. In the previous chapter we discussed extensively the factors influencing the attitudes of the actor. Probably of greatest significance, particularly where political judgments have to be made with regard to resources, is the actor's perception of the degree of threat presented by the problem in relation to other stresses in the community.

The analysis of environmental stress on the political decision-making process has been well documented by Wolpert (1966, 1968) and Kasperson (1969a, 1969b). The former (Wolpert, 1968) has analysed brilliantly the various stages of public response that result from decisions involving community disruption, particularly where minority interests are affected. In the past, when minority groups were often unrepresented, ill-organised, and inarticulate, such groups often succumbed to the opportunism of powerful vested interests. Nowadays, however, with the rise of advocacy planning (Peattie, 1968), such groups are aided in their protests by sympathetic expert opinion, and frequently a political stalemate is reached where no final decision can be made. The decision body and affected public groups confront each other with equivalent political power, so that an impasse is maintained. Wolpert (*loco cit.*) foresees a third stage, that of sophisticated trust, where all public groups are invited to express their opinions while the various alternatives are still being considered and before final decisions are made.

Kasperson (1969a, 1969b) has shown the need for fitting resource decisions into a matrix of stress-intensity perception. Perception of stress intensity depends partly upon the rapidity with which the stress becomes manifest and partly upon the manner in which it is articulated to the actor. High stress-intensity follows upon the occurrence of a rapid catastrophic event, such as a hurricane or a flood, particularly if politically important economic or social interests are affected. Low stress intensities are associated with the slow but gradual buildup of a problem, such as housing dilapidation or water quality deterioration, and is usually manifest only when important community interests are directly involved. The concept of stress-intensity perception is important, for it is usually instrumental in determining the amount of attention and the priority of action afforded any particular community issue (Figure 7.2). We have already noted that where environmental stress builds up gradually (for example, water supply shortage, water and air pollution), stress intensity perception is low in the face of more pressing community needs such as roads, schools or housing. A politician acts on the basis of threat to his position: when a particular environmental issue becomes so serious as to mobilise powerful public opinion, he will seek to resolve this threat

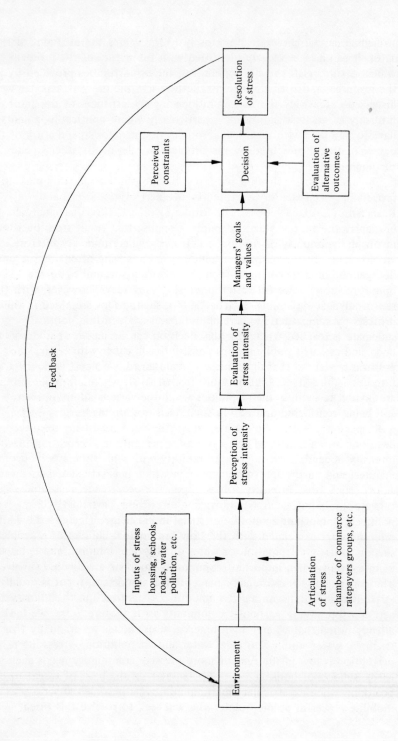

Figure 7.2. A schematic model of municipal stress management (after Kasperson, 1969a; MacIver, 1969).

through some form of mollifying action. Both Kasperson (1969b) and Dales (1968) have shown that such action is almost always too late and too little but it is usually sufficient to temper political stress.

The decision setting is also important in determining the final choice. We have already discussed the role of the professional in the decision process, but where the decision maker is an elected representative and hence where his technical knowledge is often meagre, the influence of technical advice, the clarity with which he sees the problem, his confidence in making judgments and his role in the decision hierarchy are important factors in affecting his final choice. Indeed, psychologists have shown that an actor is quite capable of choosing a strategy contrary to his own personal beliefs under certain decision situations, and that he will rationalise his action by gross simplification of problem complexity into rather simple and somewhat naive symbolic relationships, and by deliberate repression of his own contrary opinions (Festinger, 1957; Henry and Schlien, 1958).

Obviously personality and role identification play an important part here, particularly the degree of confidence that the decision maker holds in his own competence for judgment. Empirical evidence is but patchy, but Strodtbeck (Strodtbeck and White, 1968) has found that a man displaying strong male characteristics is more likely to act if he is told the problem is capable of solution, while a man identifying himself with more female characteristics tends to take action when the problem is more complex. But when an individual is placed in a group decision setting, should he regard his authority as weak vis à vis other members of the group, his final choice will be influenced by majority opinion or by the views of the dominant personality, despite any inner confidence he may have regarding his decision-making competence.

Small group psychology also plays its part in influencing final decision, though there is an urgent need for vigorous empirical investigation in this respect. The author (T.O'Riordan, 1969b) investigated the decisions of three municipal councils in British Columbia, regarding the method of treatment and disposal of sewage. Each community was located beside a lake that was threatened by eutrophication or accelerated biological ageing. He found that where the decision unit felt threatened by external political pressures, or was seeking to save face, individual differences of opinion within the council were suppressed in order to maintain group solidarity. Likewise, a desire to create a sense of community leadership may override individual disagreement. In the same study, the author found that a wish to choose a course of action which was unusual, 'progressive', or simply different tended to restrict the decision group to a very narrow range of choice and blind them to the merits of other possibly more valid alternatives.

Decision evaluation

The decision process is not complete once the final choice is made. A critical stage is the comparison and evaluation of the differences between expected and actual outcomes against some standard of acceptability (policy), for ideally this procedure should initiate feedback. In reality it is rare to see a careful appraisal of actual versus expected benefits, for this requires an expenditure of time, money, and manpower which few agencies are willing to permit. But where such studies have been undertaken, often quite disturbing and fundamental questions have been raised (Buckley and Tihanyi, 1967). Certainly there is a need to sharpen our tools of analysis in this respect.

Empirical studies

Recently, a number of empirical studies have focused on the processes by which individual resource users appraise the resource, scan the range of choice, and adopt or reject alternative strategies, according to their perception of the various technical and economic efficiences and the nature of possible external effects under the influence of various social guides (Kates, 1962; Sewell, 1965; White, 1964; Saarinen, 1966; Wong, 1968). These studies have contributed enormously to our understanding of the processes through which individuals appraise resources and make choices. Their findings also contain important implications for public policy because they help to illuminate the various factors which inhibit 'optimum' resource use as defined by the experts, and which widen the gap between the scientific knowledge of optimal methods and their practical implementation by specific resource users such as foresters, irrigators, industrial water users, and so on (White, 1966a; J.O'Riordan, 1969). Certainly, the recent thrust of research effort towards promoting the efficiency of resource use and of equating the costs more closely with those who are benefitting has been concerned with closing this gap and with aiding individual management decisions (see Chapter 4 and 5).

Much interest has also been displayed in analysing the forces and processes behind public decisions, especially where political judgment is involved. Of particular interest here is the analysis of the attitudes and political articulation of the various interest groups concerned. These studies have evolved out of earlier attempts at understanding the influence of the wider political process in resource development (Maass, 1951; Huffman, 1953; Leuchtenberg, 1953; Ostrom, 1953; Wengert, 1955; Hart, 1957b, 1961; Foss, 1960; Martin *et al.*, 1960).

More recent studies in line with the work of Wolpert (1968) have pointed out the discrepancy between political judgment and public preferences when assessing the desirability of various alternatives. For example, when analysing a water supply decision for a community in Massachusetts, Kasperson (1969b) found that politically-motivated interest groups informed themselves of the issues (usually in a highly-biased manner, which was reflected in local newspaper accounts) and, in the absence of public dialogue, used this as an important political lever to influence decision in their favour at the expense of the apathetic and uninformed majority. In the comparative analysis of three municipal councils mentioned earlier, the author (T. O'Riordan, 1969) pointed out that public groups were not kept abreast of the various alternatives surveyed for the treatment and disposal of sewage, and thus were unable to express their preference for different solutions until confronted with a 'take it or leave it' in the ballot box. This same study also showed that where the gradual buildup of a resource management problem is involved, particularly where the evidence is conflicting and there is inconsistent testimony by experts, municipal councils tend to hesitate and procrastinate in the absence of serious political stress. When crisis (in this case water pollution) does occur, decisions are rushed and are dependent upon the judgments of a few consultant experts who are not always able to pinpoint the broader issues nor consider the wider community interest. At this point studies of the attitudes and preferences for outcome held by professionals, administrators, and politicians are of crucial significance, for it is clear that these preferences play an important part in determining the final decision. For example. in this same study the author discovered that attitudes to environmental quality in general were closely related to a concern for future lake quality. Municipal councillors who expressed concern over environmental deterioration were cautious about the future ability of the lake to absorb additional polluting effluents. Councillors with less concern for environmental quality were highly optimistic regarding future lake recovery and expressed faith in technological solutions.

Such studies involving what Kasperson (1969b) calls "the political economy of resource management", can benefit enormously from the contribution by the geographer, particularly where resource management decisions involving environmental quality are concerned. In such cases choice has to be made on the basis of political value judgments where the threat exerted by groups who find they may be affected adversely by a possible decision enters the decision calculus (Wildawsky, 1966). So an analysis of the complex relationships between decision makers and decision receivers in relation to perceived effects upon groups and the landscape is not only rewarding, but also particularly geographical in flavour.

Studies of decision making in resource management are significant in that they attempt to relate and to assess the *totality* of forces in operation and aid the understanding of the processes involved in the spatial variation of phenomena on the landscape. In many ways they integrate the whole discipline of resource management, for they provide the focus into which many of the research thrusts described earlier can be directed. In addition, it is the opinion of the author that analyses of this sort provide the best means of identifying and evaluating the external social costs and benefits associated with most major resource development programmes at the present time. For, ultimately, it is only through the political process of group bargaining and group conflict that value judgments can be made involving such qualitative concepts as pollution, congestion, hazard loss reduction, and ecological preservation.

Future perspectives in resource management

In this final chapter, we shall try to bring together a number of diverse threads that have only been touched upon in previous chapters, yet which provide the greatest promise for future research. The student of resource management is living in an exciting age. Increasing public concern and involvement with resource issues, probing new scientific and technical discoveries, breakthroughs in new administrative and institutional forms, dynamic and dramatic shifts in resource legislation, and exciting reports by interdisciplinary research teams point clearly to the rapid changes taking place all around him. The research task is enormous. Complex and unforeseen problems require a new arsenal of anticipatory and highly-imaginative solutions that will test scholars, administrators, technical experts, and politicians alike. The 'ideal' or optimal solution will always evade us, for the adequacy of our problem-solving apparatus is determined by the values and perspectives of the viewer and the participant. The search is endless for desirable combinations of adjustments to minimise what we can best define as social costs and maximise what we can best evaluate as social benefits, while seeking the most equitable distribution of gains and losses.

We live in an age of dichotomies. We are armed with better technical and scientific knowledge than man has ever known, yet we are increasingly aware that we cannot control our environment. We live in an age where personal hygiene is regarded as almost sacred, yet we surround ourselves with increasing quantities of undesirable waste discharges (Kates, 1966b); we preserve the highest standards of order and tidiness in our private space, yet tend to misuse and ill-treat our public space; we attempt to devise models that maximise quantities of throughput, while we are really more interested in maintaining the quality of total capital stock (Boulding, 1966); we seek to optimise environmental quality, but to optimise we need to quantify, and we cannot quantify quality. Somehow we must get our perspectives right. Let us look at future research thrusts under the general headings of technical, administrative, institutional, legal, and social needs.

Technical research needs

The major focus for future technical research is to devise means that will change radically the present concept of waste. We have stressed that 'resource' and its antonym 'waste' are culturally derived concepts that relate to man's appraisal of his environment and his preferences for certain values and outcomes. Thus attitudes towards waste, like those towards resources, will vary from one individual to another, depending upon his aspirations and his social conscience. A well-known law of thermodynamics states that matter (including energy) can neither be created nor destroyed: it is simply converted into new forms and transferred across time and space in response to man's needs. This view can be termed the 'materials balance' approach and is excellently described by Ayres and Kneese (1969a) (Figure 8.1). The materials balance concept visualises an open system of energy and matter input, throughput, and output, and underlines the fact that the total materials throughput necessary to maintain a given level of production and consumption decreases as the efficiency of utilisation (that is, minimisation of waste) increases. This view also helps to point out the important, but not always realised, fact that the sink for residual discharges can be interchanged between water, air, and land: for example, a firm may reduce its water-receiving effluent discharge but may transfer this to increase its air-receiving emissions; or control over petrochemical car exhausts may lead to increased sulphur dioxide emissions if steam generated by coal-burning plants becomes the primary source of automotive power.

Where technology is most urgently required, therefore, is in the area of devising new methods of process efficiencies and economical means of utilising waste discharges. Kneese and Bower (1968) have presented a thorough theoretical statement of optimal waste discharge reduction, whereby individual waste dischargers are given the choice of paying a fine or seeking alternative means of reducing emissions. It is important to direct technology along lines that would assist them in this choice. For example, in the food and forest products industries potentially valuable organic products are at present being discharged as waste, which in many areas is creating a serious pollution problem (Ayres and Kneese, 1969a).

An example of this problem can be found in the British Columbia forest industry. Wood shavings and sawdust wasted as a result of inefficient cutting tools account for 17% of the volume of a log and reduce the potential value of the province's forestry by $100 million annually (Fletcher, 1969). Technological improvements which might reduce this wastage by half include finer cutting edges, less vibration during cutting, improved cutting guides, and increased strain on band saws. At present much of the sawdust and slash is burned, creating a widespread problem of air pollution. However, given the necessary incentives, managers could be induced to convert this material into valuable by-products such as pressed logs and chip-board. Likewise in the pulp industry only 60% of the tree is used. The other 40% represented by branches, foliage, stems, and roots is deliberately burned at the logging site to reduce potential fire hazard. Experiments have shown that much of this can be used for pulp processing, again assuming that incentives, which at present do not exist, are provided.

Ayres and Kneese (*loco cit.*) also estimate that 10% of the live weight of slaughtered animals (a conservative calculation) is lost in waste; that

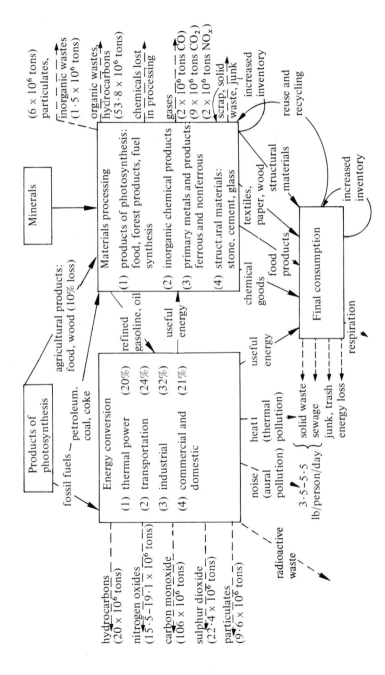

Figure 8.1. A materials balance schema (after Ayres and Kneese, 1969a, p.37). Emission figures in tons per annum for the United States.

in the pulp and paper industry at best only 15% of the lignin waste
liquors are recovered; that somewhere between 1% and 5% of the final
weight of chemical products finds its way into air, water, and the land;
and that the average household will generate between 35 and 45 lbs of
solid waste per day. Kneese (1965) and a number of his associates
(Cootner and Löf, 1966; Kneese and Bower, 1968; Löf and Kneese,
1968; Bower, 1968) have shown how, provided with incentives (effluent
controls, effluent fees) industrial managers will seek greater process
efficiencies. For example, the BOD formation by the sugar beet industry
(formerly a major polluter in the United States) has been reduced by
70% through substitution of dry for wet beet pulp during storage,
by-product utilisation and recirculation of water, with very little addition
of potentially harmful gases or inert solids (Löf and Kneese *loco cit.*).
Ayres and Kneese (1969a) have also shown that costs of collection and
distribution of both liquid and solid wastes in urban areas account for
over two-thirds of the costs of waste disposal, which in turn are ranked
third in local government expenditures after schools and roads. New
technical processes for the collection and transfer, particularly of solid
waste, might well result in significant cost savings, despite increased
expenditures in treatment (Figure 8.2). In a preliminary empirical study
of solid waste generation and disposal in the San Francisco Bay area,
Rao (1968) discovered that only 25% of the total waste found its way
to offical disposal sites. He cautioned that, should collection systems
become more efficient, existing disposal sites would soon become
overloaded. He also pointed out how collection costs were unnecessarily
high owing to the administrative fragmentation of collection systems.
The answer obviously lies in regional, integrated waste disposal systems,
but whether this solution will surmount the political and bureaucratic
hurdles strung across its path is doubtful. Improved technology for waste
separation, biodegradable packaging, incineration, scrap automobile
breakdown, and sealed land disposal methods, is urgently needed (Ellis,
1967). Certainly there is an important area of research here, using the
combined skills of the technical expert and the social scientist to produce
more comprehensive management strategies in cases where the
interdependencies of environmental inputs and outputs with regard to
social benefits and costs are considered.

Interdisciplinary research needs
The previous discussion has pointed to the need for liaison between
economists and engineers. In fact, the effects of resource management,
both beneficial and detrimental, penetrate so deeply into our everyday
lives that satisfactory solutions can only be achieved through large-scale
interdisciplinary studies involving the ingenuity and cooperation of the
world community of scientists. Considerable disparities of viewpoint
regarding research interest and relevance may have to be overcome, but

as the effects of man's use and misuse of his environment enlarge and become more serious, so a world-wide commitment is necessary and is spurred. To help fill this gap, the United Nations is sponsoring an important conference on the Human Environment in 1972; the International Geographical Union is also scheduling a symposium dealing

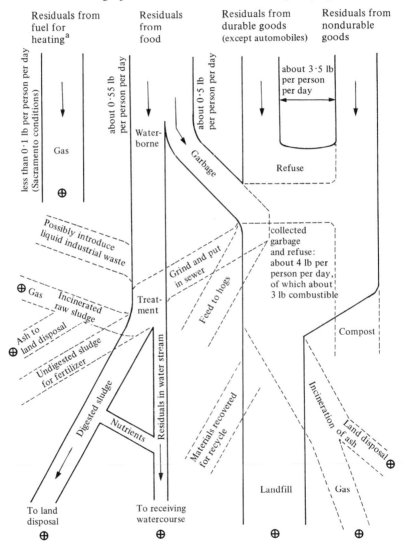

a This stream is cut if electricity is used. The waste stream then appears in the electric power sector.

⊕ Potential for external cost
---- Alternative flows

Figure 8.2. A materials flow diagram for the disposal of household wastes. (Source, Ayres and Kneese, p.63).

with the same problem in 1972, while the International Union for the Conservation of Nature and Natural Resources based in Strasbourg is strenghtening its interdisciplinary research activities.

At present the development of large-scale interdisciplinary research has barely reached the discussion stage, far less that of implementation. Apart from the problems of communication and consensus, the questions of financing and administrative responsibility will also not prove easy to resolve. Rarely is massive funding available at a private level, though some privately endowed research organisations are actively involved in resource management research (for example, Resources for the Future Inc. in Washington D.C.). Most large-scale research efforts are directed through government agencies or through public funds at the university level. Immediately, issues of fragmented agency responsibility and inconsistent programme goals become dominant, and legitimate questions have been raised as to the manner in which research funds are allocated and the purposes for which they are used (National Academy of Sciences – National Research Council, 1968; White, 1969). For example, White (1969) has probed deep into the controversy over the efficacy of upstream land management (small dams and soil conservation measures) versus downstream river control (large dams) in the reduction of flood damages, and has concluded that in the absence of clearly coordinated research and specific incontestable results the various resource development agencies involved have failed to reach agreement regarding a uniform management strategy. In the meantime, policy and resulting legislation have fluctuated between the two viewpoints and have been reflected in inconsistent patterns on the landscape (Leopold and Maddox, 1954; Morgan, 1966).

Another example of uncertain large-scale interdisciplinary research is weather modification (Sewell, 1966, Sewell *et al.,* 1968). Numerous attempts directed at altering weather patterns have been made, and proposals have ranged from small-scale local effects to possible hemispherical variations in climatic processes. But again the research effort is clouded by doubt and inconsistent interpretation of results, particularly where rainfall stimulation and storm dissipation have been attempted. Another area of some concern relates to the possible short-term and long-term repercussive effects on the landscape and upon man's use of it when such a delicate systems balance as the hydrologic cycle is altered. Here again there is an urgent need for clarifying goals and agency responsibilities and for uniting the research findings of an international interdisciplinary body (Corbridge and Moses, 1968).

A third research frontier where the interdisciplinary abilities of the physical and social scientists are necessary is that of large-scale desalination. Techniques are being developed to produce potable water, not only from seawater, but also from brackish water and polluted waste water. A surprisingly large amount of engineering and economic data are available from Britain (Burley and Collinge, 1967), Canada (Collier and Fulton, 1967), and the United States (Clawson *et al.*, 1969). Though becoming more favourable, costs at source still do not compare with the costs of fresh water supplies except in water-poor locations. In Britain, the Water Resources Board is collaborating with the Atomic Energy Authority on research into flash distillation and electrodialysis. Costs for multistage flash distillation run approximately 5·7s. (1966 prices) per 1000 gallons ($4·54 \times 10^3$ l) compared with 3·0s. per 1000 gallons ($4·54 \times 10^3$ l) for potable surface water supplies. Clawson and his colleagues (*loco cit.*) caution against any optimism over the production of nuclear-powered seawater desalination in the United States for a number of reasons. (1) Nuclear power production, despite its promising technology, is still unproven. (2) Plant investment costs are rising astronomically, so large initial payments must be made and subsequent interest payments will be high. In addition, the cost of nuclear fuel is rising. (3) Seasonal peaking of water production (so desirable for agriculture) in impracticable. (4) Losses due to evaporation and leakage and the costs of pumping and distributing water from the coastline plants to farms may raise water costs by 20%. (5) At present irrigators would appear to be willing to pay up to $30 per acre foot ($1 \times 10^5$ l) for water under fairly efficient management practices, yet it seems improbable that the on-farm price of nuclear-powered desalted seawater will drop below $130 per acre foot ($1 \times 10^5$ l) over the coming twenty years. (6) Considerable opposition is building up against the very idea of nuclear power plants, partly because of the radiation hazard, but more particularly because of the vast amounts of thermal pollution generated by their cooling processes. However, nearly 20% of US federal research in water resources is directed at desalination, particularly the more expensive form of seawater distillation, despite evidence that greater efficiency of present water use could drastically reduce estimated demands for fresh water (Brown, 1968). Again commitment to agency goals, the need to justify agency appropriations, and the traditional belief that the construction solution outweighs economic or social alternatives foster this research and present a powerful buttress, against which economic and social reason fall foul. A more comprehensive and coordinated interdisciplinary approach is necessary, preferably along international lines, to permit rational decision.

The principal focus of future interdisciplinary research will be to determine the long-term *assimilability* of the environment (or *environmental index*). Included in this effort will be research to help understand the tolerance of different environmental media (air, water, land, and the various species of plant and animal life, including man) to a broad spectrum of waste discharges (inputs) acting singly and in combination over time. There is no doubt that it will be extremely difficult to produce meaningful results, especially as time is not an ally and a significant number of new kinds of discharge (often untested) enter the environment every year. But however stumbling and incremental this research may prove to be, its findings will probably be fundamental in aiding the decision maker to establish minimal standards to guide future policy in environmental quality management.

Administrative research needs

At a time when man's scientific technological abilities are producing both challenges and resistances that place great pressures on his organisational ingenuity, research into the administrative, legal, and institutional arrangements of resource management should be both rewarding and fruitful. As resource uses become more varied over space and time, and as assessment and evaluation of environmental quality are increasingly necessary with the growing realisation of the tremendous interdependence between human activity and the total environmental milieu, so new thinking, new policies, and new institutional forms should be regarded with top priority in resource management. New foci of resources management research should be directed towards integrating the management process over a number of resource uses and across space at various levels.

Functional integration

The increasing emphasis upon social externalities in resource management decisions has drawn attention to the need for new administrative forms that recognise the linkages involved in multiple resource management. It is no longer possible to devise meaningful policies with regard to the segmental or single-purpose use of resources, though there is a legacy of narrowly focused administrative forms at all levels of government, where closely-related resource uses are artificially separated in bureaucratic enclaves. This unnatural segmentation has long been recognised by students of resource administration, but institutional and administrative changes take place at best slowly, and not always in the desired direction (Felser, 1965; Henning, 1968; Shad and Boswell, 1968). Accordingly, reaction has been slow despite the weighty arguments advanced. However, with the impetus of various environmental crises and the growing political concern by the general public over the undesirable side effects of man's use of his environment, important developments are taking place, particularly the creation of new executive agencies and high-level liaison between related groups of agencies.

The list is long and still growing. In the United Kingdom, the National Environmental Research Council (NERC) was formed to coordinate all the research and data-collecting services of the various agencies concerned with the biophysical environment (Institute of Hydrology, Geological Survey, Nature Conservancy). In addition, NERC sponsors and supervises relevant university research in the physical and biological sciences. A similar organisation, the Countryside Commission, which evolved from the National Parks Commission in 1968, coordinates all data collection and research effort in recreation and is primarily responsible for the formulation of outdoor recreation policy (Countryside Commission, 1968). The Water Resources Board, created under the 1963 Water Resources Act, is charged with the responsibility of coordinating water management policy over the whole of England and Wales as it is implemented at the regional level by the thirty-two river authorities, for coordinating all hydrologic data, and for sponsoring and instigating research in various aspects of water resource management (Institution of Water Engineers, 1967; Lloyd, 1968; Craine, 1969; Association of River Authorities, 1969). In addition, it integrates the functions of water supply and water disposal and maintains a close operational relationship with regional economic development and planning organisations (Water Resources Board, 1968).

In the United States a similar pattern is discernible. The President's Water Resources Council is a cabinet-level, coordinating body, linking the various executive agencies whose activities impinge upon water resources management. Its functions include reports to the President regarding national and regional water supply and demand needs, formulating and guiding Federal water resource management policy, and linking agency operations in the development of coordinated river basin plans (Cauldfield, 1968). All responsibility for funding and supervising research is vested with the Office of Water Resources Research which maintains close cooperation with universities. The US equivalent of NERC is the Environmental Sciences Services Administration (ESSA), which coordinates the data-collecting and research programmes of a number of agencies dealing with the biophysical environment (Hahn, 1968). In addition, ESSA is concerned with the linkages between man and his nonhuman surroundings and is sponsoring research at this most important interface. Similar to the British Countryside Commission is the US Bureau of Outdoor Recreation, created out of the recommendations of the Outdoor Recreation Resources Review Commission (1962) and responsible for research funding and policy in the general field of outdoor recreation. Recently, President Nixon has established a President's Environmental Quality Council, which seeks to devise coordinated policies and supervise the activities of all agencies where responsibilities have regard for the total environment. (At the time of writing it appears that a similar body is being formed in Britain.)

In Canada, the trend towards functional integration has been slightly slower, partly owing to the peculiar constitutional relationships between the Federal government and the Provinces (Sewell and Burton, 1967). However, an important arena of research and policy communication is the Canadian Council of Resource Ministers, which is composed of Federal and Provincial representatives in resource management, and which

has sponsored a number of important conferences and research reports
(Canadian Council of Resource Ministers, 1961, 1966a, 1966b). At the
Federal level the Department of Energy, Mines and Resources is extending
its coordinating efforts, particularly in water management, though progress
is slow and difficult. In the case of large-scale resource management
programmes which cross the US–Canadian border, the International
Joint Commission (1969) has played an important coordinating and
policy-making role and has produced some important fact-finding analyses
(*loco cit.*, 1969).

Spatial integration
Inevitably and properly the integration of resource functions is linked to
the need for a wide spatial compass in resource management programmes.
Implementation has lagged behind recognition of this need, for it has long
been realised that resource use does not respect artificially created
administrative boundaries and that more efficient and more equitable
management can only be achieved where the spatial units, in so far as is
possible, encompass technological, pecuniary, and social externalities.
This point has been best developed by Kneese and Bower (1968) in their
proposal for regional management agencies in the field of water quality
control. Spatial integration in resource management leads to economies
of scale and to an enlarged and more secure financial base. Because it
includes both the gainers and losers of a resource management programme
it is capable of devising more embracing plans and of facilitating
compensation between gainers and losers. Wider spatial units also focus
more upon the needs and preferences of the people, encourage a more
meaningful dialogue between the administration and the affected parties,
and enhance the more political and efficacious decentralisation of choice.

River basin organisation
The classical spatial form in resource management is the river basin.
There has, in the past, been some controversy as to whether the basin or
the service area benefitting from water management functions should
constitute the appropriate spatial unit for water management (Martin
et al., 1960; Hart, 1961; Fox and Craine, 1962; Bower, 1963; Craine,
1969). However, within the past six years a number of countries have
firmly established the river basin as the prime functional unit for water
management. Thus in 1963 the British created River Authorities (Lloyd,
1968), in 1964 the French established River Basin Boards (Kneese,
1967), in 1965 the US legislated River Basin Planning Commissions
(Cauldfield, 1968), and in 1969 Canada announced Water Management
Areas, while the United Nations have sponsored River Basin Management
Agencies in India, Vietnam, and Africa (UN, Department of Economic
and Social Affairs, 1958). In each case the prime emphasis lies in river
control via various forms of structural facilities, though to varying

degrees nonstructural efficiency alternatives and broader planning considerations are also included. Closely associated and usually co-spatial with river basin planning units has been the recent formation and development of regional water quality management agencies specifically tooled to operate and finance water quality programmes. Kneese (1967) and Kneese and Bower (1968) have described a number of these in considerable detail and have further evaluated and compared a number of international examples of regional water quality management institutions from the theoretical and operational standpoints.

A number of river basin management organisations should be singled out for special mention, for they provide very comprehensive case studies. The outstanding example of integrated land and water management within a river basin framework is the Tennessee Valley Authority (TVA) (Lilienthal, 1944; Clapp, 1955; Martin, 1957). Straddling seven states, the TVA is responsible for flood control, navigation, and power production, though it also provides water supplies, low flow augmentation, recreation, and mosquito control. Its functions extend to the tributaries (Wells, 1964), and include soil conservation, farm and forestry management demonstration projects, industrial and urban rehabilitation, manpower training, and the enhancement of employment opportunities. In essence TVA uses the tools of total resource management to promote regional economic development (Figure 8.3).

The Columbia River Treaty is another example of spatial and functional linkage in water management, and is particularly interesting because it crosses an international boundary and attempts to fuse the very different approaches to water management that are found in the United States and Canada. The contributions by Krutilla (1960, 1967c) are most valuable in this respect. The Delaware River Basin Commission is a further example of integrated spatial and functional water and land management and owes much of its present structure to the work of Martin and his colleagues at Syracuse (Martin et al., 1960).

The Delaware River Basin Commission also provides an interesting analysis of regional water quality management (US, Federal Water Pollution Control Administration, 1966; Kneese, 1967), as does the Potomac (Kneese and Bower, 1968; Davis, 1968) and the Ohio (Cleary, 1967). Cleary's account of the Ohio River Valley Water Sanitation Commission (ORSANCO) is especially interesting, for it includes an excellent chapter on the success of a massive education programme to garner public support for a massive cleanup campaign. Cleary also provides some very illuminating insights into the bargaining that took place between the pollution control agency and the industry. Truly the Ohio River story is one of patience and optimistic incrementalism.

Functional linkage between river basins is liable to become more common as regional disparities in water availability become more pressing.

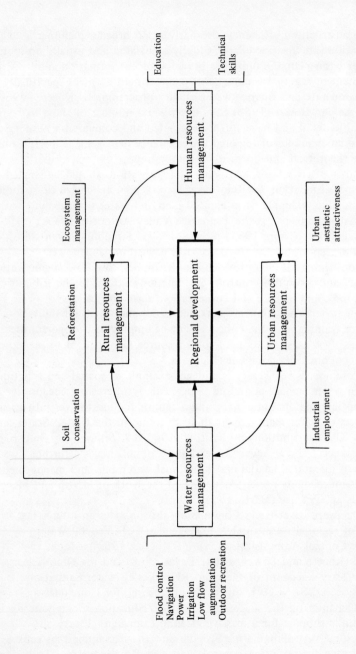

Figure 8.3. The complex of resource management projects involved in regional economic development.

The classic case is the California Water Plan (Bain *et al.*, 1966), which is intended ultimately to cost $4 billion and to convey up to 4000 cubic feet ($113 \cdot 25$ m^3) of water per second from the north to the south of the State. In fact, as a number of writers have pointed out, the California Water Plan is an excellent example of political expediency and misuse of the benefit–cost analysis technique (Hirshleifer *et al.*, 1960; G. Brown, 1968). Not only was it impossible to plan optimally when physical, legal, and institutional constraints are insurmountable, but it is highly doubtful whether lower-cost alternative solutions were ever properly examined in the original proposal (G. Brown, 1968). In fact, it is questionable whether water resource development of this magnitude is really a valid means to spur economic growth. Brown (*loco cit.*) concedes that the Plan is based on more rigorous economic criteria than most US federal water resource schemes, but states that the investment would have been better made in education and human resources development (Becker, 1964), if state economic growth and increased social welfare are to be the objectives.

Metropolitan organisation

Functional and spatial integration in resources management is not entirely confined to river basins, however. Recently, considerable interest has been expressed in improving the quality of urban services, particularly with regard to the improvement of living patterns and the quality of the urban environment (*Daedalus*, 1967; Schmandt and Bloomberg, 1969; Connery and Caralay, 1969; Perloff, 1969). Resource management in the urban context is an enormously complicated and complex function, and involves a tremendous amount of administrative skill and operational dexterity. Of prime importance is the formulation of goals—guidelines by which to establish priorities and design action. As we have already seen, because of their inherent vagueness, ambiguity and instability, goals are not easy to formulate in operational terms, and in the case of large metropolitan regions, where many complex economic subsystems and sociocultural environments conflict, this difficulty is compounded.

But attempts have been made to canvass public opinion, to create participation in the planning process by citizens' groups, and to inform, educate, and communicate with the public (Regional Plan Association, 1967; Reynolds, 1969; UK, Skeffington Committee, 1969). Tentative results have pointed to a broad-based public concern over deteriorating environmental quality issues, especially those relating to air and water pollution and solid-waste disposal, traffic congestion, and the paucity of regional and urban parks. Perloff and his colleagues (Perloff, 1969), have focused on a number of these issues and conclude that wide-ranging new administrative forms are necessary to meet the complex demands of rapidly-changing urban environments, particularly in the arena of regional metropolitan cooperation. But the almost insurmountable complexities of metropolitan political fragmentation and the public antipathy toward regionalism, which this fragmentation fosters at present, appear to be blocking the attainment of this desirable administrative objective (Bollens and Schmandt, 1965).

The one major example of metropolitan resource management is the work of the Northeastern Illinois Planning Commission (1966, 1967) which centred its attention on air and water resource planning in Metropolitan Chicago. Under the guidance of highly-qualified consultants, the Commission attempted to produce a multiple-goal–multiple-strategy approach, where the widest possible variety of means would be employed to bring about an array of desired objectives while preserving the maximum flexibility for future choice. The Commission's studies were comprehensive and penetrating (amongst its achievements were a comprehensive flood-hazard map and a highly-sophisticated water demand projection), but if found difficulty in overcoming entrenched bureaucratic and professional interests, the indifference and apathy of an uninformed public, and the enormous political hurdles inhibiting interagency and intermunicipal cooperation (White, 1969). Despite these obstacles, the Commission has retained its primary objectives and has stimulated a fresh approach to traditional thinking and modes of operation. However, the lessons learnt by the Commission point to the tremendous difficulties of implementing novel and unconventional resource management programmes against the spatial and jurisdictional fragmentation of large-scale metropolitan regions, and over the conservatism of appropriation-conscious agencies.

Regional environmental planning
Parallel to metropolitan resource management analyses is a growing field of research in regional planning where environmental and ecological processes are studied and established as controls. This approach, which is most particularly associated with McHarg (1966), is attempting to link the principles of planning, landscape architecture, and environmental design with the biophysical processes that pattern basic ecological relationships. The essence of this work emphasises man's harmony with nature and the need to understand and enmesh the tactics and strategies of man with those of nature. By following these principles of what he calls 'ecological determinism', McHarg (1966) has shown how nature can set limits, provide guidelines, and assist man in solving environmental planning problems in a manner which is entirely consistent with natural processes. An example of this philosophy would be the zoning of flood plain use in accordance with probable flood hazard estimation. [For a case study see O'Riordan (1967).]

McHarg's starting point is a region-wide ecological inventory where the various processes and relationships found in nature are studied and assessed. To McHarg, nature provides opportunities but also sets limits.

Man's will is not free: his choice is guided by possibilities and
prohibitions. Thus McHarg's work is a landscape designer's interpretation
of Leopold's land ethic philosophy (Leopold, 1949), and its impact has
been profound on regional planning and resource management strategy,
for it has linked the two disciplines of planning and resource management
and has created a new contribution in resource management research for
public policy.

Hills (1961) and Hills et al. (1967) have attempted to assess the
'productivity' of land and water based on their biological and ecological
capabilities with respect to agricultural, forestry, wildlife, and certain
recreational uses. Lewis (1964) developed the concept of 'environmental
corridors' on the basis of topography, soil capability, water availability,
and certain unique or unusual natural and cultural features. His work is
important, for it established basic guidelines for the future regional
planning of the State of Wisconsin and helped enormously to create a
widespread public awareness of the need to protect sites of environmental
interest.

Examples of environmental planning are not confined to North America.
The Lea Valley Regional Park (Civic Trust, 1964) is an outstanding case
study of the possibilities for the rehabilitation of derelict landscapes using
similar principles to those described above. A similar approach was taken
by the Nature Conservancy in its Report on Broadland (Nature
Conservancy, 1965), and has subsequently been embodied in Broadland
Plan (Norfolk County Council, 1970). Another important study is the
bid to redevelop the lower Swansea Valley from semiderelict industrial
wasteland to a desirable amenity area (UK, Ministry of Housing and Local
Government, 1963; Hilton, 1965; Arvill, 1967).

Institutional research needs

One of the least touched upon, but possibly one of the most fundamental,
research needs in resource management is the analysis of how institutional
arrangements are formed, and how they evolve in response to changing
needs and the existence of internal and external stress. There is growing
evidence to suggest that the form, structure, and operational guidelines
by which resource management institutions are formed and evolve clearly
affect the implementation of resources policy, both as to the range of
choice adopted and the decision attitudes of the personnel involved (see
Chapters 5, 6, 7). It would be a useful exercise, therefore, to compare
and evaluate different institutional forms, particularly with regard to
similar resource management problems (for example, river management,
water quality control, recreation, forest management, pest control),
and to show in each case how the various policies and operating
procedures have developed, the outcome of which in turn is reflected
spatially as various features on the landscape. An example of such an
approach is the study by Hartman and Seastone (1963) of comparative

water legal institutions in Colorado and New Mexico. Little in the way
of research design or operational theory has yet been developed, though
Jarrett (1961), Bower (1963), Kneese and Bower (1968), and Craine
(1969) have made notable introductory contributions.

One approach is to analyse the processes underlying the evolution of
resource management institutions, especially those processes affecting the
manner in which managerial innovations are diffused, interpreted, and
modified to suit differing institutional environments. There is a valuable
body of methodological literature dealing with the processes of spatial
diffusion to draw upon here (Rogers, 1962; L. A. Brown, 1968): the
need now is to relate this theory to the specific framework of resource
management institutions. For example, in drawing up their water
resource legislation, Britain, France, and the USA studied the Ruhr
Genossenschaften (Water Management Agencies) in Germany. Yet the
various political forms and established professional and administrative
attitudes encountered at the destination node created conflicts and
resistances that were only resolved by cautious modification of indigenous
institutional forms, rather than by large-scale adoption of the original
model. Of interest here are the forces creating the need for institutional
change in resource use, which might be regarded as 'permissive' or
'attracting' forces. Included here would be the notion of stress intensity,
the amount of articulation by various interest groups, and the range of
search for alternative solutions considered by responsible officials. Of
equal interest would be the factors (resistances) modifying and tempering
the willingness to accept diffused stimuli, such as the indigenous political
and legal framework, existing professional and administrative attitudes to
new ideas, the economic and social structure of the decision unit in
question, and to some extent the location and 'centrality' of the
destination node in relation to the origin node (Rogers, 1962). This kind
of analysis would involve the combined talents of the political scientist
and the behavioural scientist and should prove most rewarding. For
example, management studies of administrative structure, the decision
hierarchy, issue conflict, and the role of individual personalities would be
of particular relevance, though it is readily admitted that such studies are not
easy to assess nor to analyse (Simon, 1957a, 1957b, 1960; Pondy, 1967).

Legal research needs
A branch of resource management research that has received scant
attention, particularly from geographers, is that dealing with the role of
law and property in influencing the allocation of scarce resources.
Traditionally, the law has always regarded resources as property, either
owned by the public sector or leased by it to private operators or
purchased outright by private companies. The right to develop and use
a resource was invested as a property right, though such rights were always
subject to certain conditions, particularly where effects of misuse impinged

upon legitimate holders of other property rights. So the law of property was devised (as were market rights) to enable the orderly exchange of goods and services. However, such rights were established at a time when resource use was considered isolated both in function and in space, and little in the way of safeguards were built in to protect third parties from undesirable external effects.

Some attempts were made. For example, both the riparian and appropriative doctrines of water use include provisions whereby 'unreasonable use' can be challenged by a damaged party, and all water abstracted must be put to 'beneficial use', that is, it should be used in such a way as not to show unnecessary waste (Wisdom, 1962; Sax, 1968). However, the courts have never been consistent in their interpretation of what is 'unreasonable' or 'beneficial', with the result that the law regarding externalities is imprecise, cumbersome, tortuous, and grossly inadequate to deal with the economic and spatial components of externalities in the modern age (Milliman, 1959).

Kneese and Bower (1968), Baldwin (1969), and Pollack (1968) have admirably listed the shortcomings of existing legal devices to remedy third-party damages in air and water quality management in general. A particular difficulty lies in the fact that costs are spread over a large number of individuals whose individual loss is small, but whose aggregated costs are large. Moreover, if litigation is attempted, the individual plaintiff must show (1) that he has incurred material harm, (2) that the pollution which caused this harm was unreasonable, (3) that it was especially injurious to himself and not to others, (4) that a particular pollution source can be identified and that the harm he incurred incontestibly stemmed from this single source. The courts usually judge solely on the basis of evidence presented by the plaintiff and the defendant and little heed is paid to the wider public interest. In particular, the courts are reluctant to litigate where the polluter exerts a powerful economic influence in the local community. Generally, the courts are more concerned with equity than efficiency, they move slowly, often so slowly that external effects may have become irreversible, their guidelines are vague and ill-defined, and they are unable to cope with stochastic variations in environmental conditions, while the problems of external effects crossing jurisdictional boundaries compound the difficulties. Dales (1968) and Ayres (1969) have attempted to overcome this problem by advocating a system of pollution rights where the right to pollute is removed from the ambiguous interpretations of common law and conferred upon property rights (see Chapter 4).

Certainly the influence of the law relating to resource use and misuse must be visualised as an inhibiting factor in the optimal allocation of resources over space and time, though the exact nature of the distortions that it creates still requires more probing analysis. For example, Gaffney

(1961) and Brewer (1965) have exposed the inefficiencies of western water laws which tend to favour the excessive use of irrigation. The appropriative doctrine, by stipulating beneficial use, tends to encourage wasteful practices, since sufficient water must be used even in wet years to justify the necessary abstractions for the driest possible year. For, if the water is not used, junior irrigators will appropriate excess supplies and deny its availability to the senior user, should he wish to augment his supplies in the future. Transfers of abstraction points on a stream are almost impossible to achieve, and water rights naturally remain with the owner regardless of possible changes in water use between different owners (Hartman and Seastone, 1966). Frequently, groundwater law is separate from surface water law, despite the obvious hydrological realities. which link the two. Gaffney's study showed clearly how existing water law not only encouraged wasteful misallocations of water, but inhibited the transfer of water use from one function to another (say from agricultural to domestic use), despite the economic disparities in the relative values in use. Gaffney concluded that because the existing legislation permitted excessive wasteful practices, it was a contributory cause favouring the development of large-scale water transfers as an easy solution when water shortage inevitably threatened. This important point is substantiated in studies by Smith (1965), Parr (1967), and Gardner and Fullerton (1968).

The research need here is not simply to point out the distorting features, but to seek means for streamlining legal tools in resource management. Seckler (1969) has shown that increased water-use efficiencies brought about by improved irrigation techniques in the western USA may be offset by the legal tangle surrounding the transfer of excess water rights. In similar vein, the author (O'Riordan, 1970) has shown how a legacy of the riparian law was built into the British Water Resources Act through the system of prescriptive licenses of right. These licenses permit long-established water abstractors to continue potentially wasteful water-using practices, and thus help perpetuate inefficiencies of use which are not reflected in the scheme of charges set against all abstractions. It will be interesting to see whether these discrepancies continue to exist as the means for resolving them are embodied in the Act through provisions of licence revocation and subsidy (Lloyd, 1968).

Studies of resource management and the law touch upon a field of important but delicate research. It extends into the jurisdictional rights of resource use, and probes into the need for spatial integration of linked resource sectors where legal guides are as yet muddy and confused. It impinges upon investigations into administrative forms and decision-making processes owing to the prominence of legal controls for · establishing the decision framework and for guiding the range of choice.

Analysis of various cross-cultural and cross-institutional legal devices in comparative resource situations is much needed yet barely begun.

Social research needs

In the last analysis, however, resource management is a human problem involving values, preferences, and aspirations whose general form is moulded out of human nature and whose details are sculptured by human behaviour and action. As we enter the last three decades of the twentieth century we are becoming increasingly aware that the physical technology of science and technical progress is not only unable to solve human problems, but in fact is probably instrumental in creating them (Forbes, 1968). It is fair to say that, while science has rendered near miracles in the fields of human health and mechanistic prowess, it has also brought about more complex social issues which it has neither the means nor the understanding to solve (Dubos, 1968a, 1968b).

The emphasis must therefore swing towards social technology, towards the better understanding of the biological and social needs of man (Dubos, 1968a), towards improved socioinstitutional arrangements to meet the growing challenge of integrated spatial and functional resource management, and towards a reappraisal of the present system of values within which society judges its courses of action and sets its policies.

This will not be easy. Social and political changes take place at best slowly, and innovative institutional forms are rarely born free of agonising birth pains. Furthermore, to create political awareness, we need widespread public awareness and a positive statement of broad-based public concern. In the absence of such a forum (Caldwell, 1966) in the light of multifaceted public preferences, without meaningful social institutions for evaluating common property resource use and with few controls concerning the use and misuse of public property, the chance for opportunism and expediency are rife regardless of the longer-term repercussions.

According to the rules of most democratic societies, the public is supposed to guide the judgment of its political representatives through upward consensus-forming processes, and the politicians in turn legislate in the public interest by means of downward controlling factors, such as power and superior knowledge (Maass et al., 1962; Etzioni, 1967). If we are to play by these rules, we must concentrate on increasing public awareness across a wider spectrum of public opinion. This raises the rather ticklish question of whether the public should simply be told what is good for it and should be forced to accept 'desirable' institutional and legal forms 'for the long-run common good', or whether it should be 'educated' by means of a massive public information campaign, after which it will demand change along lines largely desired in the first place by the 'educators'.

There is no simple answer to this dilemma. That the broad mass of the public can be 'indoctrinated' is sadly all too true, given time and determination. The issue hinges upon the questions of whose values are 'right', and whether the bulk of the public really desires change and is prepared to accept sacrifices in its present pattern of living, but being largely uninformed and imperfectly represented is unable to express its preferences. The issue also hinges upon the question of time. If we do accept that public education is a necessary prerequisite to a change in social values, is there enough time, in view of the warnings by an impressive array of scientists, to allow for this change, yet to provide sufficient flexibility in present resource management decisions to permit desirable anticipatory action for the future? Possibly the increased threat of environmental collapse will spur public awareness: but decisions made under crisis are seldom the most desirable in the long run.

There is no doubt that optimal resource management decisions require the necessary ingredients of (1) an informed public, (2) two-way communication between the public and decision makers, (3) anticipatory action in the form of alternative proposals and public discussion of preferential solutions *before* decisions are made, and (4) a willingness to accept new institutional, legal, and economic arrangements which may involve some degree of individual sacrifice and some alterations to the present patterns of living.

However, these conditions may be impossible to achieve. Social change requires dedicated political leadership which has not been forthcoming in the past. Few politicians can afford the luxury of telling the people what they must accept and still remain in office. The State of California recently attempted to ban the internal combustion engine by 1975, but the Bill was blocked by the powerful automobile industry and a general public uneasiness about transferring to more expensive methods of propulsion or less personal forms of transportation. It does not appear to be human nature to anticipate rationally when environmental crises are not imminent, where there is widespread faith in untested technology, and where other more personal issues must be confronted. It is also not human nature to band together for a common cause until such a common cause is desperately urgent and clearly delineated. We are all willing to take risks to enjoy short-term pleasures at the expense of only probabilistic long-term costs, whether we smoke (Landsberg, 1967), locate on a flood plain (White, 1964), build on a hurricane-prone coastline (Burton *et al.*, 1968a) or ignore the opportunity of free vaccination (Wisner, in preparation). It may well be that it is the human condition to act and to progress only when spurred by environmental stress and external threat (Wolpert, 1966), and that decision making by careful participatory analysis of multiple strategy in advance of manifest stress is simply an idealistic dream.

There is probably more to this concept of action to resolve stress than is generally realised. On the widely-differing fields of art and sport, for example, it is well known that the supreme effort that is so necessary is the outcome of challenge, social and psychic stress, and competition. It is also true that catastrophic national disasters (earthquake in Skopje, 1964, flood in Florence, 1966) or great personal tragedies do more to unite a nation or a family, respectively, than lengthy rational debate. A sobering conclusion reached by the Natural Hazards Research group (Burton *et al.*, 1968b) is that, even assuming adoption of optimal hazard adjustments, residual damages would still exceed 50% of present damages for North America as a whole, and a much higher proportion of world-wide damage costs. Hazard-prone areas provide opportunities, and so will always be attractive for human occupancy. For many people it is human nature to play down the threat, to transfer the responsibility to some higher power, or simply to eliminate all thought of risk. Bereft of any kind of social, physical or natural stress, or conflict most human beings would probably become listless and apathetic.

But there are grounds for some optimism. Major changes of resource management policy have been brought about by massive campaigns of public information and involvement (League of Women Voters, 1966; Cleary, 1967). The techniques utilised are many and varied, but broadly the aim is to appraise a broad cross section of public opinion on the environmental implications of their present demands (sewage disposal and nearby water quality, increased housing on a flood plain, or subdivision speculation in a potential recreation area), to inform them of possible alternatives, and to involve them directly by encouraging them to learn more, to involve others, and to inform the proper authorities when broken bylaws result in some form of environmental damage.

Another cause for optimism is the tremendous influence and proliferation of public action groups concerned with improving environmental quality. These groups are arming themselves with facts, interdisciplinary expertise and funds, and are making important inroads into existing public policy by the use of careful strategies including the threat or use of legal action. The elements of success are (1) group action (individual acts are usually politically negligible), and (2) focus on a simple, clear-cut issue, provided by a broad interdisciplinary research team. By adopting such strategies, a group called 'Pollution Probe' based in the University of Toronto in the short space of five months achieved governmental bans on the use of the insecticide DDT, first in the Province of Ontario and subsequently for Canada as a whole.

Such groups are using a variety of political and legal weapons in their fight for better environmental management. For example, they may delay public exposure of a certain issue until close to election time and run a slate of candidates using their evidence as a political weapon, or they may go to court. The Sierra Club in the United States has won a number of notable injunctions against US Federal agencies whose proposals threatened a river or a park. Along with a recently formed action group, the Environmental Defence Fund, the Sierra Club has been instrumental in establishing a number of notable precedents in US environmental law, namely (1) that an aggrieved or adversely-affected party does not require to prove personal economic interest to bring suit (in other words that environmental issues can stand on their own merits), (2) that a developer must provide proof that his proposal will not result in serious environmental damage and that no reasonable alternative exists (in other words, the burden of proof falls on the defendant and not the plaintiff), and (3) that there may be a constitutional right to environmental quality, or at least that public land should be held in trust for the public good and not for private gain (Cahn, 1969).

A number of exciting research fronts are exposed here.

Opinion and attitude studies

These studies should continue to be used, but there is an urgent need for improved, more sensitive techniques to measure the intensity of public awareness and the direction of public preferences. When surveying public attitudes towards slowly-deteriorating water quality in a community whose economy is largely based on tourism, the author (T. O'Riordan, 1969b) discovered that there was a surprising lack of basic information and a considerable sense of optimism (based on faith rather than fact) as to the assimilative capacity of the nearby lake. This faith, based on ignorance, largely accounted for a general lack of public concern; yet careful probing of the public's values indicated its potential concern for deteriorating water quality.

A distinction should be made in resource management research between public opinion and public behaviour (Figure 8.4). Public opinion usually involves a questionnaire survey of residents in their homes and solicits a statement of potential interest and concern. White (1966b) has outlined some of the techniques involved, such as content analysis (Berelson, 1952) and attitude scaling (Edwards, 1957; Osgood et al., 1957), and Kasperson (1969b) has demonstrated the use of these methods in a case study. It would appear that surveys of public opinion regarding the environment have two main uses. First, they may be employed to assess the amount of public knowledge (or lack of it) regarding one or a number of environmental issues. With the assistance of a communications expert, this information can then be used to discover the best means of alerting public awareness and concern by sounding out potential allies and focusing on groups most likely to be resistant. These studies can thus be helpful in ascertaining through what media, with what frequency, and in what manner information can best be disseminated to achieve the greatest community impact. Secondly, public opinion surveys can be of value as political levers with which to influence impending decisions regarding a particular environmental issue. Judicious use of sound questionnaire surveys can exert considerable political impact, particularly if an election is near.

Public opinion surveys at best indicate the likely behaviour of people regarding resource use (for example, attendance at a crowded recreation site, choice of swimming location from a number of nearby lakes or rivers, or voting in a referendum). However, such studies must be taken as guides and not as predictive tools. It is important to probe carefully into the processes by which people choose the location, manner, and timing of resource use, and in particular how they evaluate the capacity of the environment to satisfy their needs. We have already shown how people can adapt and adjust to changing environmental conditions through physiological, psychological, and behavioural processes, for sound results will be of tremendous value in assessing the better management of the environment. (For a case study, see Warriner, 1961; Cox, 1969.)

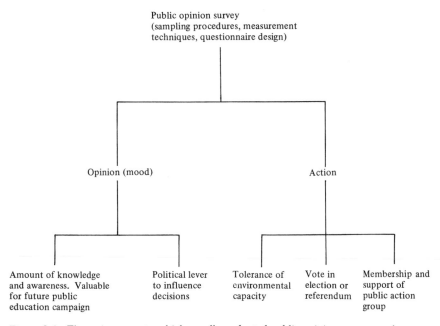

Figure 8.4. The various uses to which a well-conducted public opinion survey can be put.

Academic involvement

It may also be necessary for the resource geographer to become actively involved in the dissemination of public information, possibly to the extent of coordinating citizen's action groups into a citizens' environmental council. Such councils are already emerging in the United States, and have begun to exert considerable legal and political pressures on the decision-making process. Unfortunately, their activities are recorded more in newspapers than academic circles, though some journals provide useful information (see Appendix).

In addition, the academic resource manager may become involved in a technical-level environmental resources commission which would be advisory to the government, interdisciplinary in scope and responsible for undertaking research, defining strategy, and recommending alternative solutions for public discussion. It is envisaged that in the crucial arena of setting standards and establishing goals the citizens' environmental councils and the technical environmental resources commissions might fuse, and this in turn might help to create a better understanding between government and people.

Individual responsibility
Leopold (1949) has expressed most clearly the need for a social land ethic where every individual is aware of his responsibilities and obligations towards his social and biophysical environment when undertaking any environmental use. Codes of behaviour to guide individual action in public places may have to be determined and adhered to (Arvill, 1967). The success of this venture would largely depend on creating a new awareness towards the environment in the young. There is an urgent need for resource management education in the classroom, and for conservation schools where the land ethic can be developed and made more relevant in the field (Christian, 1966). It may also be necessary to involve students in active participatory public information campaigns to create a sense of individual responsibility and social relevance. Perhaps it might be possible to reincarnate the Civilian Conservation Corps created by President F. D. Roosevelt in the 1930's, when a large number of unemployed men planted trees, constructed dams, and cleared recreational land (Salmond, 1967). Involved and aware young people today should lead to better community acceptance tomorrow of the costs of environmental quality programmes. Thus for industry to reduce pollution we may have to pay a little more for their products, for a municipality to control its sewage outfall we may have to accept higher sewerage rates, to reduce solid-waste disposal costs we may have to pay more for biodegradable and/or combustible containers and for returnable bottles, and so on. If we are serious about improving environmental quality, we must also be prepared to pay the costs involved, both in terms of money and reduced individual licence in the use of public goods (via legal sanctions).

The research front in social technology and resources management is perhaps less tangible, but possibly more relevant and certainly at least as rewarding as more 'hard' forms of research in this field. Out of a more aware public must emerge more aware decision makers. And it is the process of decision making concerning the nature, amount, timing, and location of resource use as it affects individuals and groups on the landscape within a certain institutional, legal, and political–economic framework that constitutes resource management in the modern world.

References and bibliography

Note. This list is not exhaustive but is intended to guide the interested reader to most of the major sources of literature in resource management. Ancillary references can be found from the sources cited below.

Ackerman, E. A., 1959, "Population and natural resources", in *The Study of Population,* Eds. P. Hauser, O. D. Duncan (University of Chicago Press, Chicago), pp.621–48.

Ackerman, E. A., Löf, G. O., 1959, *Technology in American Water Development* (Johns Hopkins University Press, Baltimore), 710 pp.

Ad Hoc Water Resources Council, 1964, *Evaluation Standards for Primary Outdoor Recreation Benefits,* Supplement No.1, Senate Document No.97 (Government Printing Office, Washington), 9 pp.

Allen, S. W., Leonard, J. W., 1966, *Conserving Natural Resources* (McGraw-Hill, New York), 432 pp.

Allport, F. H., 1955, *Theories of Perception and the Concept of Structure* (John Wiley, New York), 709 pp.

Allport, G. W., 1955, *Becoming: Basic Considerations for a Psychology of Personality* (Yale University Press, New Haven), 106 pp.

Altouney, E. G., 1965, *The Role of Uncertainties in the Economic Evaluation of Water Resource Projects* (Stanford University Press, Stanford, California).

American Academy of Arts and Sciences, 1967, "America's changing environment", *Daedalus,* **96**, 1003–210.

American Institute of Chemical Engineers, 1967, "Water reuse", *Chem. Engng. Prog. Symp. Ser.,* **63**, 261

American Journal of Agricultural Economics, 1968, "Symposium on the economics of natural resource use", *Am. J. Agric. Econ.,* **50**, 1600–701.

An Foras Forbartha, 1967, *Planning for Amenity and Tourism* (An Foras Forbartha, Dublin), 110 pp.

Appleyard, D., Lynch, K., Meyer, J., 1964, *The View from the Road* (MIT Press, Cambridge, Mass.), 64 pp.

Ardern, F. L., Kavanagh, N. J., 1968, "Modern management techniques", *J. Instn Wat. Engrs,* **22**, 415–65.

Arrow, K. J., 1966, "Discounting and public investment criteria", in *Water Research,* Eds. A. V. Kneese, S. C. Smith (Johns Hopkins University Press, Baltimore), pp.13–32.

Arvill, R., 1967, *Man and Environment: Crisis and the Strategy of Choice* (Penguin Books, London), 317 pp.

Association of River Authorities, London, 1969, "The future of our rivers", Proceedings of Congress, London, May 1969.

Atkisson, A. A., Robinson, I. M., 1969, "Amenity resources for urban living", in *The Quality of the Urban Environment Essays on the 'New Resources' in an Urban Age,* Ed. H. S. Perloff (Johns Hopkins University Press, Baltimore), pp. 179–204.

Ayres, R. U., 1969, "Air pollution in cities", *Natn. Resources J.,* **9**, 1–23.

Ayres, R. U., Kneese, A. V., 1969a, "Pollution and environmental quality", in *The Quality of the Urban Environment: Essays on the 'New Resources' in an Urban Age,* Ed. H. S. Perloff (Johns Hopkins University Press, Baltimore, pp.35–74.

Ayres, R. U., Kneese, A. V., 1969b, "Production, consumption and externalities", *Am. Econ. Rev.,* **59**, 282–97.

Bain, J. S., Caves, R. E., Margolis, J., 1966, *Northern California's Water Industry: The Comparative Efficiency of Public Enterprise in Developing a Scarce Natural Resource* (Johns Hopkins University Press, Baltimore), 784 pp.

Baker, G. W., Chapman, D. W. (Eds.), 1962, *Man and Society in Disaster* (Basic Books, New York), 442 pp.

Baldwin III, B. B. (Ed.), 1969, "Legal control of water pollution" *Davis, University of California Law Rev.,* **1**, 274 pp.

Barker, M. L., 1968, "The perception of water quality as a factor in consumer attitudes and space preferences in outdoor recreation", unpublished M.A. Thesis, University of Toronto, Department of Geography.

Barker, M. L., Burton, I., 1968, "Differential response to stress in natural and social environments: an application of a modified Rosenzweig picture frustration test", University of Toronto, Department of Geography, Natural Hazard Research Working Paper No.5, 18 pp.

Barker, R. G., 1963, "On the nature of the environment", *J. Social Issues,* **19**, 17–38.

Barker, R. G., 1965, "Exploration in ecological psychology", *Am. Psychol.,* **20**, 1–14.

Barnett, H. J., Morse, C., 1963, *Scarcity and Growth: The Economics of Natural Resource Availability* (Johns Hopkins University Press, Baltimore), 288 pp.

Barrows, H. H., 1923, "Geography as human ecology", *Ann. Ass. Am. Geographers,* **13**, 1–14.

Bates, F. L., 1963, "The social and psychological consequences of a natural disaster: a longitudinal study of hurricane Audrey", National Academy of Sciences–National Research Council, Washington, Disaster Research Group Study No.18.

Bates, M., 1961, *Man in Nature* (Prentice-Hall, Englewood Cliffs, N.J.), 116 pp.

Bauman, D. D., 1969, "Perception and public policy in the recreational use of domestic water supply reservoirs", *Wat. Resources Res.,* **5**, 543–55.

Baumol, W. J., 1952, *Welfare Economics and the Theory of the State* (Cambridge University Press, Cambridge), 212 pp.

Baumol, W. J., 1961, *Economic Theory and Operations Analysis* (Prentice-Hall, Englewood Cliffs, N.J.), 438 pp.

Beasley, R., 1967, "Conservation decision-making: a rationalisation", *Natn. Resources J.,* **7**, 345–60.

Beck, R., 1967, "Spatial meaning and the properties of the environment", in "Environmental perception and behaviour", Ed. D. Lowenthal, University of Chicago, Department of Geography, Research Paper No.109, pp.18–29.

Becker, G. S., 1964, *Human Capital: A Theoretical and Empirical Analysis with Special Reference to Education* (Columbia University Press, New York), 187 pp.

Berelson, B., 1952, *Content Analysis in Communication Research* (Free Press, Glencoe), 220 pp.

Bevan, W., 1958, "Perception: evolution of a concept", *Psychol. Rev.,* **65**, 34–55.

Beyers, W. B., Sommarstrom, A. R., 1968, "Problems in the study of the economic impact of national parks upon local communities", unpublished paper presented at the B.C. Meeting of the Canadian Association of Geographers, Burnaby, B.C., March 1968, 11 pp.

Black, J. D., 1968, *The Management and Conservation of Biological Resources* (Davis, Philadelphia), 339 pp.

Blaut, J., 1959, "A study of the cultural determinants of soil erosion and conservation in the Blue Mountains of Jamaica", *Social Econ. Stud.,* **8**, 402–20.

Bollens, J.C., Schmandt, H.J., 1965, *The Metropolis. Its People, Politics and Economic Life* (Harper and Row, New York), 643 pp.

Bonhem, G. W., 1968, "On the marginal cost pricing of municipal water", *Wat. Resources Res.,* **4**, 191–3.

Borgstrom, G., 1965, *The Hungry Planet: The Modern World at the Edge of Famine* (Macmillan, New York), 487 pp.

Boulding, K. E., 1964, "The economist and engineer: economic dynamics and water resource development", in *Economics and Public Policy in Water Resource Development,* Eds. S. C. Smith, E. N. Castle (Iowa State University Press, Ames), pp.82–92.

Boulding, K. E., 1966, "The economics of the coming spaceship Earth", in *Environmental Quality in a Growing Economy: Essays from the 1966 RFF Forum,* Ed. H. Jarrett (Johns Hopkins University Press, Baltimore), pp. 3–14.

Bowden, L. W., 1965, "Diffusion of the decision to irrigate: simulation of the spread of a new resource management practice in the Colorado Northern High Plains", University of Chicago, Department of Geography, Research Paper No.97, 146 pp.

Bower, B. T., 1963, "Some physical, technological, and economic characteristics of water and water resources systems: implications for administration", *Natn. Resources J.,* **3**, 215–38.

Bower, B. T., 1966, "The economics of industrial water utilisation", in *Water Research,* Eds. A. V. Kneese, S. C. Smith (Johns Hopkins University Press, Baltimore), pp. 143–74.

Bower, B. T., 1968, "Industrial water demands", in *Forecasting the Demands for Water,* Eds. W. R. D. Sewell, B. T. Bower (Queen's Printer, Ottawa), pp.85–125.

Boyer, W. E., Tolley, G. S., 1966, "Recreation projection based upon demand analysis", *J. Fm Econ.,* **48**, 984–1001.

Bramhall, D. F., Mills, E. S., 1966, "An alternative method of improving stream quality: an economic and policy analysis", *Wat. Resources Res.,* **2**, 355–63.

Braybrooke, D., Lindblom, C. E., 1963, *A Strategy for Decision: Policy Evaluation as a Social Process* (Free Press, Glencoe), 268 pp.

Brewer, M. F., 1965, "The economics of water transfer", *Natn. Resources J.,* **4**, 522–36.

Brewer, M. F., Bordner, B., 1966, "Organizational alternatives for recreational resource management", *Natn. Resources J.,* **6**, 560–79.

Brown, G., Jr., 1968, "The California water project: is public decision making becoming more efficient?", *Wat. Resources Res.,* **4**, 463–70.

Brown, G., Jr., McGuire, C. B., 1967, "A socially optimum pricing policy for a public water agency", *Wat. Resources Res.,* **3**, 33–43.

Brown, G., Jr., Mar, B., 1968, "Dynamic economic efficiency of water quality standards or charges", *Wat. Resources Res.,* **4**, 1153–60.

Brown, H. S., 1954, *The Challenge of Man's Future* (Viking, New York), 290 pp.

Brown, H. S., Bonner, J., Weir, J., 1957, *The Next Hundred Years: A Discussion Prepared for Leaders of American Industry* (Viking, New York), 193 pp.

Brown, L. A., 1968, *Diffusion Processes and Location. A Conceptual Framework and Bibliography* (Regional Science Research Institute, Philadelphia), 177 pp.

Bruce, J. P., Maasland, D. E. L., 1968, *Water Resources Research in Canada,* Science Secretariat, Special Study No.5 (Queen's Printer Ottawa), 167 pp.

Bryson, R. A., Kutzbach, J. E., 1968, *Air Pollution,* Association of American Geographers Commission on College Geography, Washington, Report No.2, 42 pp.

Buchanan, J. M., 1968, *The Demand and Supply of Public Goods* (Rand McNally, Chicago), 214 pp.

Buchanan, J. M., Stubblebine, W. C., 1962, "Externality", *Economica,* **29**, 371–84.

Buckley, H., Tihanyi, E., 1967, *Canadian Policies for Rural Adjustment: A Study of the Economic Impact of ARDA, PFRA and MMRA* (Queen's Printer, Ottawa), 268 pp.

Bultena, G. L., Taves, M. J., 1961, "Changing wilderness images and forestry policy", *J. For.,* **59**, 167–70.

Burley, M. S., Collinge, V. K., 1967, "Desalination and the future in the U.K.", *Ass. River Auth. Yb.,* **14**, 16–21.

Burton, I., 1965, "Investment choices in public resource development", in *The Prospect of Change,* Ed. A. Rotstein (McGraw-Hill, Toronto), pp. 149–73.

Burton, I., 1967, "A preliminary report on flood damage reduction", *Geogr. Bull.,* **7**, 161–85.

Burton, I., 1968, "The quality of the environment: a review", *Geogr. Rev.*, **58**, 472–81.

Burton, I., Kates, R. W., 1964a, "Canadian resources and American requirements", *Can. J. Econ. Polit. Sci.*, **30**, 265–9.

Burton, I., Kates, R. W., 1964b, "The perception of natural hazards in resource management", *Natn. Resources J.*, **3**, 412–41.

Burton, I., Kates, R. W., 1964c, "The flood plain and the seashore: a comparative analysis of hazard zone occupance", *Geogr. Rev.*, **54**, 366–85.

Burton, I., Kates, R. W. (Eds.), 1965, *Readings in Resource Management and Conservation* (University of Chicago Press, Chicago), 609 pp.

Burton, I., Kates, R. W., Snead, R., 1968a, "The human ecology of coastal flood hazard in megalopolis", University of Chicago, Department of Geography, Research Paper No.115, 196 pp.

Burton, I., Kates, R. W., White, G. F., 1968b, "The human ecology of extreme geophysical events", University of Toronto, Department of Geography, Natural Hazard Research Working Paper No.1, 25 pp.

Burton, T. L., Wibberley, G. P., 1965, "Outdoor recreation and the British countryside", Wye College, London, Department of Economics, 51 pp.

Cahn, R., 1969, "Law and environment", *Christian Sci. Monitor*, Oct., 3, 4, 8, 18, 20, 24.

Caldwell, L. K., 1963, "Environment: a new focus for public policy", *Publ. Adm. Rev.*, **23**, 132–9.

Caldwell, L. K., 1964, *Biopolitics: Science, Ethics and Public Policy* (Yale University Press, New Haven).

Caldwell, L. K., 1966, "Administrative possibilities for environmental control, in *Future Environments of North America*, Eds. F. F. Darling, J. Milton (Natural History Press, New York), pp.648–72.

Caldwell, L. K. (Ed.), 1967, *Environmental Studies*, 4 volumes (Indiana University, Institute of Public Administration, Bloomington), 223 pp.

Caldwell, L. K. (Ed.), 1968, "Symposium: environmental policy: new directions in Federal action", *Publ. Adm. Rev.*, **28**, 301–48.

Calef. W. C., 1960, *Private Grazing and Public Lands: Studies of the Local Management of the Taylor Grazing Act* (University of Chicago Press, Chicago), 292 pp.

Calhoun, J. B., 1962, "Population density and social pathology", *Scient. Am.*, **206**, 139–48.

Campbell, R., 1968, "Personality as an element in regional geography", *Ann. Ass. Am. Geographers*, **58**, 748–59.

Campbell, T. H., Sylvester, R. O. (Eds.), 1968, *Water Resources Management and Public Policy* (University of Washington Press, Seattle), 296 pp.

Canada, Department of Energy Mines and Resources, 1968, *Air Pollution: Causes and Control* (Queen's Printer, Ottawa), 25 pp.

Canadian Council of Resource Ministers, 1961, *Resources for Tomorrow*, 3 volumes (Queen's Printer, Ottawa).

Canadian Council of Resource Ministers, 1966a, *National Conference on Pollution and Our Environment*, 3 volumes (Queen's Printer, Ottawa).

Canadian Council of Resource Ministers, 1966b, *The Administration of Water Resources in Canada* (Queen's Printer, Ottawa).

Carlin, A., 1968, "The Grand Canyon controversy: lessons for Federal cost benefit practice", *Land Econ.*, **44**, 219–28.

Carson R. L., 1962, *Silent Spring* (Houghton Mifflin, Boston), 308 pp.

Castle, R., Kelso, M., Gardner, D., 1963, "Water resources development: a review of the new Federal evaluation procedures", *J. Fm Econ.*, **45**, 693–704.

Cattell, R. B., 1965, *The Scientific Analysis of Personality* (Penguin Books, London), 400 pp.

Cattell, R. B., Warburton, F. W., 1967, *Objective Personality and Motivation Tests: A Theoretical Introduction and Practical Compendium* (University of Illinois Press, Urbana), 687 pp.

Catton, W., Jr., 1969, "Motivations of wilderness users", unpublished paper presented at the National Forest Fire Conference Winnipeg, Manitoba, April 1969.

Cauldfield, H. P., 1968, "Environmental management: water and related land", *Publ. Adm. Rev.,* **28**, 306–10.

Chevalier, M., Cartwright, T. J., 1966, "Towards an action framework for the control of pollution", in *National Conference on Pollution and Our Environment,* Canadian Council of Resource Ministers (Queen's Printer, Ottawa), Paper D 30–1, 52 pp.

Christian, G., 1966, *Tomorrow's Countryside: The Road to the Seventies* (John Murray, London), 229 pp.

Churchman, C. W., 1961, *Prediction and Optimal Decision* (Prentice-Hall, Englewood Cliffs, N.J.), 394 pp.

Ciriacy-Wantrup, S. V., 1952, *Resource Conservation* (University of California Press, Berkeley), 395 pp.

Ciriacy-Wantrup, S. V., 1964, "Benefit-cost analysis and public resource development", *J. Fm Econ.,* **37**, 676–89.

Ciriacy-Wantrup, S. V., Parsons, J. J. (Eds.), 1967, *Natural Resources: Quality and Quantity* (University of California Press, Berkeley), 217 pp.

Civic Trust, 1964, *A Lea Valley Regional Park: An Essay on the Use of Neglected Land for Recreation and Leisure* (Civic Trust, London), 48 pp.

Clapp, G. R., 1955, *The T. V. A.: An Approach to the Development of a Region* (University of Chicago Press, Chicago), 206 pp.

Clawson, M., 1959, "Methods for measuring the demand for and value of outdoor recreation", Resources for the Future, Washington, Reprint No.10, 36 pp.

Clawson, M., 1963, *Land and Water for Recreation* (Rand McNally, Chicago), 160 pp.

Clawson, M., 1966, *Insurance and Other Programs for Financial Assistance to Flood Victims* (Department of Housing and Urban Development, Washington).

Clawson, M., 1969, "Open (uncovered) space as a new urban resource", in *The Quality of the Urban Environment: Essays on the 'New Resources' in an Urban Age,* Ed. H. S. Perloff (Johns Hopkins University Press, Baltimore), pp.139–78.

Clawson, M., Held, R. B., 1965, *Soil Conservation in Perspective* (Johns Hopkins University Press, Baltimore), 344 pp.

Clawson, M., Knetsch, J. L., 1963, "Outdoor recreation research: some concepts and suggested areas of study", *Natn. Resources J.,* **3**, 250–75.

Clawson, M., Knetsch, J. L., 1966, *Economics of Outdoor Recreation* (Johns Hopkins Press, Baltimore), 328 pp.

Clawson, M., Landsberg, H. H., Alexander, L. T., 1969, "Desalted seawater for agriculture: is it economic?", *Science,* **166**, 1141–8.

Cleary, E. J., 1967, *The ORSANCO Story: Water Quality Management in the Ohio Under an Interstate Compact* (Johns Hopkins University Press, Baltimore), 352 pp.

Clement, R. C., 1968, "The pesticide problem", *Natn. Resources J.,* **8**, 11–22.

Clough, D. J., 1969, "A multi-agency decision model framework for benefit cost analysis", *Can. Op. Res. Soc. J.,* **7**, (3), 193–203.

Clough, D. J., Bayer, M. B., 1968, "Optimal waste treatment and pollution abatement benefits on a closed river system", *Can. Op. Res. Soc. J.,* **6**, (3), 153–62.

Coase, R. H., 1960, "The problem of social cost", *J.Law Econ.,* **3**, 1–44.

Collier, E. P., Fulton, J. F., 1967, *Water Desalination* (Queen's Printer, Ottawa), 23 pp.

Collinge, V. K., 1967, "Changes in water conservation in England and Wales", in
Symposium on the Conservation and Reclamation of Water (Institute of Water
Pollution Control, London), 8 pp.

Commoner, B., 1969, *Science and Survival* (Viking, New York), 150 pp.

Conley, B. C., 1967, "Price elasticity of the demand for water in Southern California",
Ann. Reg. Sci., **1**, 180–9.

Connery, R. H., Caraley, D. (Eds.), 1969, *Governing the City: Challenges and
Options for New York* (Praeger, New York), 230 pp.

Conrath, D. W., 1967, "Organisational decision making behaviour under varying
conditions of uncertainty", *Mgmt Sci.,* **13**, B487–500.

Cooley, R. A., Wandesforde-Smith, G., 1970, *Congress and the Environment*
(University of Washington Press, Seattle), 260 pp.

Cootner, P. H., Löf, G. O. G., 1966, *Water Demand for Steam Electric Generation*
(Johns Hopkins University Press, Baltimore), 156 pp.

Coppock, J. T., 1968, "The countryside (Scotland) act and the geographer",
Scott. Geogr. Mag., **84**, 201–11.

Corbridge, J. N., Jr., Moses, R. J., 1968, "Weather modification: law and
administration", *Natn. Resources J.,* **8**, 207–35.

Coser, L. A., 1956, *The Functions of Social Conflict* (Free Press, New York), 188 pp.

Cotner, M. L., 1969, "A policy for public investments in natural resources", *Am. J.
Agric. Econ.,* **51**, 87–99.

Countryside in 1970, 1963, 1965, "Proceedings of the two study conferences",
2 volumes (Nature Conservancy and HMSO, London).

Cox, P. T., 1969, "Success of watershed development in local communities",
Natn. Resources J., **9**, 24–34.

Craik, K. H., 1968, "The comprehension of the everyday physical environment",
J. Am. Inst. Planners, **34**, 29–38.

Craik, K. H., 1970a, "Environmental psychology" in *New Directions in Psychology,*
Ed. K. H. Craik (Holt Reinhart and Winston, New York), 222 pp.

Craik, K. H., 1970b, "The environmental dispositions of environmental decision
makers", *Ann. Am. Acad. Pol. Soc. Sci.,* May 1970.

Craine, L. C., 1957, "The Muskingum watershed conservancy district: a study in local
control", *Law Contemp. Probl.,* **22**, 378–404.

Craine, L. C., 1969, *Water Management Innovations in England* (Johns Hopkins
University Press, Baltimore), 123 pp.

Crocker, T. D., 1968, "Some economics of air pollution control", *Natn. Resources J.,*
8, 236–58.

Crowe, S., 1956, *Tomorrow's Landscape* (Architectural Press, London), 207 pp.

Crowe, S., 1960, *The Landscape of Roads* (Architectural Press, London), 136 pp.

Crutchfield, J. A., 1962, "Valuation of fishery resources", *Land Econ.,* **38**, 145–54.

Daedalus, 1967, "America's changing environment", *J. Am. Acad. Arts. Sci.,* **95**,

Dahl, R. A., Lindblom, C. E., 1953, *Politics, Economics and Welfare* (Harper and Row,
New York), 557 pp.

Daiute, R. J., 1966, "Methods for the determination of the demand for outdoor
recreation", *Land Econ.,* **42**, 327–38.

Dales, J. H., 1968, *Pollution, Property and Prices: An Essay in Policymaking and
Economics* (University of Toronto Press, Toronto), 111 pp.

Danserau, P. (Ed.), 1970, *Challenge for Survival: Land, Air and Water for Man in
Megalopolis* (Columbia University Press, New York), 235 pp.

Darling, F. F., Milton, J. (Eds.), 1966, *Future Environments of North America*
(Natural History Press, New York), 767 pp.

Darling, F. F., 1967a, " A wider environment of ecology and conservation", *Daedalus*, **96**, 1003–19.

Darling, F. F., 1967b, *Man and Nature in National Parks, Reflections on Policy* (Natural History Press, New York), 80 pp.

Dasmann, R. F., 1964, *Environmental Conservation* (John Wiley, New York), 307 pp.

Dasmann, R. F., 1966a, "Man in North America", in *Future Environments of North America,* Eds. F. F. Darling, J. Milton (Natural History Press, New York), pp.326–34.

Dasmann, R. F., 1966b, *The Destruction of California* (Collier, New York), 247 pp.

Dasmann, R. F., 1968, *A Different Kind of Country* (Macmillan, New York), 278 pp.

David, E. J. L., 1968, "Lakeshore property values: a guide to public investment in recreation, *Wat. Resources Res.,* **4**, 697–708.

David, E. J. L., 1969, "The exploding demand for recreational property", *Land Econ.,* **45**, 206–17.

Davidson, P., Adams, F. G., Seneca, J., 1966, "The social value of water recreational facilities resulting from an improvement in water quality", in *Water Research,* Eds. A. V. Kneese, S. C. Smith (Johns Hopkins University Press, Baltimore), pp. 175–214.

Davis, K. P., 1969, "What multiple forest land use and for whom?", *J. For.,* **67**, 718–21.

Davis, L. S., Bentley, W. R., 1967, "The separation of facts and values in resource policy analysis, *J. For.,* **65**, 612–20.

Davis, O., Whinston, A., 1962, "Externalities, welfare and the theory of games", *J. Polit. Econ.,* **60**, 241–62.

Davis, O., Whinston, A., 1967, "Piecemeal policy in the theory of second best", *Rev. Econ. Statist.,* **98**, 323–31.

Davis, R. K., 1963, "Recreation planning as an economic problem", *Natn. Resources J.,* **3**, 239–49.

Davis, R. K., 1965, "Some economic aspects of advanced water treatment", *J. Wat. Pollution Control Fed.,* **37**, 1617–28.

Davis, R. K., 1968, *The Range of Choice in Water Management* (Johns Hopkins University Press, Baltimore), 230 pp.

Davis, R. K., Knetsch, J. L., 1966, "Comparisons of methods for recreation evaluation", in *Water Research,* Eds. A. V. Kneese, S. C. Smith (Johns Hopkins University Press, Baltimore) pp.121–43.

Day, H. J., Bugliarello, G., Ho, P. H. P., Houghton, V. T., 1969, "Evaluation of benefits of a flood warning system", *Wat. Resources Res.,* **5**, 937–46.

Deutsch, K. W., 1966, *The Nerves of Government*(Free Press, London), 316 pp.

Devine, E. S., 1966, "The treatment of incommensurables in cost benefit analysis", *Land Econ.,* **42**, 383–7.

Dorfman, R., 1953, "Mathematical or linear programming: a non-mathematical exposition", *Am. Econ. Rev.,* **43**, 797–825.

Dorfman, R., 1965a, "Formal (mathematical) models in the design of water resource systems", *Wat. Resources Res.,* **1**, 329–36.

Dorfman, R. (Ed.), 1965b, *Measuring Benefits of Government Investments* (Brookings Institution, Washington), 429 pp.

Dorfman, R. (Ed.), 1970, *Models for Regional Water Management* (Harvard University Press, Cambridge, Mass.), in the press.

Dorst, J., 1969, *Before Nature Dies* (Collins, London), 329 pp.

Downey, G. T., 1968, "The significance of government policies and attitudes in water pollution control: a case study of the Merrimack river valley", unpublished PhD. Thesis, Clark University, Worcester, Mass.

Downing, P. B., 1969, *The Economics of Urban Sewage Disposal* (Praeger, New York), 195 pp.

Dubos, R., 1965, *Man Adapting* (Yale University Press, New Haven), 527 pp.

Dubos, R., 1968a, *Man, Medicine and Environment* (Praeger, New York), 125 pp.

Dubos, R., 1968b, *So Human An Animal* (Charles Scribner, Boston), 267 pp.

Duerr, W. A., 1967, "The changing shape of forest resource management", *J. For.,* **65,** 526-9.

Duncan, C., 1962, "Resource utilisation and the conservation concept", *Econ. Geogr.,* **38,** 113-21.

Eckstein, O., 1958, *Water Resource Development: The Economics of Project Evaluation* (Harvard University Press, Cambridge, Mass), 300 pp.

Edwards, A. L., 1957, *Techniques of Attitude Scale Construction* (Appleton–Century–Crofts, New York), 256 pp.

Ehrlich, P. R., Ehrlich, A. H., 1970, *Population Resources Environment Issues in Human Ecology* (Freeman, San Francisco), 383 pp.

Ellis, H. M., 1967, *Solid Waste Disposal: Problems Raised by the Treatment of Litter, Refuse and other Kinds of Non Soluble Waste Materials* (Council of Europe, Conservation of Nature and Natural Resources, Strasbourg), 18 pp.

Ellis, W. H., 1966, "Water transfer problems: law", in *Water Research,* Eds. A. V. Kneese, S. C. Smith (Johns Hopkins University Press, Baltimore), pp.233-50.

Etzioni, A., 1967, "Towards a theory of societal guidance", *Am. J. Sociol.,* **73,** 173-87.

Etzioni, A., 1968, *The Active Society: A Theory of Societal and Political Processes* (Free Press, New York), 698 pp.

Ewald, W. R. (Ed.), 1967, *Environment for Man—The Next Fifty Years* (University of Indiana Press, Bloomington), 308 pp.

Ewald W. R. (Ed.), 1968a, *Environment and Policy: The Next Fifty Years* (University of Indiana Press, Bloomington), 459 pp.

Ewald, W. R. (Ed.), 1968b, *Environment and Change: The Next Fifty Years* (University of Indiana Press, Bloomington), 397 pp.

Fair, G. M., 1961, "Pollution abatement in the Ruhr District", in *Comparisons in Resource Management: Six Programs in Other Countries and Their Possible U.S. Application,* Ed. H. Jarrett (Johns Hopkins University Press, Baltimore), pp.142-72.

Fair, G. M., Geyer, J. C., Okun, D. A., 1966, *Water and Wastewater Engineering,* 2 volumes (John Wiley, New York).

Fairchild, W. B., 1949, "Renewable resources: a world dilemma. Recent publications in conservation", *Geogr. Rev.,* **39,** 89-98.

Farber, S. M., 1966, "Quality of living—stress and creativity", in *Future Environments of North America,* Eds. F. F. Darling, J. Milton (Natural History Press, New York), pp.342-54.

Farina, J., 1961, "The social and cultural aspects of recreation", in *Resources for Tomorrow,* Canadian Council of Resource Ministers (Queen's Printer, Ottawa), 11 pp.

Farvar, M. Z. (Ed.), 1969, "The unforeseen international ecologic boomerang", *Nat. Hist.,* **70,** 44-72.

Feldstein, M. S., 1964, "The social time preference discount in cost benefit analysis, *Econ. J.,* **74,** 360-79.

Felser, J. W., 1965, "National water resources administration", in *Economics and Public Policy in Water Resource Development,* Eds. S. C. Smith, E. N. Castle (Iowa State University Press, Ames), pp.368-402.

Festinger, L., 1957, *A Theory of Cognitive Dissonance* (Row Peterson, Evanston), 241 pp.

Festinger, L., 1964, *Conflict, Decision and Dissonance* (Stanford University Press, Stanford, California), 164 pp.

Fiering, M. B., 1967, *Streamflow Synthesis* (Macmillan, London), 139 pp.

Fines, K. D., 1967, "Landscape evaluation: a research project in East Sussex", *Reg. Stud.,* **2,** 41-5.

Firey, W. I., 1945, "Sentiment and symbolism as ecological variables", *Am. Sociol. Rev.*, **10**, 140–8.

Firey, W. I., 1960, *Man, Mind and Land: A Theory of Resource Use* (Free Press, Glencoe), 256 pp.

Fisher, J. L., Potter, N., 1964, *World Prospects for Natural Resources: Some Projections of Demand and Indications of Supply to the Year 2000* (Johns Hopkins University Press, Baltimore), 73 pp.

Fleischman, P., 1969, "Conservation: the biological fallacy", *Landscape*, **18**, 23–7.

Fletcher, W., 1969, "Researchers cut sawmill waste", *Vancouver Sun*, December 4, p.40.

Fonaroff, S. L., 1963, "Conservation and stock reduction on the Navajo tribal range", *Geogr. Rev.*, **53**, 200–23.

Forbes, R. J., 1968, *The Conquest of Nature: Technology and Its Consequences* (Praeger, New York), 98 pp.

Foss, P. O., 1960, *Politics and Grass* (University of Washington Press, Seattle), 236 pp.

Foss, P. O., 1965, "Problems in Federal management of natural resources for recreation", *Natn. Resources J.*, **5**, 62–94.

Fox, D. J., 1965, "Man–water relationships in metropolitan Mexico", *Geogr. Rev.*, **55**, 523–45.

Fox, I. K., 1965, "New horizons in water resources administration", *Publ. Adm. Rev.*, **25**, 61–9.

Fox, I. K., 1966a, "Policy problems in the field of water resources", in *Water Research*, Eds. A. V. Kneese, S. C. Smith (Johns Hopkins University Press, Baltimore), pp.271–90.

Fox, I. K., 1966b, "Trends in river basin development", Resources for the Future, Washington, Reprint No.37, 11 pp.

Fox, I. K., 1966c, "We can solve our water problems", *Wat. Resources Res.*, **2**, 617–25.

Fox, I. K., Craine, L. E., 1962, "Organisational arrangements for water development", *Natn. Resources J.*, **2**, 1–44.

Fox, I. K., Herfindahl, O. C., 1964, "Attainment of efficiency in satisfying demands for water resources", *Am. Econ. Rev.*, **54**, 198–208.

Frake, C. O., 1962, "Cultural ecology and ethnography", *Am. Anthrop.*, **64**, 53–9.

Frake, C. O., 1964, "Notes and queries on ethnography", in "Transcultural studies in cognition", Eds. A. K. Romney, R. G., D'Andrade, *Am. Anthrop.*, **66**, 132–45.

Frankel, R. J., 1965, "Water quality management: engineering economic factors in municipal waste disposal", *Wat. Resources Res.*, **1**, 173–86.

Frankel, R. J., 1967a, "Reviewing water renovation and reuse in regional water resources systems", *Wat. Resources Res.*, **3**, 57–62.

Frankel, R. J., 1967b, "Economics of artifical recharge for municipal water supply", Resources for the Future, Washington, Reprint. No.62, 12 pp.

Frederickson, H. G., Magnas, H., 1968, "Comparing attitudes towards water pollution in Syracuse", *Wat. Resources Res.*, **4**, 877–89.

Freeman, A. M., III, 1967, "Six Federal reclamation projects and the distribution of income", *Wat. Resources Res.*, **3**, 319–32.

Freeman, A. M., III, 1969, "Advocacy and resource allocation decisions in the public sector", *Natn. Resources J.*, **9**, 166–75.

Frey, J. C., Gamble, H. B., 1967, "Policy issues and problems in outdoor recreation", *J. Farm Econ.*, **49**, 1307–20.

Gaffney, M. S., 1961, "Diseconomies inherent in Western water laws: a California case study", *Water and Range Resources and Economic Development of the West*, Report No.9, Western Agricultural Economics Research Council, pp.55–82.

Gaffney, M. S. (Ed.), 1967, *Extractive Resources and Taxation* (University of Wisconsin Press, Madison), 450 pp.

Gaffney, M. S., Hibbs, G., 1968, *Social Sciences and the Environment* (University of Wisconsin Press, Madison), 450 pp.

Galbraith, J. K., 1958a, *The Affluent Society* (Houghton Mifflin, Boston), 368 pp

Galbraith, J. K., 1958b, "How much should a country consume?", in *Perspectives on Conservation: Essays on America's Natural Resources*, Ed. H. Jarrett (Johns Hopkins University Press, Baltimore), pp.89–99.

Gardner, B. D., Fullerton, H. H., 1968, "Transfer restrictions and misallocations of irrigation water", *Am. J. Agric. Econ.,* **50**, 556–71.

Garnsey, M. S., Hibbs, G., 1968, *Social Sciences and the Environment* (University of Colorado Press, Boulder), 320 pp.

Gehardt, P. H., 1968, "Incentives to air pollution control, *Law Contemp. Probl.,* **33**, 358–68.

Gillespie, G. A., Brewer, D., 1968, "Effects of non-priced variables upon participation in water-oriented outdoor recreation", *Am. J. Agric. Econ.,* **50**, 82–90. Critique, *ibid,* **50**, 192–5, **51**, 942–5.

Glacken, C. J., 1956, "Changing ideas of the habitable world, in *Man's Role in Changing the Face of the Earth*, Ed. W. L. Thomas, Jr. (University of Chicago Press, Chicago), pp. 70–92.

Glacken, C. J., 1965, "The origins of the conservation philosophy", in *Readings in Resource Management and Conservation*, Eds. I. Burton, R. W. Kates (University of Chicago Press, Chicago), pp.158–63.

Glacken, C. J., 1966, "Meditations on the man–nature theme as a subject for study", in *Future Environments of North America*, Eds. F. F. Darling, J. Milton (Natural History Press, New York), pp.355–71.

Glacken, C. J., 1967, *Traces on the Rhodian Shore: Nature and Culture in Western Thought from Ancient Times to the End of the Eighteenth Century* (University of California Press, Berkeley), 763 pp.

Gloyna, E. A. (Ed.), 1968, *Advances in Water Quality Improvement* (University of Texas Press, Austin), 513 pp.

Golant, S., Burton, I., 1968, "Avoidance response to the risk environment", University of Toronto, Department of Geography, Natural Hazard Research Working Paper No.6, 31 pp.

Golant, S., Burton, I., 1969, "The meaning of a hazard: application of the semantic differential", University of Toronto, Department of Geography, Natural Hazard Research Working Paper No.7, 14 pp.

Goldman, M. L., 1967, *Controlling Pollution: The Economics of a Cleaner America* (Prentice-Hall, Englewood Cliffs, N.J.), 175 pp.

Gordon, M., 1963, *Sick Cities: The Pathology of Urban Life* (Macmillan, New York), 366 pp.

Gore, W. J., 1964, *Administrative Decision-Making: A Heuristic Model* (John Wiley, New York), 191 pp.

Gore, W. J., Dyson, J. W., 1964, *The Making of Decisions: A Reader in Administrative Behaviour* (Free Press, New York), 440 pp.

Gould, P. R., 1963, "Man against his environment: a game theoretic network", *Ann. Ass. Am. Geographers,* **53**, 290–7.

Grant, E. L., Ireson, W. G., 1964, *Principles of Engineering Economy* (Ronald Press, New York), 574 pp.

Grava, J., 1969, *Urban Planning Aspects of Water Pollution Control* (Columbia University Press, New York), 223 pp.

Gregory, P., 1965, "Polluted homes", Occasional Papers in Social Administration, London, No.15, 90 pp.

Griffith, E. S., 1958, "Main lines of thought and action", in *Perspectives on Conservation: Essays on America's Natural Resources*, Ed. H. Jarrett (Johns Hopkins University Press, Baltimore), pp.3-23.

Hagevik, G., 1968, "Legislating for air quality management: reducing theory to practice", *Law Contemp. Probl.*, **33**, 369-99.

Hahn, W. A., 1968, "Providing environmental science services", in "Symposium: environmental policy: new directions in Federal action", *Publ. Adm. Rev.*, **28**, pp.326-41.

Hall, F. T., 1966, *The Hidden Dimension* (Doubleday, Garden City), 201 pp.

Hamill, L., 1968, "The process of making good decisions about the use of the environment for man", *Natn. Resources J.*, **8**, 279-302.

Hamilton, H. R., Goldstone, S. E., Milliman, J. W., Pugh, H. C., III, Roberts, E. R., Zellner, H., 1969, *Systems Simulation for Regional Analysis to River Basin Development* (MIT Press, Cambridge, Mass.), 407 pp.

Hamming, E., 1958, "Water legislation", *Econ. Geogr.*, **34**, 42-6.

Hammond, R. J., 1966, "Convention and limitation in benefit-cost analysis", *Natn. Resources J.*, **6**, 195-222.

Hardin, G., 1968, "The tragedy of the commons", *Science*, **162**, 1243-8.

Hardin, G., 1969, "The economics of wilderness", *Nat. Hist.*, **78**, 21-6.

Hart, H. C., 1957a, "Crisis, community and consent in water politics", *Law Contemp. Probl.*, **22**, 510-37.

Hart, H. C., 1957b, *The Dark Missouri* (University of Wisconsin Press, Madison), 260 pp.

Hart, H. C., 1961, *Administrative Aspects of River Valley Development* (Asia Publishing House, New York), 112 pp.

Hart, W. J., 1966, *A Systems Approach to Park Planning* (International Union for Conservation of Nature and National Resources, Morges), 134 pp.

Hartman, L. M., Holland, D., Giddings, M., 1969, "Effects of hurricane storms on agriculture", *Wat. Resources Res.*, **5**, 555-63.

Hartman, L. M., Seastone, D. A., 1963, "Alternative institutions for water transfers: the experience in Colorado and New Mexico", *Land Econ.*, **34**, 31-43.

Hartman, L. M., Seastone, D. A., 1966, "Regional economic interdependencies and water use", in *Water Research*, Eds. A. V. Kneese, S. C. Smith (Johns Hopkins University Press, Baltimore), pp 215-31.

Harvey, D., 1969, *Explanation in Geography* (Arnold, London), 521 pp.

Haveman, R. H., 1965, *Water Resource Investment and the Public Interest* (Vanderbilt University Press, Nashville), 199 pp.

Haveman, R. H., 1969, "The opportunity cost of displaced private spending and the social discount rate, *Wat. Resources Res.*, **5**, 947-57.

Haveman, R. H., Krutilla, J. V., 1968a, *Unemployment, Idle Capacity and the Evaluation of Public Expenditures* (Johns Hopkins University Press, Baltimore), 159 pp.

Haveman, R. H., Krutilla, J. V., 1968b, "Unemployment, excess capacity and benefit cost investment criteria", Resources for the Future, Washington, Reprint No.70, 12 pp.

Havighurst, G. C., 1969, *Air Pollution Control: Law and Contemporary Problems* (Oceania Press, Dobbs Ferry, New York), 230 pp.

Hays, S. P., 1959, *Conservation and the Gospel of Efficiency* (Harvard University Press, Cambridge, Mass.), 277 pp.

Headley, J. C., Lewis, J. N., 1967, *The Pesticide Problem: An Economic Approach to Public Policy* (Johns Hopkins University Press, Baltimore), 141 pp.

Helliwell, P. R., 1969, "Valuation of wildlife resources", *Reg. Stud.*, **3**, 41-7.

Hendee, J. C., Catton, W. R., Jr., Marlow, L. D., Brockman, C. F., 1968, "Wilderness users in the Pacific Northwest—their characteristics, values and management preferences", U.S.D.A. Forest Service Research Paper PNW-61 Portland, 92 pp.

Henning, D. H., 1968, "The politics of natural resources adminstration", *Ann. Reg. Sci.,* **2**, 239–48.

Henry, W. E., Schlien, J. M., 1958, "Affective complexity and psychotherapy: some comparisons of timelimited and unlimited treatment", *J. Projective Tech.,* **22**, 153–62.

Herfindahl, O. C., 1961, "What is conservation?", Resources for the Future, Washington, Reprint No.30, 11 pp.

Herfindahl, O. C., Kneese, A. V., 1965, *Quality of the Environment: An Economic Approach to Some Problems in Using Land, Water and Air* (Johns Hopkins University Press, Baltimore), 104 pp.

Hewings, J. M., 1968, "Water quality and the hazard to health: placarding public beaches", University of Toronto, Department of Geography, Natural Hazard Research Working Paper No.3, 72 pp.

Highsmith, R. M., Jensen, J. G., Rudd, R. D., 1969, *Conservation in the United States* (Rand McNally, Chicago), 407 pp.

Hill, M., 1968, "A goals–achievement matrix for evaluating alternative plans", *J. Am. Inst. Planners,* **34**, 19–29. Critique, *ibid,* **35**, 139–42.

Hills, G. A., 1961, "The ecological basis for land use planning", Department of Lands and Forests, Ontario, Research Report No.46, 204 pp.

Hills, G. A., Lewis, P. H., McHarg, I. L., 1967, *Three Approaches to Environmental Resource Analysis* (The Conservation Foundation, Washington), 102 pp.

Hilton, K. J., 1965, "The Lower Swansea Valley project", *J. Tn Plann. Inst.,* **51**, 106–8.

Hirshleifer, J., DeHaven, J. C., Milliman, J. W., 1960, *Water Supply: Economics, Technology and Policy* (University of Chicago Press, Chicago), 386 pp.

Hirshleifer, J., Milliman, J. W., 1967, "Urban water supply: a second look", *Am. Econ. Rev.,* **57**, 169–78.

Hodges, R. C., 1967, "Maximum efficiency of exploitation: a pragmatic theory of resource development", *Can. Geogr.,* **11**, 166–71.

Holden, M., Jr., 1966, *Pollution Control as a Bargaining Process* (Cornell University Water Resources Centre, Ithaca), Publication No.9, 53 pp.

Hotelling, H., 1949, *Economics of Public Recreation* (U.S. National Park Service Government Printing Office, Washington).

Howe, C. W., 1966, "Broad horizons in water resource planning and investment", *Wat. Resources Res.,* **2**, 843–8.

Howe, C. W., 1968, "Water pricing—residential areas", *J. Am. Wat. Wks Ass.,* **60**, 497–501.

Howe, C. W., Linaweaver, F. P., 1967, "The impact of price in residential water demand and its relation to system design and price structure", *Wat. Resources Res.,* **3**, 13–32.

Huffman, R. E., 1953, *Irrigation Development and Public Water Policy* (Ronald Press, New York), 336 pp.

Hufschmidt, M. M., 1965a, "Research on comprehensive planning of water resource systems", *Natn. Resources J.,* **5**, 223–35.

Hufschmidt, M. M., 1965b, "The methodology of water resource system design", in *Readings in Resource Management and Conservation,* Eds. I. Burton, R. W. Kates (University of Chicago Press, Chicago), pp.558–74.

Hufschmidt, M. M., 1966, "The Harvard program: a summing up", in *Water Research,* Eds. A. V. Kneese, S. C. Smith (Johns Hopkins University Press, Baltimore), pp.441–56.

Hufschmidt, M. M., 1967, "Environmental aspects of river basin planning", *J. Hydraul.,* **93,** 323–33.

Hufschmidt, M. M., Fiering, M. B., 1966, *Simulation Techniques for Design of Water Resource Systems* (Harvard University Press, Cambridge, Mass.), 212 pp.

Hufschmidt, M. M., Krutilla, J. V., Margolis, J., Marglin, S., 1961, *Standards and Criteria for Formulating and Evaluating Federal Water Resources Developments,* Report of a panel of Consultants to the Bureau of the Budget (Government Printing Office, Washington).

Hughes, J., Mann, L., 1969, "Systems and planning theory", *J. Am. Inst. Planners,* **35,** 330–3.

Huirichs, H. H., Raynor, G. M., 1969, *Program Budgeting and Benefit Cost Analysis,* (Goodyear, Pacific Palisades), 420 pp.

Hunker, H. L. (Ed.), 1964, *Introduction to World Resources* (Harper and Row, New York), 220 pp.

Hutchins, W. A., 1962, "Background and modern developments in water law in the United States", *Natn. Resources J.,* **2,** 416–44.

Hutchison, S. B., 1969, "Bringing resource conservation into the mainstream of American thought", *Nat. Resources J.,* **9,** 518–536.

Huth, H., 1957, *Nature and the American: Three Centuries of Changing Attitudes* (University of California Press, Berkeley), 275 pp.

Innis, H., 1938, "The economics of conservation", *Geogr. Rev.,* **28,** 137–140.

Insko, C. A., 1967, *Theories of Attitude Change* (Appleton Century Crofts, New York).

Institute of Water Pollution Control, 1968, *Symposium on the Conservation and Reclamation of Water* (Institute of Water Pollution Control, London), 374 pp.

Institution of Public Health Engineers, 1968, *Engineering Aspects of the Use and Reuse of Water* (Institution of Public Health Engineers, London).

Institution of Water Engineers, 1965, "Report on the recreational use of waterworks", *J. Instn. Wat. Engrs.,* **17,** 71–114.

Institution of Water Engineers, 1967, "British association: symposium on water resources", *J. Instn. Wat. Engrs.,* **21,** 201–330.

International Joint Commission, 1969, *Pollution of Lake Erie, Lake Ontario and the International Section of the St. Lawrence River,* Volume 1—Summary (International Joint Commission, Ottawa), 152 pp.

Isaac, P. C. G. (Ed.), 1967, *River Management* (MacLaren, London), 258 pp.

Isard, W., Bassett, K., Choguill, C., Furtado, J., Izumita, R., Kissin, J., Romanoff, E., Seyfarth, R., Tatlock, R., 1968, "On the linkage of socio-economic and ecologic systems", *Pap. Reg. Sci. Ass.,* **21,** 79–100.

Isard, W., Smith, T. E., Isard, P., Hsiung, T., Dacey, M., 1969, *General Theory Social, Political Economic and Regional* (MIT Press, Cambridge, Mass.), 1040 pp.

Ise, J., 1961, *Our National Park Policy: A Critical History* (Johns Hopkins University Press, Baltimore), 714 pp.

Jackson, C. I., Bird, P. I., 1966, "Economic methods of charging for water", *J. Br. Wat. Wks Ass.,* **48,** 171–8; **48,** 614–28.

Jackson, J. B., 1968, "Pretensions and delusions", *Landscape,* **18,** Winter, 1–3.

James, L. D., 1967, "Economic analysis of alternative flood control measures", *Wat. Resources Res.,* **3,** 333–43.

Jarrett, H. (Ed.), 1958, *Perspectives on Conservation: Essays on America's Natural Resources* (Johns Hopkins University Press, Baltimore), 272 pp.

Jarrett, H. (Ed.), 1961, *Comparisons in Resource Management: Six Programs in Other Countries and Their Possible U.S. Application* (Johns Hopkins University Press, Baltimore), 288 pp.

Jarrett, H. (Ed.), 1966, *Environmental Quality in a Growing Economy: Essays from the 1966 RFF Forum* (Johns Hopkins University Press, Baltimore), 188 pp.

Jennings, B. H., Murphy, J. E., 1966, *Interactions of Man and His Environment* (Plenum Press, New York), 168 pp.

Jewett, F. I., 1968, "The impact of a national park upon a country's economy", *Ann. Reg. Sci.,* **2**, 274-87.

Johnson, E. L., 1967, "A study in the economics of water quality management", *Wat. Resources Res.,* **3**, 291-306.

Johnson, J. F. (forthcoming), "Attitudes toward renovated waste water as an alternative source for municipal water supply", University of Chicago, Department of Geography, Research Paper.

Journal of the American Institute of Planners, 1969, "Symposium: planning and citizen participation", *J. Am. Inst. Planners,* **35**, 216-64.

Kahn, A. E., 1966, "The tyranny of small decisions: market failures, imperfections and the limits of economics", *Kyklos,* **19**, 23-46.

Kamien, M. T., Schwartz, N. L., Dolbear, F. T., 1966, "Asymmetry between bribes and charges", *Wat. Resources Res.,* **2**, 147-58.

Kapp, W., 1950, *The Social Cost of Private Enterprise* (Harvard University Press, Cambridge, Mass.).

Kasperson, R. E., 1969a, "Environmental stress and the municipal political system: the Brockton water crisis of 1961-66, in *The Structure of Political Geography,* Eds. R. E. Kasperson, J. V. Minghi (Aldine, Chicago), pp.481-96.

Kasperson, R. E., 1969b, "Political behaviour and the decision making process in the allocation of water resources between recreational and municipal use, *Natn. Resources J.,* **9**, 176-211.

Kates, R. W., 1962, "Hazard and choice perception in flood plain management", University of Chicago, Department of Geography, Research Paper No.78, 157 pp.

Kates, R. W., 1965, "Industrial flood losses: damage estimation in the Lehigh valley, University of Chicago, Department of Geography, Research Paper No.98, 76 pp.

Kates, R. W., 1966a, "The pursuit of beauty in the environment", *Landscape,* **16**, 21-5.

Kates, R. W., 1966b, "Stimulus and symbol: a view from the bridge", in "Man's response to the physical environment", Eds. R. W. Kates, J. F. Wohlwill, *J. Social Issues,* **22**, pp 19-27.

Kates, R. W., 1967, "The perception of storm hazard on the shores of megalopolis", in "Environmental perception and behaviour", Ed. D. Lowenthal, University of Chicago, Department of Geography, Research Paper No.109, pp.60-74.

Kates, R. W., Wohlwill, J. F. (Eds.), 1966, "Man's response to the physical environment", *J. Social Issues,* **22**, 19-140.

Katz, D., 1960, "A functional approach to the study of attitudes", *Publ. Opinion Q.,* **24**, 163-204.

Kaufman, H., 1960, *The Forest Ranger: A Study in Administrative Behaviour* (Johns Hopkins University Press, Baltimore), 259 pp.

Kavanagh, N. J., 1967, "The demand for water: policy issues and empirical evidence", *J. Instn Wat. Engrs.,* **21**, 305-13.

Kavanagh, N. J., 1968a, "Economics of water supply and cost benefit analysis", Institute of Municipal Treasurers and Accountants, London, 18 pp.

Kavanagh, N. J., 1968b, "The economics of the recreational uses of rivers and reservoirs", *Wat. Wat. Engng,* **72**, 401-8.

Kelso, M. M., 1967, "The 'water is different' syndrome, or what is wrong with the water industry?", *Proc. Am. Wat. Resources Ass.,* 176-83.

Kirk, W., 1963, "Problems of geography", *Geography,* **48**, 357-71.

Kleinmutz, R. B. (Ed.), 1968, *Formal Representation of Human Judgment* (John Wiley, New York), 273 pp.

Kluckhohn, F. R., Strodtbeck, F. L., 1961, *Variations in Value Orientations* (Row, Peterson, Evanston, Ill.), 437 pp.

Kneese, A. V., 1965, "Economic and related problems in contemporary water resources management", *Natn. Resources J.,* **5**, 236–58.

Kneese, A. V., 1967, "Approaches to regional water quality management", in *National Conference on Pollution and Our Environment*, Canadian Council of Resource Ministers (Queen's Printer, Ottawa), Paper D30-4, 47 pp.

Kneese, A. V., 1968, "Economics and the quality of the environment: some empirical observations", Resources for the Future, Washington, Reprint No.71, 28 pp.

Kneese, A. V., d'Arge, R. C., 1969, "Pervasive external costs and the response of society", Resources for the Future, Washington, Reprint No.80, 28 pp.

Kneese, A. V., Bower, B. T., 1968, *Managing Water Quality: Economics, Technology, Institutions* (Johns Hopkins University Press, Baltimore), 338 pp.

Kneese, A. V., Nobe, K. C., 1962, "The role of economic evaluation in planning for water resource development", *Natn. Resources J.,* **2**, 445- 82.

Kneese, A. V., Smith, S. C. (Eds.), 1966, *Water Research* (Johns Hopkins University Press, Baltimore), 534 pp.

Knetsch, J. L., 1963a, "Outdoor recreational demands and benefits", *Land Econ.,* **39**, 387–96.

Knetsch, J. L., 1963b, "Land values and parks in urban fringe areas", *J. Fm Econ.,* **44**, 1718–26.

Knetsch, J. L., 1964, "The influence of reservoir projects on land values", *J. Fm. Econ.,* **46**, 231–43.

Knetsch, J. L., 1965, "Economics of including recreation as a purpose of water resources projects", Resources for the Future, Washington, Reprint No.50, 11 pp.

Knetsch, J. L., 1969, "Assessing the demand for outdoor recreation", *J. Leisure Res.,* **1**, 85–7.

Knetsch, J. L., Parrott, C. J., 1964, "Estimating the influence of large reservoir projects on land values", *J. Fm Econ.,* **46**, 231–43.

Koenig, L., 1967, "The cost of water treatment by coagulation, sedimentation, and rapid sand filtration", *J. Am. Wat. Wks Ass.,* **59**, 290–336.

Krutilla, J. V., 1960, "Sequence and timing in river basin development", Resources for the Future, Washington, 35 pp.

Krutilla, J. V., 1961, "Welfare aspects of benefit cost analysis", *J. Polit. Econ.,* **69**, 226–35.

Krutilla, J. V., 1966a, "Is public intervention in water resource development conducive to economic efficiency?", *Natn. Resources J.,* **6**, 60–75.

Krutilla, J. V., 1966b, "An economic approach to coping with flood damage", *Wat. Resources Res.,* **2**, 183–90.

Krutilla, J. V., 1967a, "Conservation reconsidered", *Am. Econ. Rev.,* **67**, 777–86.

Krutilla, J. V., 1967b, "Environmental effects of economic development", *Daedalus,* **96**, 1058–70.

Krutilla, J. V., 1967c, *The Columbia River Treaty: The Economics of an International River Basin Development* (Johns Hopkins University Press, Baltimore), 226 pp.

Krutilla, J. V., Eckstein, O., 1958, *Multiple Purpose River Development* (Johns Hopkins University Press, Baltimore), 330 pp.

Kuiper, E., 1966, *Water Resources Development* (Butterworths, London), 483 pp.

Landsberg, H. H., 1967, "The U.S. resource outlook: quality and quantity, *Daedalus,* **96**, 1034–57.

Landsberg, H. H., Fischmann, L. L., Fisher, J. L., 1963, *Resources in America's Future: Patterns of Requirements and Availabilities, 1960-2000* (Johns Hopkins University Press, Baltimore), 1040 pp.

Law and Contemporary Problems, 1968, "Air Pollution Control", *Law Contemp. Probl., 33,* 230 pp.

League of Women Voters, 1966, *The Big Water Fight* (Stephen Greene, Battleboro, Vermont), 256 pp.

League of Women Voters, 1967, *Challenge on the Hudson* (Washington), 44 pp.

Lee, D. H. K., 1966, "The role of attitude in response to environmental stress", *J. Social Issues,* 22, 83-91.

Lee, R. R., 1964, "Local government public works decision making", Stanford University, Institute in Engineering—Economic Systems, 382 pp.

Lee, T. R., 1969, "Residential water demand and economic development", University of Toronto, Department of Geography, Research Publication No.2, 151 pp.

Leopold, A., 1949, *A Sand County Almanac* (Oxford University Press, New York), 269 pp.

Leopold, L. B., Maddox, T., 1954, *The Flood Control Controversy. Big Dams, Little Dams and Land Management* (Ronald Press, New York), 278 pp.

Leopold, L. B., Marchand, M. O., 1968, "On the quantitative inventory of the riverscape", *Wat. Resources Res.,* 4, 709-17.

Leopold, L. B., 1969, "Landscape aesthetics: how to quantify the scenics of a river valley", *Nat. Hist.,* 78, 36-45.

Leuchtenberg, W. E., 1953, *Flood Control Politics: The Connecticut River Valley Problem, 1927-1950* (Harvard University Press, Cambridge, Mass.), 339 pp.

Lewis, P. H., 1964, "Quality corridors", *Landscape Archit. Q.,* 54, 100-7.

Leyhausen, P., 1965, "The sane community—a density problem?, *Discovery,* 26, 27-33.

Lichfield, N., 1964, "Cost-benefit analysis in plan evaluation", *Tn Plann. Rev.,* 35, 159-69.

Lichfield, N., 1966, "Cost-benefit analysis in urban redevelopment. A case study—Swanley", *Urban Stud.,* 3, 215-49.

Lichfield, N., 1968, "Economics in town planning", *Tn Plann. Rev.,* 34, 5-20.

Liebman, J. C., Lynn, W. R., 1966, "The optimum allocation of stream dissolved oxygen", *Wat. Resources Res.,* 2, 581-91.

Lilienthal, D., 1944, *Democracy on the March* (Penguin Books, London), 248 pp.

Lind, R. C., 1964, "The social rate of discount and the optimal rate of investment: further comment", *Q. J. Econ.,* 77, 274-89.

Lind, R. C., 1967, "Flood control alternatives and the economics of flood protection", *Wat. Resources Res.,* 3, 345-57.

Lind, R. C., 1968, "Benefit cost analysis—a criterion for social investment", in *Water Resources Management and Public Policy,* Eds. T. H. Campbell, R. O. Sylvester (University of Washington Press, Seattle), pp.44-64.

Lindblom, C. E., 1959, "The science of muddling through", *Publ. Adm. Rev.,* 19, 78-88.

Lindblom, C. E., 1965, *The Intelligence of Democracy: Decision-Making Through Mutual Adjustment* (Free Press, New York), 352 pp.

Lindblom, C. E., 1968, *The Policy-Making Process* (Prentice-Hall, Englewood Cliffs, N.J.), 122 pp.

Linton, D., 1968, "The assessment of scenery as a natural resource", *Scott. Geogr. Mag.,* 84, 219-38.

Lipsey, R. G., Lancaster, K., 1956, "The general theory of the second best", *Rev. Econ. Stud.,* 24, 11-32.

Lloyd, J. G., 1968, "River authorities and their work", *J. Instn Wat. Engr,* **22**, 343–83.

Löf, G. O., Kneese, A. V., 1968, *The Economics of Water Utilisation in the Beet Sugar Industry* (Johns Hopkins University Press, Baltimore), 134 pp.

Lofting, E. M., McGauhey, P. H., 1968, *An Input–Output Linear Programming Analysis of California Water Requirements (Economic Evaluation of Water, Part IV)* (University of California Water Resources Centre, Berkeley), 187 pp.

Loucks, D. P., Lynn, W. R., 1966, "Probabilistic models for predicting stream quality", *Wat. Resources Res.,* **2**, 593–605.

Lowenthal, D., 1958, *George Perkins Marsh: Versatile Vermonter* (Columbia University Press, New York), 442 pp.

Lowenthal, D., 1961, "Geography, experience and imagination: towards a geographical epistemology", *Ann. Ass. Am. Geographers,* **51**, 241–60.

Lowenthal, D., 1962, "Not every prospect pleases—what is our criterion for scenic beauty?", *Landscape,* **12**, Winter, 19–23.

Lowenthal, D. (Ed.), 1967, "Environmental perception and behaviour", University of Chicago, Department of Geography, Research Paper No.109, 88 pp.

Lowenthal, D., 1968, "The American scene", *Geogr. Rev.,* **58**, 61–89.

Lowenthal, D., Prince, H. C., 1964, "The English landscape, *Geogr. Rev.,* **65**, 309–46.

Lowenthal, D., Prince, H. C., 1965, "English landscape tastes", *Geogr. Rev.,* **66**, 186–222.

Lucas, R. C., 1964, "Wilderness perception and use: the example of the boundary waters canoe area", *Natn. Resources J.,* **3**, 394–411.

Luce, R. D., Raiffa, H., 1957, *Games and Decisions* (John Wiley, New York), 509 pp.

Lynch, K., 1960, *The Image of the City* (MIT Press, Cambridge, Mass.), 194 pp.

Lyon, W. A., 1966, "Some thoughts about effluent standards, *J. Wat. Pollution Control Fed.,* **38**.

Maass, A., 1951, *Muddy Waters: The Army Engineers and the Nation's Rivers* (Harvard University Press, Cambridge, Mass.), 306 pp.

Maass, A., 1966, "Benefit–cost analysis: its relevance to public investment decisions", *Q. J. Econ.,* **76**, 208–226.

Maass, A., Hufschmidt, M. M., Dorfman, R. T., Harold, A. J., Marglin, S. A., Fair, G. M., 1962, *Design of Water Resource Systems* (Harvard University Press, Cambridge, Mass.), 620 pp.

McClellan, K., Medrich, E. A., 1969, "Outdoor recreation: economic consideration for optimal site solution and development", *Land Econ.,* **45**, 174–82.

McConnell, A., 1965, "The conservation movement—past and present", in *Readings in Resource Management and Conservation,* Eds. I. Burton, R. W. Kates (University of Chicago Press, Chicago), pp.189–201.

McGauhey, P. H., 1965, "Folklore in water quality standards, *Civ. Engng,* **35**, 70–1.

McHarg, I. L., 1966, "Ecological determinism", in *Future Environments of North America,* Eds. F F. Darling, J. Milton (Natural History Press, New York), pp.526–38.

McHarg, I. L., 1969, *Design with Nature* (Natural History Press, New York), 197 pp.

MacIver, I., 1969, "Urban water supply alternatives: perception and choice in the Grand Basin, Ontario", unpublished PhD. Thesis, University of Chicago, Department of Geography.

Mack, R. P., Meyers, S., 1965, "Outdoor recreation", in *Measuring Benefits of Government Investments* Ed. R. Dorfman (Brookings Institution, Washington), pp.71–114.

McKean, R. N., 1958, *Efficiency in Government through Systems Analysis* (John Wiley, New York), 336 pp.

McKean, R. N., 1965, "The unseen hand in government", *Am. Econ. Rev.,* **60,** 495–506.

McKinley, C., 1952, *Uncle Sam in the Pacific North West* (University of California Press, Berkeley), 673 pp.

Makino, G., 1968, "Conservation trends and the future American environment", *The Biologist,* **50,** 1–19.

Malinowski, B., 1935, *The Coral Gardens and Their Magic,* 2 volumes (American Book Co., New York).

Marglin, S. A., 1963, "The social rate of discount and the optimum rate of investment", *Q. J. Econ.,* **77,** 95–111.

Marglin, S. A., 1966, *Public Investment Criteria* (Allen and Unwin, London), 103 pp.

Margolis, J., 1957, "Secondary benefits, external economies and the justification of public investment, *Rev. Econ. Statist.,* **39,** 384–91.

Marsh, G. P., 1864, *Man and Nature, or, Physical Geography as Modified by Human Action* (Charles Scribner, New York), 472 pp.

Marshall, H., 1965, "Rational choice in water resources planning", in *Economics and Public Policy in Water Resource Development,* Eds. S. C. Smith, E. N. Castle (Iowa State University Press, Ames), pp.403–23.

Marshall, H., 1966, "Politics and efficiency in water development", in *Water Research,* Eds. A. V. Kneese, S. C. Smith (Johns Hopkins University Press, Baltimore), pp.291–310.

Martin, P., 1969, "Conflict resolution through the multiple use concept in forest service decision making", *Natn. Resources J.,* **9,** 228–36.

Martin, R. C., 1960, *Water for New York* (Syracuse University Press, Syracuse), 264 pp

Martin, R. C., 1957, "TVA—A study of Federal control", *Law Contemp. Probl.,* **20,** 351–77.

Martin, R. C., 1960, *River Basin Administration and the Delaware* (Syracuse University Press, Syracuse), 390 pp.

Martin, W. E., Young, R. A., 1969, "The need for additional water in the arid Southwest: an economist's dissent", *Ann. Reg. Sci.,* **3,** 22–31.

Marts, M. E., 1956, "Use of indirect benefit analysis in establishing repayment responsibility for irrigation projects", *Econ. Geogr.,* **32,** 132–8.

Masser, I., 1966, "The use of outdoor recreational facilities", *Tn. Plann. R.,* **37,** 41–54.

Mattern, H., 1966, "The growth of landscape consciousness", *Landscape,* **16,** 14–21.

Means, R. L., 1969, "The new conservation", *Nat. Hist.,* **78,** 16–25.

Medalia, N. Z., 1965, *Community Perception of Air Quality: An Opinion Survey in Clarkston, Washington* (Public Health Service, Washington), Publication No. 999-Ap-10.

Meggers, B. J., 1958, "Environmental limitation on the development of culture", *Am. Anthrop.,* **56,** 801–24.

Meier, R. L., 1965, *Science and Economic Development: New Patterns of Living* (John Wiley, New York), 273 pp.

Mercer, D. C., 1970, "Urban recreational hinterlands—a review and an example", *Prof. Geogr.,* **22,** 74–9.

Merewitz, L., 1966, "Recreational benefits of water resources development, *Wat. Resources Res.,* **2,** 625–46.

Merewitz, L., 1968, "Estimation of recreational benefits at selected water development sites in California", *Ann. Reg. Sci.,* **2,** 249–73.

Merton, R. K., 1957, *Social Theory and Social Structure* (Free Press, Glencoe), 645 pp.

Meyersohn, R., 1969, "The sociology of leisure in the United States: introduction and bibliography, 1945-1965", *J. Leisure Res.,* **1,** 53–68.

Millar, D. W., Starr, M., 1967, *The Structure of Human Decisions* (Prentice-Hall, Englewood Cliffs, N.J.), 174 pp.

Miller, M., 1961, "The scope and content of resource policy in relation to economic development", *Land Econ., 37*, 291-330.

Miller, M., 1962, "The developmental framework for resource policy and its judicial-administrative implications", *Can. Publ. Adm. J., 5*, 133-55.

Milliman, J. W., 1959, "Water law and private decision making", *J. Law Econ., 2*, 41-63.

Milliman, J. W., 1962, "Can people be trusted with natural resources?", *Land Econ., 38*, 199-218.

Milliman, J. W., 1963, "Policy horizons for future urban water supply", *Land Econ., 39*, 109-32.

Millward, R. E., 1968, "PPBS: problems of implementation", *J. Am. Inst. Planners, 34*, 88-93.

Mishan, E. J., 1965, "Reflections on recent developments in the concept of external effects", *Can. J. Econ. Polit. Sci., 31*, 1-34.

Mishan, E. J., 1967, *The Costs of Economic Growth* (Stables Press, London), 190 pp.

Mitchell, J. M., Mitchell, W. C., 1969, *Political Analysis and Public Policy: An Introduction to Political Science* (Rand McNally, Chicago), 685 pp.

Moreel, B., 1956, "Our nation's water resources—policies and politics" (University of Chicago Law School, Chicago), 266 pp.

Morgan, R. J., 1966, *Governing Soil Conservation: Thirty Years of the New Decentralisation* (Johns Hopkins University Press, Baltimore), 416 pp.

Munger, F., Houghton, A., 1965, "Politics and organisation in water resources administration: a comparative study of decisions", *Wat. Resources Res., 1*, 337-48.

Murphy, E. F., 1961, *Water Purity: A Study in Legal Control in Natural Resources* (University of Wisconsin Press, Madison), 212 pp.

Murphy, E. F., 1967, *Governing Nature* (Quadrangle Books, Chicago), 333 pp.

Murray, A. S., 1964, "The relationship between the administrator and the scientist in the renewable resources field", *Can. Publ. Adm., 7*, 360-70.

Musgrave, R. A., 1959, *The Theory of Public Finance: A Study in Public Economy* (McGraw-Hill, New York), 626 pp.

Nash, R., 1967, *Wilderness and the American Mind* (Yale University Press, New Haven), 236 pp.

Nash, R., 1968, *The American Environment: Readings in the History of Conservation* (Addison-Wesley, New York), 236 pp.

National Academy of Sciences, Washington, 1969, *A Program for Outdoor Recreation Research,* 90 pp.

National Academy of Sciences-National Research Council, Washington, 1962, *Desalination Research and the Water Problem,* Publication No.941, 85 pp.

National Academy of Sciences-National Research Council, Washington, 1966a, *Alternatives in Water Management,* Committee on Water Publication No.1648, 52 pp.

National Academy of Sciences-National Research Council, Washington, 1966b, *Waste Management and Control,* Publication No.1400, 258 pp.

National Academy of Sciences-National Research Council, Washington, 1968, *Water and Choice in the Colorado Basin: An Example of Alternatives in Water Management,* Committee on Water Publication No.1689, 107 pp.

National Academy of Sciences-National Research Council, Washington, 1969, *Resources and Man,* 254 pp.

National Parks Commission, 1969, *Recreation Research Register No.1* (HMSO, London), 35 pp.

National and Provincial Parks Association of Canada, Calgary, 1968, *The Canadian National Parks: Today and Tomorrow,* 2 volumes.

Natural Hazard Research, 1969, "Collaborative research on natural hazards:progress report", University of Toronto, Department of Geography, 24 pp.

Nature Conservancy, The, 1965, *Report on Broadland* (HMSO, London), 98 pp.

Neiderland, W. G., 1956, 1957, "River symbolism", *Psychoanal Q.,* Part I, **25,** 469–564; Part II, **26,** 71–85.

Nixon, M., 1966, "Economic evaluation of land drainage works", in *River Engineering and Water Conservation Works,* Ed. R. B. Thorn (Butterworths, London), pp.47–51.

Norfolk County Council, 1970, *A Plan for Broadland* (Norfolk County Offices, Norwich).

Northeastern Illinois Planning Commission, 1966, *The Water Resource in Northeastern Illinois: Planning Its Use* (Northeastern Illinois Planning Commission, Chicago), 182 pp.

Northeastern Illinois Planning Commission, 1967, *Managing the Air Resource in Northeastern Illinois* (Northeastern Illinois Planning Commission, Chicago), 111 pp.

Ogden, D. C., 1966, "Economic analysis of air pollution", *Land Econ., 42,* 137–47.

Ohlin, G., 1967, *Population Control and Economic Development* (Organisation for Economic Co-operation and Development, Paris), 138 pp.

Olson, S. H., 1966, "Some conceptual problems of interpreting the value of water in humid regions", *Wat. Resources Res., 2,* 1–11.

O'Riordan, J., 1969, "Efficiency in irrigation use: a case study in the Okanagan Valley, B.C.", Unpublished PhD.Thesis, University of British Columbia, Department of Geography, 162 pp.

O'Riordan, T., 1967, "A study in multi-purpose water resources management—what Britain can learn", *J. Instn. Wat. Engrs,* **21,** 314–21.

O'Riordan, T., 1969a, "Planning to improve environmental capacity: a case study in Broadland", *Tn. Plann. Rev., 40,* 39–58.

O'Riordan, T., 1969b, "Decision making and evironmental quality. A case study from the Okanagan Valley, B.C.", paper read at Annual Meeting of the Canadian Association of Geographers, St. Johns, Newfoundland, 1969.

O'Riordan, T., More, R. J., 1969, "Choice in water use", in *Water, Earth and Man* Ed. R. J. Chorley (Methuen, London), pp.547–73.

O'Riordan, T., 1970, "Spray irrigation and the Water Resources Act 1963", *Trans. Instn Br. Geographers,* **49,** 33–48.

Osborn, F., 1953, *The Limits of the Earth* (Little, Brown and Co., Boston), 238 pp.

Osborn, F., 1962, *Our Crowded Planet: Essays on the Pressure of Population* (Doubleday, New York), 240 pp.

Osgood, C. E., Suci, G. T., Tannenbaum, P. H., 1957, *The Measurement of Meaning* (University of Illinois Press, Urbana), 342 pp.

Ostrom, V., 1953, *Water and Politics* (Hays Foundation, Los Angeles).

Ostrom, V., 1962, "The water economy and its organisation", *Natn. Resources J.,* **2,** 55–74.

Ostrom, V., 1964, "Property proprietorship and politics—law and the structure of strategic opportunities in the California water industry", Resources for the Future, Washington, Reprint No.47, 12 pp.

Outdoor Recreation Resources Review Commission, 1962, *Outdoor Recreation for America* (Government Printing Office, Washington), contains 27 Study Reports.

Palmer, J. E., 1967, "Recreational planning: a bibliographical review, *Plann. Outlook,* **2,** 19–70.

Parker, D. S., Crutchfield, J. A., 1968, "Water quality management and the time profile of benefits and costs", *Wat. Resources Res., 4,* 233–46.

Parkins, A. E., Whitaker, J. R., 1939, *Our Natural Resources and their Conservation* (John Wiley, New York), 647 pp.

Parr, A. E., 1966, "Pathological aspects of urbanology", *J. Social Issues,* **22**, 39–45.

Parr, W. R., 1967, "Water law—legal impediments to transfers of water rights", *Natn. Resources J.,* **7**, 433–41.

Parson, R. L., 1964, *Conserving American Resources* (Prentice-Hall, Englewood Cliffs, N.J.), 521 pp.

Parsons, T., 1949, *The Structure of Social Action* (Free Press, Glencoe), 817 pp.

Patterson, R. W., 1967, "The art of the impossible", *Daedalus,* **96**, 1020–33.

Paul, B. D., Gamson, W. A., Kegeles, G. S. (Eds.), 1961, "Trigger for community conflict: the causes of fluoridation", *J. Social Issues,* **17**, 1–81.

Paulson, R. W., 1969, "The longitudinal diffusion coefficient in the Delaware river estuary as determined from a steady state model", *Wat. Resources Res.,* **5**, 59–68.

Pearse, P. H., 1966, "Public management and mismanagement of natural resources in Canada", *Queens Q.,* **43**, 86–99.

Pearse, P. H., 1968a, "A new approach to the evaluation of non-priced recreational resources", *Land Econ.,* **44**, 87–99.

Pearse, P. H., 1968b, "Water based recreational demands", in *Forecasting the Demands for Water,* Eds. W. R. D. Sewell, B. T. Bower (Queen's Printer, Ottawa), pp.161–203.

Pearse, P. H., 1969, "Toward a theory of multiple use: the case of recreation versus agriculture", *Natn. Resources J.,* **9**, 561–75.

Peattie, L. R., 1968, "Reflections on advocacy planning", *J. Am. Inst. Planners,* **34**, 80–8.

Penman, H. L., 1963, *Vegetation and Hydrology* (Commonwealth Bureau of Soils, Harpenden), 24 pp.

Perloff, H. S. (Ed.), 1969 *The Quality of the Urban Environment: Essays on the 'New Resources' in an Urban Age* (Johns Hopkins University Press, Baltimore), 332 pp.

Pigou, A. C., 1946, *The Economics of Welfare* (Macmillan, London), 876 pp.

Pinchot, G., 1947, *Breaking New Ground* (Harcourt Brace and World, New York).

Pollack, L. W., 1968, "Legal boundaries of air pollution control", *Law Contemp. Probl.,* **33**, 331–57.

Pondy, L. R., 1967, "Organisational conflict: concepts and models", *Admin. Sci. Q.,* **12**, 296–320.

Porter, P. W., 1965, "Environmental potentials and economic opportunities—a background for cultural adaptation", *Am. Anthrop.,* **67**, 409–20.

Pred, A., 1968, *Behaviour and Location: Foundations for a Geographic and Dynamic Location Theory* (Lund Studies in Geography, Lund), Part I, 128 pp.

President's Materials Policy Commission, 1952, *Resources for Freedom,* Report by the Paley Commission (Government Printing Office, Washington), 5 volumes.

President's Science Advisory Committee, 1963, *Use of Pesticides* (Government Printing Office, Washington).

President's Science Advisory Committee, 1965, *Restoring the Quality of our Environment,* Report of the Environmental Pollution Panel (Government Printing Office, Washington), 317 pp.

President's Water Resources Council, 1962, *Policies, Standards and Procedures in the Formulation, Evaluation and Review of Plans for Use and Development of Water and Related Land Resources,* Senate Document No.97 (Government Printing Office, Washington), 13 pp.

Prest, A. R., Turvey, R., 1965, "Cost benefit analysis: a survey", *Econ. J.,* **75**, 683–735.

Price, E. T., 1955, "Values and concepts in conservation", *Ann. Ass. Am. Geographers,* **45**, 65–84.

Public Administration Review, 1966, "Symposium: planning programming budgeting system", *Publ. Adm. Rev.,* **26**, 243–329.

Public Administration Review, 1969, "Symposium: alienation, decentralisation and participation", *Publ. Adm. Rev.,* **29**, 3–65.

Public Opinion Quarterly, 1950, "Symposium on processes of opinion formation", *Publ. Opinion Q.,* **14**, 667–86.

Quinn, F., 1968, "Water transfers—must the American West be won again?", *Geogr. Rev.,* **58**, 108–32.

Rao, S. A., 1968, "Regional solid wastes management—an empirical approach, *Ann. Reg. Sci.,* **2**, 313–30.

Raup, H., 1964, "Some problems in ecological theory and their relation to conservation", *J. Ecol.,* **51**, 19–24.

Regional Plan Association, 1967, *Citizen Participation in Planning* (Regional Plan Association, New York), 74 pp.

Relph, E. C., Goodwillie, S., Burton, I., Schulte, P., 1968, "Annotated bibliography on snow and ice problems", University of Toronto, Department of Geography, Natural Hazard Research Working Paper No.2, 14 pp.

Renshaw, E. F., 1958, *Toward Responsible Government* (University of Chicago Press, Chicago), 164 pp.

Resources for the Future, 1961, "A report on the planning policy making and research activities—Department of the Interior", Resources for the Future, Washington, 38 pp.

Reynolds, J. P. (Ed.), 1969, "Public participation in planning", *Tn Plann. Rev.,* **40**, 131–48.

Richards, J. H., 1965, "Provincialism, regionalism and federalism as seen in joint resource development programs", *Can. Geographer,* **9**, 205–15.

Ridker, R., 1966a, *Economic Costs in Air Pollution* (Praeger, New York), 214 pp.

Ridker, R., 1966b, "Strategies for measuring the cost of air pollution", in *The Economics of Air Pollution,* Ed. H. Wolozin (Norton, New York).

Robinson, W. C., 1967, "The simple economics of outdoor recreation", *Land Econ.* **43**, 71–84.

Rockeach, M., 1968a, *Beliefs, Attitudes and Values* (Jossey Bass, San Francisco), 214 pp.

Rockeach, M., 1968b, "The role of values in public opinion research", *Publ. Opinion Q.,* **32**, 347–59.

Rodda, M., 1967, *Noise and Society* (Oliver and Boyd, London), 113 pp.

Rogers, E. M., 1962, *Diffusion of Innovations* (Free Press, New York), 367 pp.

Rogers, P., 1969, "A game theory approach to the problems of international river basins", *Wat. Resources Res.,* **5**, 749–61.

Romain, J., 1967, "Politics, professionalism and the environment: the administration of public health services", in *Environmental Studies,* Ed. L. K. Caldwell (Indiana University, Institute of Public Administration, Bloomington), Vol.3, pp.1–21.

Rooney, J. F., 1967, "The urban snow hazard in the U.S. An appraisal of disruption", *Geogr. Rev.,* **57**, 538–59.

Rothenberg, J., 1961, *The Measurement of Social Welfare* (Prentice-Hall, Englewood Cliffs, N.J.), 357 pp.

Rudd, R. L., 1964, *Pesticides and the Living Landscape* (University of Wisconsin Press, Madison), 320 pp.

Russell, C. J., 1969, "Losses from natural hazards", University of Toronto, Department of Geography, Natural Hazard Research Working Paper No.10, 25 pp.

Russell, C. J., Arey, D., Kates, R. W., in preparation, *Drought and Water Supply: Implications of the Massachusetts Experience for Municipal Planning* (Resources for the Future, Washington).

Ruttan, V. W., 1965, *The Economic Demand for Irrigated Acreage: New Methodology and Some Preliminary Projections, 1954-1980* (Johns Hopkins University Press, Baltimore), 154 pp.

Saarinen, T. F., 1966, "Perception of the drought hazard on the Great Plains", University of Chicago, Department of Geography, Research Paper No.106, 183 pp.

Saarinen, T. F., 1969, "Perception of environment", Association of American Geographers, Washington, Resource Paper No.5, 37 pp.

Salmond, J. A., 1967, *The Civilian Conservation Corps, 1933-1942. A New Deal Case Study* (Duke University Press, Durham), 240 pp.

Samuelson, P. A., 1954, "The pure theory of public expenditure", *Rev. Econ. Statist.,* 34, 387-9.

Sapolsky, H. M., 1969, "The fluoridation controversy: an alternative explanation", *Publ. Opinion Q.,* 33, 240-8.

Sax, J., 1968, *Water Law, Planning and Policy: Cases and Materials* (Bobbs-Merrill, Indianapolis). 520 pp.

Scarato, R. E., 1969, "Time-capacity expansion of urban water systems", *Wat. Resources Res.,* 5, 929-36.

Schiff, A. L., 1962, *Fire and Water: Scientific Heresy in the Forest Service* (Harvard University Press, Cambridge, Mass.), 225 pp.

Schiff, A. L., 1966a, "Innovation and adminstrative decision-making: a study in the conservation of land resources", *Adm. Sci. Q.,* 11, 1-30.

Schiff, A. L., 1966b, "Outdoor recreation values in the public decision process", *Natn. Resources J.,* 6, 542-59.

Schmandt, H. J., Bloomberg, W., Jr., 1969, *The Quality of Urban Life.* Vol.III, Urban Affairs Annual Reviews (Sage Publications, Berkeley).

Schmoyer, R. D., 1967, "Decision-making in the development of domestic water systems in Prowers County, Colorado", unpublished Master's Thesis, University of Chicago, Department of Geography.

Schutjer, W. A., Hallberg, M. C., 1968, "Impact of water recreational development on rural property values", *Am. J. Agric. Econ.,* 50, 572-83.

Scitovsky, T., 1951, *Welfare and Competition: The Economics of a Fully Employed Economy* (Irwin, Chicago), 457 pp.

Scott, A., 1955, *Natural Resources: The Economics of Conservation* (University of Toronto Press, Toronto), 184 pp.

Sears, P. B., 1966, *The Living Landscape* (Basic Books, New York), 199 pp.

Sears, P. B., 1969, *Lands Beyond the Forest* (Prentice-Hall, Englewood Cliffs, N.J.), 206 pp.

Seckler, D. W., 1966, "On the uses and abuses of economic science in evaluating public outdoor recreation", *Land Econ.,* 42, 485-95.

Seckler, D. W., 1969, "The potential effects of sprinkler horticulture on the North American water balance", paper presented at the Third Water Resources Symposium of the American Water Resources Association, Banff, June 1969.

Segall, M. H., Campbell, D. T., Herskovits, M. J., 1966, *The Influence of Culture on Visual Perception* (Bobbs Merrill, New York), 268 pp.

Sellers, J. B., 1970, "Open geography and its enemies", in *Geography of Economic Behaviour,* by M. E. Eliot Hurst (Wadsworth, Los Angeles), Appendix A.

Sewell, W. R. D., 1965, "Water management and floods in the Fraser river basin", University of Chicago, Department of Geography, Research Paper No.100, 163 pp.

Sewell, W. R. D. (Ed.), 1966, "Human dimensions of weather modification", University of Chicago, Department of Geography, Research Paper No.105, 423 pp.

Sewell, W. R. D., 1967, "A continental water system: pipedream or practical possibility?", *Bull. Atom. Sci.,* **23,** 9–13.

Sewell, W. R. D., 1968, "The role of attitudes of engineers in water management", in *Attitudes Toward Water: An Interdisciplinary Exploration,* Eds. F. L. Strodtbeck, G. F. White (University of Chicago Press, Chicago), 67 pp.

Sewell, W. R. D., 1969, "Human response to floods", in *Water, Earth and Man,* Ed. R. J. Chorley (Methuen, London), pp.431–54.

Sewell, W. R. D., Bower, B. T. (Eds.), 1968, *Forecasting the Demands for Water* (Queen's Printer, Ottawa), 259 pp.

Sewell, W. R. D., Burton, I., 1967, "Recent innovations in resource development policy", *Can. Geographer,* **11,** 327–40.

Sewell, W. R. D., Davis, J., Ross, D. W., 1961, *Guide to Benefit-Cost Analysis* (Queen's Printer, Ottawa), 49 pp.

Sewell, W. R. D., Judy, R. W., Ouellet, L., 1969, *Water Management Research: Social Science Priorities* (Queen's Printer, Ottawa), 145 pp.

Sewell, W. R. D., Kates, R. W., Phillips, L. E., 1968, "Human response to weather and climate: geographical contributions", *Geogr. Rev.,* **52,** 262–86.

Shad, T. M., Boswell, E., 1968, "Congressional handling of water resources", *Wat. Resources Res.,* **4,** 649–84.

Shafer, E. L., Jr., 1969, "Perception of natural environments", *Environment and Behaviour,* **1,** 71–82.

Shafer, E. L., Jr., Hamilton, J. E., Schmidt, E. A., 1969, "Natural landscape preferences: a predictive model", *J. Leisure Res.,* **1,** 1–20.

Sharp, R. S., 1967, "Estimation of future demands on water resources in Britain", *J. Instn. Wat. Engrs,* **21,** 232–49.

Sheaffer, J. R., 1960, "Flood proofing: an element in a flood damage reduction program", University of Chicago, Department of Geography, Research Paper No.65, 190 pp.

Sheehan, L. Hewitt, K., 1969, "A pilot survey of global natural disasters over the past twenty years", University of Toronto, Department of Geography, Natural Hazard Research Working Paper No.11, 19 pp.

Shepard, P., 1967, *Man in the Landscape: A Historic View of the Esthetics of Nature* (Knopf, New York), 290 pp.

Shepard, P., McKinley, D. (Eds.), 1969, *The Subversive Science: Essays Toward an Ecology of Man* (Houghton Mifflin, Boston), 453 pp.

Sierra Club, 1970, *Ecotactics: The Sierra Club Handbook for Environmental Activists* (Pocket Books, New York), 278 pp.

Simmons, I. G., 1966, "Wilderness in the Mid-Twentieth Century USA", *Tn Plann. Rev.,* **36,** 249–56.

Simon, H. A., 1957a, *Administrative Behaviour* (Macmillan, New York), 259 pp.

Simon, H. A., 1957b, *Models of Man* (John Wiley, New York), 287 pp.

Simon, H. A., 1960, *The New Science of Management Decisions* (Harper and Row, New York), 50 pp.

Sims, J., Saarinen, T. F., 1969, "Coping with environmental threat: Great Plains farmers and the sudden storm", *Ann. Ass. Am. Geographers,* **59,** 677–86.

Smith, A. R., 1966, *Air Pollution,* Monograph No.22 (Society of Chemical Industry, London), 203 pp.

Smith, D., 1969, "The civic amenities act: conservation and planning", *Tn Plann. Rev.,* **40,** 149–62.

Smith, G. H. 1951, *Conservation of Natural Resources* (John Wiley, New York), 533 pp. (3rd Edn. 1965).

Smith R. J., Kavanagh, N. J., 1969, "The measurement of benefits of trout fishing: preliminary results of a study at Graffam Water, Great Ouse Water Authority, Huntingdonshire", Faculty of Commerce and Social Science, University of Birmingham, 31 pp.

Smith, S. C., 1961, "The rural–urban transfer of water in California", *Natn. Resources J.,* **1**, 41–63.

Smith, S. C., 1965, "Organisations and water rights in the rural urban transfer of water", in *Economics and Public Policy in Water Resource Development,* Eds. S. C. Smith, E. N. Castle (Iowa State University Press, Ames), pp.353–67.

Smith, S. C., Castle, E. N., 1964, *Economics and Public Policy in Water Resource Development* (Iowa State University Press, Ames), 463 pp.

Smithsonian Institution, 1968, *The Fitness of Man's Environment* (Smithsonian Institution Press, Washington), Smithsonian Annual II, 250 pp.

Snyder, R. C., 1958, "A decision-making approach to the study of political phenomena", in *Approaches to the Study of Politics,* Ed. R. Young (Northwestern University Press, Evanston), pp.3–38.

Sobell, M. J., 1965, "Water quality improvement programming problems", *Wat. Resources Res.,* **1**, 477–87.

Sommer, R., 1969, *Personal Space: The Behavioural Basis of Design* (Prentice-Hall, Englewood Cliffs, N.J.), 177 pp.

Sonnenfeld, J., 1966, "Variable values in space and landscape: an inquiry into the nature of environmental necessity", *J. Social Issues,* **22**, 71–82.

Sonnenfeld, J., 1967, "Environmental perception and adaptation level in the Arctic", in "Environmental perception and behaviour", Ed. D. Lowenthal, University of Chicago, Department of Geography, Research Paper No.109, pp.42–59.

Sonnenfeld, J., 1969, "Equivalence and distortion of the perceptual environment", *Environment and Behaviour,* **1**, 83–99.

Spoehr, A., 1956, "Cultural differences in the interpretation of natural resources", in *Man's Role in Changing the Face of the Earth,* Ed. W. L. Thomas, Jr. (University of Chicago Press, Chicago), pp.93–102.

Sprout, H., Sprout, M., 1965, *The Ecological Perspective on Human Affairs with Special Reference to International Politics* (Princeton University Press, Princeton), 255 pp.

Stamp. D., 1969, *Nature Conservation in Britain,* New Naturalist Series No.49 (Collins, London), 273 pp.

Stein, M., 1962, "Problems and programs in water pollution", *Natn. Resources J.,* **2**, pp.388–415.

Steiner, P. O., 1959, "Choosing among alternative investments in the water resources field", *Am. Econ. Rev.,* **49**, 893–916.

Steiner, P. O., 1966, "The role of alternative cost in project design and selection" in *Water Research,* Eds. A. V. Kneese, S. C. Smith (Johns Hopkins University Press, Baltimore), pp.33–51.

Stevens, J. B., 1966, "Recreation benefits from water pollution control", *Wat. Resources Res.,* **2**, 167–82.

Stoevener, H. H., Brown, W. G., 1967, "Analytical issues in demand analysis for outdoor recreation", *J. Farm Econ.,* **49**, 1255–304.

Strodtbeck, F. L., White, G. F., 1968, *Attitudes Toward Water: An Interdisciplinary Exploration* (University of Chicago Press, Chicago), forthcoming.

Thomas, H. A., Jr., Revelle, R., 1966, "On the efficient use of high Aswan Dam for hydropower and irrigation", *Mgmt Sci.,* **12**, B296–B311.

Thomas, W. L., Jr. (Ed.), 1956, *Man's Role in Changing the Face of the Earth* (University of Chicago Press, Chicago), 1193 pp.

Thoreau, H. D., 1893, *Excursions, The Writings of Henry David Thoreau,* 11 volumes (Riverside, Boston).

Thorn, R. B. (Ed.), 1966, *River Engineering and Water Conservation Works* (Butterworths, London), 520 pp.

Tippy, R., 1968, "Preserving values in river basin planning", *Natn. Resources J.,* **8,** 259–78.

Tolley, G. S., 1966, "The impacts of water investments in depressed areas", in *Water Research,* Eds. A. V. Kneese, S. C. Smith (Johns Hopkins University Press, Baltimore), pp.457–70.

Trelease, F. J., 1964, "The concept of reasonable beneficial use in the law of surface streams, in *Economics and Public Policy in Water Resource Development,* Eds. S. C. Smith, E. N. Castle (Iowa State University Press, Ames), pp.272–92.

Trelease, F. J., 1965, "Policies for water law: property rights, economic forces, and public regulation, *Natn. Resources J.,* **5,** 1–48.

Trice, A. H., Wood, S. E., 1958, "Measurement of recreation benefits", *Land Econ.,* **34,** 195–207.

Tuan, Y. F., 1961, "Topophilia, or sudden encounter with landscape", *Landscape,* **2,** 29–32.

Tuan, Y. F., 1967, "Attitudes toward environment: themes and approaches", in "Environmental perception and behaviour", Ed. D. Lowenthal, University of Chicago, Department of Geography, Research Paper No.109, pp.4–17.

Tuan, Y. F., 1968a, *The Hydrologic Cycle and the Wisdom of God: A Theme in Geoteleology* (University of Toronto Press, Toronto), 160 pp.

Tuan, Y. F., 1968b, "Discrepancies between environmental attitude and behaviour: examples from Europe and China", *Can. Geographer,* **12,** 176–91.

Turnovsky, S. J., 1969, "The demand for water: some empirical evidence on consumers' response", *Wat. Resources Res.,* **5,** 350–61.

Turvey, R., 1962, "On divergencies between social cost and private cost", *Economica,* **30,** 309–13.

Twiss, R. H., Litton, R. B., 1966, "Resource use in the regional landscape", *Natn. Resources J.,* **6,** 76–82.

Udall, S. D., 1963, *The Quiet Crisis* (Holt, Rinehart and Winston, New York), 209 pp.

Ullman, E. L., 1954, "Amenities as a factor in regional growth", *Geogr. Rev.,* **44,** 119–32.

Ullman, E. L., Volk, D. J., 1962, "An operational model for predicting reservoir attendance and benefits: implications of a location approach to water recreation", *Pap. Mich. Acad. Sci. Arts Lett.,* **47,** 473–84.

UK, Ministry of Housing and Local Government, 1963, *New Life for Dead Lands: Derelict Acres Reclaimed* (HMSO, London), 30 pp.

UK, Ministry of Housing and Local Government, 1967, *Memorandum of Advice on the Preparation of Charging Schemes as Under Section 58 of the Water Resources Act, 1963* (HMSO, London), 15 pp.

UK, Ministry of Land and Natural Resources, 1966, *Guidelines for the Recreational Use of Public Water Supply Reservoirs,* Circular No.3/66 (HMSO, London), 6 pp.

UK, Skeffington Committee, 1969, *People and Planning,* London Ministry of Housing and Local Government (HMSO, London), 71 pp.

UK, *Water Resources Act, 1963,* 11–13 Eliz.2, Chapter 38 (HMSO, London), 184 pp.

UN, Department of Economic and Social Affairs, 1958, *Integrated River Basin Development* (Department of Economic and Social Affairs, New York).

UN, Economic Commission for Asia and The Far East, 1957, *Development of the Water Resources of the Lower Mekong Basin* (Economic Commission for Asia and The Far East, Bangkok), 75 pp.

UN, Economic Commission for Asia and The Far East, 1960, *A Case Study of the Damodar Valley Corporation and its Projects* (Economic Commission for Asia and The Far East, Bangkok), 106 pp.

UN, World Health Organisation, 1969, *Urban Air Pollution With Particular Reference to Motor Vehicles.* Technical Report No.410 (United Nations, Geneva), 53 pp.

University of Michigan Law School, 1958, "Water resources and the law" (University of Michigan Law School, Ann Arbor), 614 pp.

Upton, C., 1968, "Optimal taxing of water pollution", *Wat. Resources Res.,* **4**, 865–75.

US, Ad Hoc Water Resources Council, 1964, *Evaluation Standards for Primary Outdoor Recreation Benefits,* Supplement No.1 to Senate Document 97 (Government Printing Office, Washington), 9 pp.

US, Department of Health Education and Welfare Public Health Service, 1965, *Public Awareness and Concern with Air Pollution in the St. Louis Metropolitan Area* (Government Printing Office, Washington), 82 pp.

US, Department of the Interior, 1965a, *Quest for Quality* (Government Printing Office, Washington), 96 pp.

US, Department of the Interior, 1965b, *A Report on Natural Beauty to the President* (Government Printing Office, Washington), 20 pp.

US, Department of the Interior, 1967, *The Third Wave: America's New Conservation* (Government Printing Office, Washington), 128 pp.

US, Department of the Interior, 1968, *The Cost of Clean Water*, 4 volumes (Government Printing Office, Washington).

US, Federal Interagency Committee on Water Resources, 1950, *Proposed Practices for Economic Analysis of River Basin Projects* (Government Printing Office, Washington).

US, Federal Interagency Committee on Water Resources, 1958, *Proposed Practices for Economic Analysis of River Basin Projects* (Government Printing Office, Washington).

US, Federal Water Pollution Control Administration, 1966, *Delaware Estuary Comprehensive Study: Report on Alternative Water Quality Improvement Programmes* (Government Printing Office, Washington).

US, Senate, Committee on Public Works, 1966, *Western Water Development,* special subcommittee on Western Water Development (Government Printing Office, Washington).

US, Senate Select Committee, 1960, *Senate Select Committee on National Water Resources* (Government Printing Office, Washington), contains 32 Committee Prints.

US, Water Resources Council, 1968, *The Nation's Water Resources*, 8 volumes (Government Printing Office, Washington).

US, Water Resources Council, 1969, *Procedures for Evaluation of Water and Related Land Resource Projects,* Report by Special Task Force (Government Printing Office, Washington), 122 pp.

Vajda, S., 1961, *The Theory of Games and Linear Programming* (Methuen, London), 106 pp.

Vajda, S., 1962, *Readings in Mathematical Programming* (John Wiley, New York), 130 pp.

Van Arsdol, M. D., Jr., Sabagh, G., Alexander, F., 1964, "Reality and the perception of environmental hazards", *J. Health and Hum. Behaviour,* **5**, Winter, 144–53.

Van Burkalow, A., 1959, "The geography of New York City's water supply: a study of interactions", *Geogr. Rev.,* **49**, 369–86.

Van Hise, C. R., 1910, *The Conservation of Natural Resources in the United States* (Macmillan, New York).

Verleger, P. K., Crowley, J. M., 1969, "Air pollution, water pollution, industrial co-operation and the Antitrust Laws", *Land Wat. Law Rev.,* **4**, 476–85.

Vernon, M. D., 1962, *The Psychology of Perception* (Penguin Books, London), 261 pp.

Vogt, W., 1948, *Road to Survival* (Sloane, New York), 335 pp.

Waggoner, P. E., Bravdo, B. A., 1967, "Stomata and the hydrologic cycle", *Proc. Natn. Acad. Sci.,* **57**, 1096–102.

Walton, K., 1968, "The approach of the physical geographer to the countryside", *Scott. Geogr. Mag.,* **84**, 212–8.

Warford, J. J., 1966, "Water 'requirements': the investment decision in the water supply industry", *Manchr Sch. Econ. Social Stud.,* **37**, 87–112.

Warner, A. W., Morse, D., Cooney, T. E. (Eds.), 1969, *The Environment of Change* (Columbia University Press, New York).

Warriner, C. K., 1961, "Public opinion and collective action: formation of a watershed district", *Adm. Sci. Q.,* **6**, 333–59.

Water Resources Board, 1966, *Water Supplies in South East England*, 2 volumes (HMSO, London).

Water Resources Board, 1968, *Fifth Annual Report* (HMSO, London), 72 pp.

Water and Water Engineering, 1967, "Editorial on water metering", *Wat. Wat. Engng.,* **71**, 348–9.

Watson, R. A., Watson, P. J., 1969, *Man and Nature: An Anthropological Essay in Human Ecology* (Harcourt Brace and World, New York), 172 pp.

Watt. K. E. F., 1968, *Ecology and Resource Management: A Quantitative Approach* (McGraw-Hill, New York), 450 pp.

Weaver, J. C., 1965, "Conservation: more ethics than economics", in *Readings in Resource Management and Conservation*, Eds. I. Burton, R. W. Kates (University of Chicago Press, Chicago), 259–61.

Wells, D. T., 1964, "The T.V.A. tributary area development program", University of Alabama, Arburn, Bureau of Public Administration, 168 pp.

Wengert, N., 1955, *Natural Resources and the Political Struggle* (Doubleday, New York), 71 pp.

Wengert, N., 1961, "Resource development and the public interest: a challenge for research", *Natn. Resources J.,* **1**, 207–23.

Wennergren, E. B., 1964, "Valuing non-market priced recreation resources", *Land Econ.,* **40**, 303–14.

Whipple, W., Jr., 1966, "Economic basis for effluent charges and subsidies", *Wat. Resources Res.,* **2**, 159–64.

Whipple, W., Jr., 1968, *Economic Basis for Water Resources Analysis,* Rutgers University Water Resources Research Institute, New Brunswick, 116 pp.

Whipple, W., Jr., 1969, "Optimizing investment in flood control and floodplain zoning", *Wat. Resources Res.,* **5**, 761–7.

Whitaker, J. R., 1941, "Sequence and equilibrium in destruction and conservation of natural resources", *Ann. Ass. Am. Geographers,* **31**, 129–44.

Whitaker, J. R., Ackerman, E. A., 1951, *American Resources: Their Management and Conservation* (Harcourt and Brace, New York), 497 pp.

White, A. U., 1968, "Social cost and individual decision in domestic water use in East Africa", unpublished paper presented at Annual Meeting, American Association of Geographers, Washington, August 1968, 13 pp.

White, G. F., 1949, "Toward an appraisal of world resources: new views of conservation problems", *Geogr. Rev.,* **39**, 625–39.

White, G. F., 1957, "A perspective of river basin development", *Law Contemp. Probl.,* **22**, 157–87.

White, G. F. (Ed.), 1960, "Papers on flood problems", University of Chicago, Department of Geography, Research Paper No.70, 234 pp.

White, G. F., 1961, "The choice of use in resource management", *Natn. Resources J.,* **1**, 23–40.

White, G. F., 1963, "Contributions of geographical analysis to river basin development, *Geogr. J.*, **124**, 412–36.

White, G. F., 1964, "Choice of adjustment to floods", University of Chicago, Department of Geography, Research Paper No.93, 150 pp.

White, G. F., 1966a, "Optimal flood damage management: retrospect and prospect", in *Water Research*, Eds. A. V. Kneese, S. C. Smith (Johns Hopkins University Press, Baltimore), pp.251–70.

White, G. F., 1966b, "Formation and role of public attitudes, in *Environmental Quality in a Growing Economy: Essays from the 1966 RFF Forum*, Ed. H. Jarrett (Johns Hopkins University Press, Baltimore), pp.105–27.

White, G. F., 1969, *Strategies of American Water Management* (University of Michigan Press, Ann Arbor), 192 pp.

White G. F., White, A. U., forthcoming, *Drawers of Water: Domestic Water Use in East Africa* (University of Chicago Press, Chicago).

White, L., Jr., 1967, "The historical roots of our ecologic crisis", *Science*, **155**, 1203–7.

Whyte, W. H., 1968, *The Last Landscape* (Doubleday, New York), 376 pp.

Wildawsky, A., 1966, "The political economy of efficiency: cost benefit analysis, systems analysis and program budgeting, *Publ. Adm. Rev.*, **26**, 292–310.

Willcox, J. C., Ferries, C. H., 1955, *A Comparison of Furrow and Sprinkler Irrigation in the Okanagan Valley* (Canada Department of Agriculture, Ottawa), Publ. No.954.

Williams, G. H., 1962, *Wilderness and Paradise in Christian Thought* (Harper and Row, New York), 245 pp.

Wisdom, A. S., 1962, *The Law of Rivers and Watercourses* (Shaw, London).

Wisner, B., forthcoming, "Tropical biological hazards", University of Toronto, Department of Geography, Natural Hazard Research Programme.

Wohwill, J. F., 1966, "The physical environment: a problem for a psychology of stimulation", *J. Soc. Issues*, **22**, 29–38.

Wolfe, R. I., 1964, "Perspective on outdoor recreation", *Geogr. Rev.*, **54**, 203–38.

Wollman, N., 1962, *The Value of Water in Alternative Uses* (University of New Mexico Press, Albuquerque), 426 pp.

Wollman, N., 1968, *The Water Resources of Chile: An Economic Method for Analysing a Key Resource in a Nation's Development* (Johns Hopkins University Press, Baltimore), 296 pp.

Wolozin, H. (Ed.), 1966, *The Economics of Air Pollution* (Norton, New York), 318 pp.

Wolpert, J., 1966, "Migration as an adjustment to environmental stress", *J. Social Issues*, **22**, 92–102.

Wolpert, J., 1968, "The transition to interdependence in locational decisions", paper presented at the Annual Meeting of the American Association of Geographers, Washington, 1968.

Wong, S. T., 1969, "Perception of choice and factors affecting industrial water supply decisions in Northeastern Illinois", University of Chicago, Department of Geography, Research Paper No.117, 96 pp.

Wright, C., 1969, "Some aspects of the use of corrective taxes for controlling air pollution emissions", *Natn. Resources J.*, **9**, 63–83.

Wright, T. K., 1947, "Terrae incognitae: the place of imagination in geography", *Ann. Ass. Am. Geographers*, **37**, 1–15.

Young, R. A., Martin, W. E., 1967, "The economics of Arizona's water problem", *Ariz. Rev.*, **16**, 9–18.

Zimmermann, E. W., 1951, *World Resources and Industries* (Harper and Row, New York), 220 pp.

Zobler, L., 1962, "An economic–historical view of natural resource use and conservation", *Econ. Geogr.*, **38**, 189–94.

Appendix

Journals with articles relevant to resource management research

Social sciences
Administrative Science Quarterly
American Academy of Political and Social Science Annuals
American Behavioural Scientist
American Economic Review
American Institute of Planners Journal
American Journal of Agricultural Economics
American Journal of Economics and Sociology
American Journal of Psychology
American Journal of Sociology
American Political Science Review
American Psychologist
American Sociological Review
Annals of the Association of American Geographers
Behavioural Science
British Journal of Sociology
British Journal of Psychology
Canadian Farm Economics
Canadian Geographer
Canadian Journal of Agricultural Economics
Canadian Journal of Economics and Political Science
Canadian Journal of Economics and Sociology
Canadian Public Administration
Canadian Review of Sociology and Anthropology
Daedalus
Econometrics
Economic Development and Cultural Change
Economic Geography
Economic Journal
Economica
Ekistics
Environment and Behaviour
Environment and Planning
Forum
Geographical Review
Journal of Agricultural Economics
Journal of Conflict Resolution
Journal of Environmental Design
Journal of Farm Economics
Journal of Law and Economics
Journal of Leisure Research
Journal of Management Studies
Journal of Political Economy
Journal of Social Issues

Land Economics
Landscape
Landscape Architecture
Law and Contemporary Problems
Management Science
Manchester School of Economic and Social Studies
Milieu
National Parks Magazine
Natural History
Natural Resources Journal
Park Administration
Parks and Recreation
Parks and Recreation in Canada
Plan
Planning Outlook
Professional Geographer
Public Administration
Public Administration Review
Public Affairs Quarterly
Public Interest
Public Opinion Quarterly
Quarterly Journal of Economics
Recreation
Regional Science Association Papers and Proceedings
Regional Studies
Review of Economic Studies
Review of Economics and Statistics
Scottish Journal of Political Economy
Social Forces
Sociometry
Southern Economic Journal
Town and Country Planning
Town Planning Institute Journal
Town Planning Review
Transaction
Urban Affairs Quarterly
Urban Studies

Technical

Environment generally
Environment
Environmental Science and Technology
Natural History
Nature
Science
Scientific American

Air and water pollution
Air Pollution Control Association Journal
Air and Water Pollution
Environmental Health
Institute of Public Health Engineers Journal
Institute of Sewage Purification Journal
Journal of Environmental Health
Water and Pollution Control
Water Pollution Control Federation Journal
Water and Sewage Works
Water Treatment and Examination
Water and Waste Treatment
Water and Wastes Engineering

Water engineering
American Society of Civil Engineers, Hydraulics Division; Irrigation and Drainage Division
American Waterworks Association Journal
British Waterworks Association Journal
Desalination
Industrial Water Engineering
Institute of Civil Engineers Proceedings
Institution of Water Engineers Journal
Journal of Hydrology
Journal of the New England Water Works Association
Journal of Soil and Water Conservation
Water Power
Water Resources Research
Water and Water Engineering

Ecology
American Forests
Audobon Magazine
Bioscience
California Fish and Game
Canadian Journal of Plant Science
Ecological Monographs
Journal of Agronomy
Journal of Applied Ecology
Journal of Ecology
Journal of Forestry
Journal of Wildlife Management
Quarterly Journal of Forestry
Sierra Club Bulletin
Society of American Forestry Proceedings
Soil Science Society of America Proceedings
Transactions of the American Fisheries Society

Index